THE LATIN AMERICANS

Translated from the French by Ivan Kats

Carlos Rangel

THE LATIN AMERICANS

Their Love-Hate Relationship
with the United States

A Helen and Kurt Wolff Book

Harcourt Brace Jovanovich

New York and London

Printed in the United States of America

Library of Congress Cataloging in Publication Data

Rangel Guevara, Carlos.
The Latin Americans.

"A Helen and Kurt Wolff book."
Translation of Du bon sauvage au bon révolutionnaire.
Includes bibliographical references and index.
1. Latin America—Civilization.   2. Latin America—Politics and government.   3. Latin America—Relations (general) with the United States.   4. United States—Relations (general) with Latin America.   I. Title.
F1408.3.R3513   301.29'8'073   77-73121

ISBN 0-15-148795-2

First edition

B C D E

For, and because of, Sofia

Contents

Contents

Contents

Foreword

This is the first contemporary study of Latin-American civilization that discusses that continent in truly original and, to my mind, accurate fashion. Like any accurate assessment, it begins by doing away with the false interpretations, trumped-up images, and easy excuses that are common coin today. It follows that *The Latin Americans* is required reading for anyone who wishes to understand not only Latin America but also that much larger area of the contemporary world that exhibits the same failures, the same impotence, the same illusions. We can read Rangel's book either as an in-depth study of a specific civilization, or as the model of a more widespread phenomenon; a study contrasting what a society really *is* with its self-image. How far can a country allow the gap to grow, between what it is and what it thinks of itself, before it loses its grip on reality? This is the question that the history of Latin America, and the confrontation of its "myths" and "realities," allow us to answer.

Alien observers are chiefly responsible for the myths of Latin America. Europe has been the most prolific myth-maker in this case, and no wonder, since the colonizing power that shaped Latin-American society was European. Today, Europe no longer sends over its soldiers and priests, but it continues to send over its own obsessions.

For the Europeans have not been primarily concerned with understanding the two Americas; they have used the New World for their own ends. Their needs have been economic, imperial, ideological; they have craved adventure, dreams, the picturesque; they have needed to convert, to encourage, or to hate; and their narcissism has created an untold number of false images along the way.

These images are projections of ourselves; it was Europe that peopled the American continent, governed and directed it for centuries, brought African slaves to it, took over control of the Indian populations, or massacred them. Thus, we want to forget that the American civilizations, as they exist today, are the outcome of European colonialism, either of conquest or of what we may call imperialism-by-flight: the imperialism of millions of immigrants driven from Europe by hunger and persecution.

Whatever the blend of competitiveness, inferiority complexes, and smug paternalism that has gone into our conception of the two Americas, we must admit that in general this kind of mixture tends to engender myths. At the same time, a powerful mental block keeps even the most basic information about these countries from reaching us. In the twentieth century, we may simplify the picture by saying that the myths have crystallized around two main axes: North America is reactionary; Latin America is revolutionary.

It is true that the "myths and realities" of *North* America are constantly under discussion, so that some measure of reality, some sound perceptions, manage to survive. But *Latin* America is almost exclusively the domain of legend. From the start, the wish to know these societies, to understand them, or simply to describe them has been crushed under the need to use them as handy props for the European visionary's crystal ball.

The harm done would not be quite so great if, all along the path of history, our legends had not become a drug on which the Latin Americans we observed have loved to feed. Not that they are innocent of making up and propagating their own myths. But they are enormously encouraged in such counterfeiting when the figments of their imagination and their illusions about themselves are sent back to them duly authenticated, bearing the stamp of recognition bestowed by the high priests of the European intelligentsia.

My trouble in writing this foreword at the author's friendly request stems from the fact that I know I owe him whatever I shall think of Latin America from now on. Usually, forewords are written by the masters, not by the disciples.

Perhaps the following quote from a letter Carlos Rangel wrote me while he was working on his book and coming to grips with his basic theory will be more helpful than my own Eurocentric comments:

"As I told you when we met in Caracas, a job of demystification needs to be done. Not that every single thing one hears about Latin America is untrue: but the sum of it gives a false impression. . . . Columbus himself laid the first stone of this house of myths; his own reasons for his quest and his first relations of it bear witness to this. We know he thought he had discovered the Earthly Paradise. Then came Father Las Casas and other monks who built up the image of the 'noble savage,' still much alive today, and launched the 'Black Legend' of the absolute evils of Spanish colonization. This proved useful to Holland, England, and France, the powerful rivals of Spanish colonization, as a tool in criticizing Spain: a job made simpler by the fact that until 1800 the Spanish did all they could to isolate the American provinces from the rest of the world."

Whatever its excesses and abuses may have been, it is untrue that Spanish colonization was nothing but one endless chain of oppression lasting over three centuries. Alexander von Humboldt, who visited the Spanish empire in the last years of his life, was surprised by the degree of progress, culture, and knowledge that he found in a city as unimportant as Caracas was at the time. This explains why here, as elsewhere on the continent, there should have arisen men as exceptional as Bolívar or Miranda. When discussing their thought, Carlos Rangel shows that they were on a par with the most remarkable contemporary theoreticians and statesmen of Europe and North America. But in Europe and North America, the new ideas generally gave rise to institutions, mores, methods of government. This development failed to take place in Spanish America.

Why the failure? For we must make no mistake on this score. Latin America's history since the beginning of the nineteenth century is a story of failure, just as the history of North America is a story of success. Why this difference? This is the question Rangel sets out to answer; for failure and its causes have perpetuated themselves to the present day, even though the myth that was at the origin of the first misunderstanding has evolved: the myth of the noble savage has developed into the myth of the good revolutionary.

The significance of this book reaches well beyond the borders of Latin America. Surely, Latin America is in itself a distinct, significant, and interesting field of study, but its problems and its fantasies are common to other continents as well.

Foreword

Its resentment and fear of the United States are an exacerbated version of passions that Europe shares. Latin America's difficulties in fitting liberal democracy to local conditions; the failure of Chilean "democratic socialism," the resurgence of "national-military socialism," which helps to disguise and gain acceptance for a new form of *caudillismo*—all these conditions parallel those in other parts of the world. Will Latin America, with its Western cultural heritage and its relatively favorable position, be able to find workable solutions to its problems without giving up the ideals and gains of the great liberal revolution? Its failure to do so would be a bad omen for the rest of the world: it would imply that the greater part of humanity cannot be governed other than by authoritarianism and terror.

JEAN-FRANÇOIS REVEL

In politics and history, if one takes accepted statements at face value, one will be sadly misled.

JOSÉ ORTEGA Y GASSET

The [true] revolution—which under varied names has been moving man since the dawn of history—aims at freeing man from the myths that oppress him, in order that he may attain full being. . . . Propaganda, on the contrary, aims to enslave man . . . to alter him, to alienate him. We are told that the goal is Revolution or freedom, but the result is paralysis, domination, slavery.

HECTOR A. MURENA

I am appalled that the ideas that the rest of the world has about the United States are to such a great extent false; this injects a dose of error into every aspect of life on earth, so that men therefore (although not only for that reason) live in a state of permanent misunderstanding.

JULIAN MARIAS

In Spanish America . . . the political lie established itself almost constitutionally. The moral damage it has caused is incalculable; it has affected profound areas of our existence. We move about in this lie with complete naturalness. . . . Hence the struggle against the official, constitutional lie must be the first step in any serious attempt at reform.

OCTAVIO PAZ

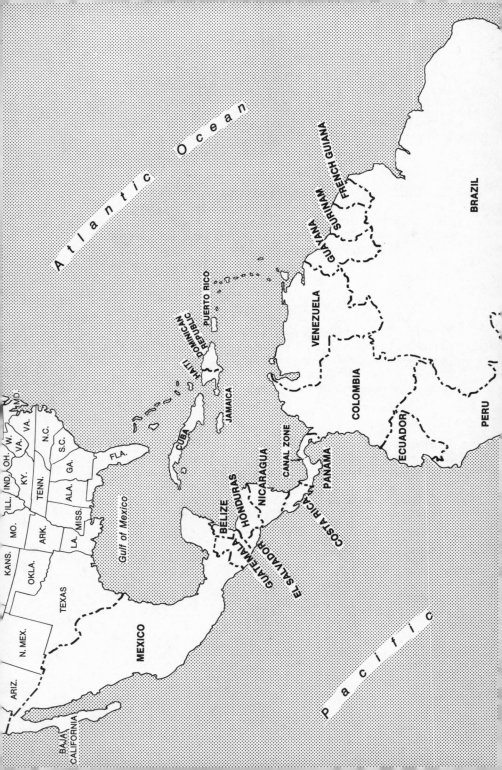

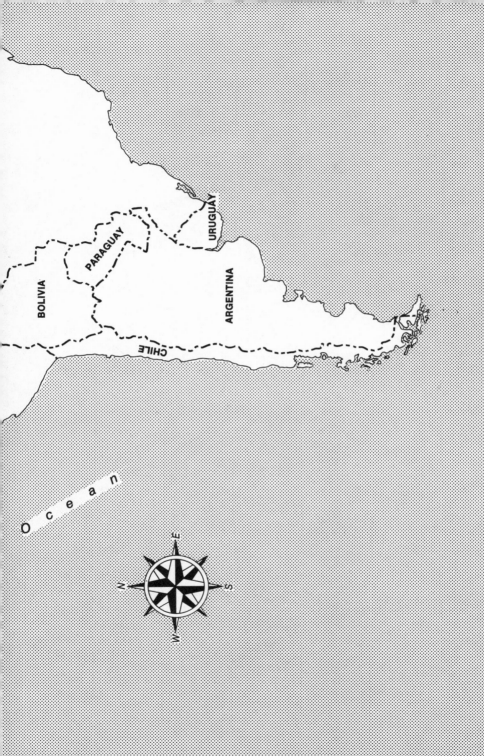

THE LATIN AMERICANS

Introduction

"Spanish" America, Not "Latin" America

We Latin Americans are not happy with ourselves, with what we are. But, then, what are we? And what do we want to be, what do we want to become? There is no agreement among us on these questions. This Latin-American world of ours, stretching from the Rio Grande to Patagonia, just exactly what is it? One possible answer is that there is not one Latin America, but about twenty, including Brazil as one of the different parts, and even Haiti. But the fact is that any *Spanish* American knows perfectly well that Brazilians are different from us, and that we and they look at the world from different and even potentially incompatible perspectives. On the other hand, where Spanish America is concerned, the ten thousand kilometers that separate the northern border of Mexico from the southern tip of Chile and Argentina are a geographic distance, not a spiritual discontinuity.

It is true that the Spanish American countries contain a number of marginal peoples who live as strangers within the dominant culture. These are the descendants of the pre-Columbian population, of the "legitimate owners" of the land; the blood of these slaves runs in the veins of an enormous proportion of the Spanish American population, and is therefore one of the main components of the vast ethnic mix that is Latin America. Like their ancestors, they are the victims of foreign conquest and domination. All these factors have tended to blur the continent's self-awareness by giving rise to myths—myths that encompass and apologize for a tendency to racism, guilt, inferiority complexes, and other self-deceptive reactions.

We may for the time being limit this urgent issue, which has tortured Latin America since the Conquest, by stressing that its discussion has been carried on by *Spanish* America only: the indigenous civilizations and the individuals who are heirs to those civilizations have stood by passively.

The conscience (one might say the *bad* conscience) of Latin America depends to a significant degree on the treatment of these native inhabitants, the Indians. There are several reasons for this. The Indians were, of course, witnesses to the discovery of the continent; many elements of their culture were assimilated, often unwittingly, by the Hispanic societies that developed through conquest, colonization, and evangelization; they contributed to forming the mestizo stock; and, finally, they have endured and are still on the scene. But the cult of the native, now in fashion, must not hide from us the fact that Argentina, Bolivia, Cuba, Colombia, Costa Rica, Chile, Ecuador, El Salvador, Guatemala, Honduras, Mexico, Nicaragua, Panama, Paraguay, Peru, Puerto Rico, Santo Domingo, Uruguay, and Venezuela all belong to a single, Spanish American culture, which has now been implanted in eighteen independent nations plus one commonwealth (Puerto Rico) that is politically under the tutelage of the United States.

On landing, the Spaniards found the continent occupied by native societies in various states of evolution, some quite advanced. They then imported African blacks. Later, immigrants from different European countries were integrated in various proportions, to form the populations of each of the countries. The Anglo-Saxon hegemony in the Western Hemisphere (and later in the entire world) has had a deep impact on Latin America—an impact that was felt everywhere, though it varied from one country to another. Notwithstanding these variations, there is but *one* Spanish America, and we may look on it as a unit, not as divided into twenty or even into three or five different parts.

On the other hand, when we speak of one "Latin America" it is awkward to think of it as including Brazil. Brazil is set apart from Spanish America, not only by its Portuguese origin and language, but by other factors as well: by the manner of its conquest and colonization; by the fact that for many years it was the metropolis of the Portuguese empire; by the methods through which its separation from the empire was achieved—a non-traumatic experience, a governmental decree that left intact the political and administrative structures set up by the metropolis from which Brazil was freeing itself.

In short, Brazil and Spanish America have points of resemblance and a certain kinship, but the points on which they differ are far more significant. This is particularly evident if we consider the astonishing consolidation of Brazil into one giant nation bordering on all the Latin-American countries of South America except Ecuador and Chile: a sharp contrast to the fragmentation of Spanish America into nineteen pieces.

This wide continental extension of Brazil has in itself great significance and now holds the seed of ever-greater differences and even possible conflicts between Spanish America and Brazil. If we wish to understand Latin America, we can no more leave out Brazil than we can disregard the United States. But to Spanish America, Brazil appears as a neighbor—potentially friendly, potentially threatening, but in any case different, a distinct entity, whereas Spanish America's own vast extension and apparent heterogeneity do not keep it from being an identifiable whole, displaying common traits and a basic unity, a clear and distinct division of the globe.

Spanish America can be seen as a whole because its parts share the stamp of the same conquerors, colonizers, and evangelists. There is no agreement concerning the exact number of these "Pioneers of the Indies," the handful of sailors, soldiers, and churchmen who brought about this extraordinary development. But what is certain is that in fewer than sixty years, from 1492 to 1550, this small band of men (no more than thirty thousand) explored vast territories, vanquished two empires, founded almost all those cities still extant today as well as others that have since disappeared, and spread the Catholic faith and the language and culture of Castile in a manner more than merely durable—indeed, ineradicable.

The name "Latin America," fashioned by Frenchmen or Anglo-Saxons, has imposed itself to such a degree that it would be pedantic either not to use it or to insist at every step that it does not encompass Brazil. Let the reader be warned, however, that unless I specify otherwise, the "Latin" America that I am concerned with is the Spanish-speaking area of the continent.

From Failure to Compensation Through Myth

Almost five hundred years have elapsed since 1492: half a millennium. If we try to summarize those five centuries of

Latin-American history, going to the heart of the matter and leaving analyses, anecdotes, controversies, and inferences for later, one all-encompassing fact stands out: the history of Latin America, to the present day, is a story of failure. I am not saying this to be shocking. It is the simple truth, and we Latin Americans are quite aware of it. It is a truth that hurts and that we seldom mention, but it crops up whenever we take an honest look at ourselves. We perceive our history as one of frustration. Simon Bolívar, Latin America's greatest hero, wrote in 1830:

"I was in command for twenty years, and during that time came to only a few definite conclusions: (1) I consider that, for us, [Latin] America is ungovernable; (2) whosoever works for a revolution is plowing the sea; (3) the most sensible action to take in [Latin] America is to emigrate; (4) this country [Great Colombia, later to be divided into Colombia, Venezuela, and Ecuador] will ineluctably fall into the hands of a mob gone wild, later again to fall under the domination of obscure small tyrants of every color and race; (5) though decimated by every kind of crime and exhausted by our cruel excesses, we shall still not be tempting to Europeans for a reconquest; (6) if any part of the world were to return to a primeval chaos, such would be the last avatar of [Latin] America."

These six pithy sentences summarize in the most lucid fashion the Latin American's pessimism and the jaundiced view he takes of his own society. Some of Bolívar's prophecies came true to the letter—and even if we consider them to reflect the depressive mind of a man advancing in years, disillusioned, and embittered, they also show the clarity of the Liberator's sociological insight and his political realism.

Since Bolívar formulated so succinctly his views on the political future of Latin America, the picture has been expanded by additional facts and points of comparison: (1) the disproportionate success of the United States in the same "New World" during a parallel period of history; (2) Latin America's inability to evolve harmonious and cohesive nations, capable of redeeming, or at least reasonably improving, the lot of vast marginal social and economic groups; (3) Latin America's impotence in its external relations—military, economic, political, cultural, et cetera—and hence its vulnerability to outside action or influences in each of these areas; (4) the notable lack of stability of the Latin-American forms of government, other than those founded on dictatorships and repression; (5) the absence of noteworthy Latin-American contributions in the sciences or the arts (the exceptions I could quote merely prove the rule); (6) its population growth rate, the highest in the world; (7) Latin America's feeling that it is of little if any use to the world at large. In moments of depression (or insight) we suspect that the rest of the world would hardly be affected if the ocean were to swallow up the Latin-American continent overnight.

Almost a century and a half after Bolívar, Carlos Fuentes, one of the foremost Spanish American intellectuals of our day, could write:

"A much more alarming prospect exists [for Latin America]: as the gap widens between the technocratic world, which grows in geometric progression, and our ancillary societies, which grow in arithmetic progression, Latin America gradually becomes a *useless* entity in the eyes of imperialism. Traditionally, we have been exploited societies. Soon we will not even be that: it will no longer be necessary to exploit us, because technology will have learned (and it has already learned to a high degree) to manufacture industrial substitutes for the poor offerings of our one-crop economies. Will we stretch out our hand to pick up the crumbs of North American, European, or Soviet charity? Will we then become the India of the Western world? Will our economy be a simple fiction, kept alive out of sheer philanthropy?"[1]

Like Bolívar's, Fuentes's pessimism is more than the self-esteem of Latin Americans can bear. He moves from these sobering remarks to a defense of revolutionary action. Only through such action can Latin America hope to redeem or to create its own true personality, develop its own program of action, and someday play, in the world at large, if not an indispensable or even distinguished role, at least the role of an independent entity.

At any rate, from Bolívar to Carlos Fuentes, any Latin American honestly facing up to the problem has either admitted or at least marginally alluded to the failure of Latin America throughout its history.

Human societies confronted with the achievements of rival societies will tend either to emulate them or to deprecate the values that have made them possible and that they envy. If

1. *La nueva novela hispanoamericana*, Mexico, Cuadernos de Joaquín Mortiz, 1969.

they have tried the way of emulation and failed, they may seek consolation in a mythology that will explain their own failure and hold out the prospect of some miraculous future reversal of action. This is the case in Latin America.

1

From Noble Savage to Good Revolutionary

The Indies as the Earthly Paradise

The basic myths of America are not American, but have sprung from the imagination of Europeans. Take one further step and you can trace them to Judeo-Christian or Asian antiquity, reformulated by Europeans in their delight at having discovered a "New World."

When the peoples of Latin America awoke to national consciousness in the nineteenth century, they found a ready-made mythical base to help them claim the pre-Columbian past as their own. Later the same myth was to help them excuse or cover up the relative failure of Latin America, the land that is daughter to the noble savage, wife to the good revolutionary, predestined mother to the new man.

Once they had charted their inland sea and sailed on beyond Gibraltar to discover the ocean, the Mediterranean peoples intuited that there must be something beyond these seemingly endless waters. This is clear from Plato's well-known Atlantis, "an island greater than Libya and Asia together," as from Seneca's prophecy in his *Medea*: "In some years a day will come when the Ocean will open the gates of the world and reveal a land unknown; Tethys will then reveal a new world to us, and Thule will no longer be the end of the earth."

The fifteenth century could hardly fail to know that the Indies—that is to say, the Far East, including China, Japan, Malacca, Java, and Sumatra—lay at the other side of the world. As early as two thousand years before the discovery of America, the Greeks had observed that ships setting out to sea disappeared beyond the horizon, while to the seaborne traveler the earth seemed to sink away. Similarly, they noted that during eclipses of the moon, the earth's shadow fell as a circle on its satellite. They had guessed that the earth was round.

It followed that to reach the East, a ship could sail into the setting sun or into the rising sun. But the distance westward was reckoned, rightly, as much greater. If there was only water between Europe's western coast and Asia's eastern coast, sailing such light vessels through so immense an ocean understandably seemed sheer madness.

Christopher Columbus, following his intuition, persevered in holding out, against the generally held opinion, that the earth was not only round (which was not seriously in dispute), but also very much smaller than it really is. He set sail for certain death, and accidentally discovered America.

The New World: Utopia

The Europeans' initial illusion that they had reached Asia did not stay long with them. Had Columbus not been so set in his conviction, he would have inferred from what he could see and touch that he had accomplished far more than reaching the Old World in a new way. Believing himself near Japan, he viewed as illusory or supernatural certain signs that, had they been interpreted by a less medievally circumscribed mentality, would have told him he was near a vast new continent.

"When he reached the mouth of the Orinoco, he thought he had reached the Earthly Paradise. . . . The violent stream of fresh water that almost destroyed his caravels in the Gulf of the Whale, with its Serpent's Mouth and its Dragon's Mouth, should have led him to infer that he was near large forests and mountains. . . . He thought instead that he was near the fountain that springs from Earthly Paradise. . . . For theologians affirmed that God had not destroyed Paradise, but removed it to a land or Blessed Isle which knew neither sickness, nor old age, nor death, nor fear."[1]

At the meeting point of the Middle Ages and the Renaissance, it was quite possible for medieval-minded men like Columbus to find and to see with their own eyes things foretold by the learned authorities and duly recorded by them in their books.

[1]. Angel Rosenblat, *La primera visión de América y otros estudios*, Caracas, Ministerio de Educacion, 1965.

But the perenniality of ancestral myths manifested itself equally in the thought of those of Columbus's contemporaries who had moved beyond the medieval level and looked at the future through Renaissance eyes. Thomas More, in his *Utopia,* took his point of departure in the age-old story or myth of the Blessed Isle, as reinvigorated by Columbus's discovery. More's fiction combined the vision of Plato's *Republic* with enthusiasm over a New World as yet uncorrupted by civilization. This was where the ideal society might be found or else be launched, with its promise of eternal bliss, peace, equality, plenty, freedom, security. The title of the book clearly reflects the modern skepticism of Henry VIII's Chancellor, but its contents attest the hold of old illusions, especially as taken up and reactivated by that catalyst, the New World.

The Fountain of Youth, the Amazons, El Dorado

Soon after their arrival, the conquistadors exerted intense and poignant efforts to find the Fountain of Youth. This was an old myth, which has much in common with that of the Earthly Paradise; the Tree of Life can be identified with the Fountain of Life, immortality, beatitude. Belief in it fills a need that rises out of the subconscious, a symbolic identification of life itself with fountains and springs, with "the eternal human thirst for pleasure, youth, and happiness as the visionary realization of man's power over death and destiny."[2]

As they did with the better-known myth of El Dorado, the American natives, realizing that the white invaders were seeking a magic fountain, nourished this illusion in order to lure them on ever farther from their bases.

The conquistadors were no less myth-driven when they set out on their search for the Amazons. Two names on the map stand as reminders of their obstinacy in finding in the West Indies what medieval tradition placed in the true Indies, in the Far East. One of the books of Amadis of Gaul tells us that "to the right hand of the Indies an island is to be found, called *California,* neighboring on the Earthly Paradise, peopled with black women, manless, and whose style of life much resembled that of the Amazons . . . for their tall stature, their generous and warm hearts, their great strength. . . . Their weapons were all of gold, as was their horses' tackle . . . for in all the island there is no other metal. . . ."

2. *Ibid.*

The navigators and conquistadors who came after Columbus eagerly sought these fabled Amazons and their country full
of gold. We see that the myth of El Dorado is linked to very
ancient legends. In this as in other instances, the discovery of
America brought nothing to European mythology that was not
already there; it only rekindled old dreams of a Golden Age
and the State of Innocence that preceded the Fall. It fed the
equally ancient hope that Paradise had not been lost, but only
removed to an unknown place; perhaps to the fatherland of
Prester John, that legendary Christian emperor of an old Oriental kingdom; perhaps to "the Indies." There still dwelt men
free from original sin, whose touch could help sinners redeem
themselves far more surely and rapidly than through the
anguish of awaiting the distant resurrection promised by
Christ.

The Noble Savage

The newcomers, in their search, created the most powerful
myth of modern times: that of the noble savage. This is the
"Americanized" version of the myth of man's innocence before
the Fall, and that new version of the ancient myth was to have
an immense impact on the history of ideas.

The myth of the noble savage responded far more adequately to the characteristic anguishes of Western European,
Christian, traditional civilization than earlier myths of a related nature. The belief that man is innately good and that
civilization corrupted him, that there was once a Golden Age
followed by the present-day Age of Bronze or Iron, would find
its confirmation in the discovery of men allegedly living in a
state of nature, uncorrupt and uncivilized.

It was in these terms that Columbus saw the natives of the
Caribbean Sea, and so he described them in his letters to the
Catholic Kings: "I certify to their Highnesses that there is no
better land anywhere, that there are no better people: they love
others as themselves and speak the sweetest language in the
world."

One native, to whom Columbus was offering his sword, could
not understand what this object was: he seized it by the blade
and cut himself, which led Columbus to conclude that these
people knew neither weapons nor war. Their readiness to give

away gold trinkets made him think that they were equally ignorant of avarice.[3]

The conquistadors endowed even the land with supernatural qualities. Soon after the year 1500, a Sevillian priest, following Columbus's reports and also quoting him, informed his readers that the New World appeared to have been made in the image of its inhabitants. The steep mountains, which even today stand as an often insurmountable obstacle, he describes as being "very tall," or "elevated." But he interprets this adjective in the sense of "grand," which they certainly are, and imaginatively assures the reader that they are "quite traversable." The trees are so tall that "they seem to touch the sky"; as they never lose their leaves, the Sevillian concludes that the weather is invariably like Europe's in the month of May. "In the island [of Hispaniola] there are pine woods, cultivated fields and pasture . . . mines of gold-bearing ore." And all this about a region that was as inhospitable then as it is now. Those Spaniards who, instead of dreaming about the New World without leaving Seville, decided to come and look for themselves, suffered the heat, the razor-sharp grasses, and the stinging insects, and they dubbed Columbus "Admiral of the Mosquitoes."

Civilization as Corrupter

But Europe had set its mind on believing in the "noble savage," the native of a New World. By the middle of the sixteenth century the myth had taken root and was ravaging Europe far more insidiously than syphilis—another import, we are told, from the New World. Montaigne endorses the myth and puts the full weight of his authority behind it: "They are even savage,[4] as we call those fruits wilde, which nature of her selfe,

3. Why did Europeans not encounter the noble savage in Africa? Quite certainly because the African savages had been known since antiquity and were not, therefore, truly exotic. Europe found no noble savages in Africa because it was not seeking them there. And this is why the blacks were perceived by Western consciousness simply as savages—without qualification, in the exact, pejorative meaning of the word.
4. Montaigne is referring to the New World Indians, whom he calls cannibals without being unduly shocked. He even finds some good arguments for occasionally eating human flesh. He holds this a less reprehensible practice than the Europeans' custom of torturing to death their condemned criminals.

and of her ordinarie progresse hath produced. . . . In those are the true and most profitable vertues, and natural properties most lively and vigorous, which in these we have bastardized. . . . The lawes of nature doe yet command them, which are but little bastardized by ours . . . for me seemeth that what in those nations we see by experience, doth not only exceed all the pictures wherewith licentious Poesie hath proudly imbellished the golden age, and all her quaint inventions to faine a happy condition of man, but also the conception and desire of Philosophy. They could not imagine a genuitie so pure and simple, as we see it by experience; not ever beleeve our societie might be maintained with so little art and humane combination. It is a nation, would I answer Plato, that hath no kinde of traffike, no knowledge of Letters, no intelligence of numbers, no name of magistrate, nor of politike superioritie; no use of service, of riches or of povertie; no contracts, no successions, no partitions, no occupation but idle; no respect of kinred, but common, no apparell but naturall, no manuring of lands, no use of wine, corne, or mettle. The very words that import lying, falshood, treason, dissimulations, covetousnes, envie, detraction, and pardon, were never heard of amongst them. . . . They live in a country of so exceeding pleasant and temperate situation, that as my testimonies have told me, it is verie rare to see a sicke body amongst them; and they have further assured me, they never saw any man there, either shaking with the palsie, toothlesse, with eyes dropping, or crooked and stooping through age. . . . Their language is a kinde of pleasant speech, and hath a pleasing sound, and some affinitie with the Greeke terminations. [They are] ignorant how deare the knowledge of our corruptions will one day cost their repose, securitie, and happinesse, and how their ruine shall proceed from this commerce."[5]

Rousseau had nothing to add to this two hundred years later. But it is even more surprising to meet in the same essay by Montaigne the idea that European society deserved a bloody revolution which would bring it back to its pristine state of natural goodness, to the Golden Age; or which, at least, would bring rightful restitution to the greater part of the people, wronged as they had been by the "antinatural" inequality to which civilization had led Europe:

5. "Of the Caniballes," in *The Essayes of Montaigne,* trans. John Florio, New York, Modern Library, n.d., pp. 163–64, 170. Reprinted by permission of Random House, Inc.

"They [three Indians come to the court of Charles IX in Roanne] had perceived, there were men amongst us full gorged with all sortes of commodities, and others which hunger starved, and bore with need and povertie, begged at their gates; and found it strange, these moyties so needy could endure such an injustice, and that they tooke not the others by the throte, or set fire on their houses."[6]

Because of this myth of the noble savage, the West today is afflicted with an absurd feeling of guilt, convinced that its civilization has corrupted the other peoples of the world, grouped as the "Third World," who, had they not been exposed to Western culture, would have remained happy as Adam and flawless as diamonds. But our present interest lies in retracing the road traveled in Latin America by this particular myth.

The Good Revolutionary

To understand how the noble savage was transmuted into the good revolutionary, we have to understand the supposed relation between man before the Fall and man after redemption. These two states are not merely related: they are *identical*. The stage in between is a parenthesis, an interruption in man's natural beatitude. The first days will be like the last; the end of history will be a return to the Golden Age.

Some of the first Christians were convinced that, after his second coming, Christ would establish a perfect Kingdom on earth, and that it would last a thousand years. Since then this millenarian expectation has been a recurrent fever in society. At a time when man's eternal myths have everywhere become degraded and desacralized, this millenarianism has evolved into a secular revolutionism, with the "Fall" consisting in the institution of private property. Before this "antinatural" institution existed, all men are supposed to have been happy and free; and so they will be again when private property has been abolished.

"Millenarian" (or revolutionary) sects invariably conceive redemption as absolute, in the sense that, through some transformation, life on earth will suddenly be changed, returned to the perfection it enjoyed before the Fall. Furthermore, millenarian outbreaks have invariably been accompanied by the sudden appearance of prophets and martyrs endowed with

6. *Ibid.*

special qualities: eloquence, courage, personal magnetism, charisma.

No doubt millenarianism and revolutionism do not fit in with the rationalist spirit in which the West found its greatness. But, on the other hand, they are supremely attractive to all those who feel outcast, marginal, frustrated, beaten, dispossessed of their *natural* right to enjoy the goods of the earth—with which, it is supposed, the noble savages of America were amply provided before the arrival of the fateful caravels.

This explains why successful America (the United States) has little use for the myth of the noble savage and is putting up a healthy resistance (certainly greater than Europe's) to the myth of the good revolutionary. And it explains why frustrated America (Latin America) is so vulnerable to both.

The noble savage plays as unimportant a role in the psyche of North Americans as it has played in their history. "The last of the Mohicans" is noble, to be sure, but he is alien and nearly extinct. The Anglo-Saxon colonizers were looking more for land and liberty than for gold and slaves. Having expelled the natives from the land, or exterminated them, they felt no need either to reject or to assimilate those natives socially or psychologically.

By contrast, this need has been the crucial factor, and persists in being the cancer, of Latin America. There the conquistadors created a society in which the Indians were reduced to servitude, made an integral and indispensable part of society, men filling the need for labor, and women filling the need for sex. As a result, we Latin Americans are the descendants of both the conquerors and the conquered, of both the masters and the slaves; we are the sons of the women who were ravished and of the men who ravished them. The myth of the noble savage is our personal business, our pride and our shame.

In the extremity of our frustration and irrationality, we will not admit to any other parentage; and even if we are the children or grandchildren of recent European immigrants we will consider ourselves "Tupamaros" (so called after the Túpac Amaru who headed an Indian uprising in Peru in the eighteenth century).

So the noble savage is turned into the good revolutionary, the "romantic adventurer, Red Robin Hood, the Don Quixote of communism, the new Garibaldi, the Marxist Saint-Just, the Cid Campeador of the wretched of the earth, the Sir Galahad of the

Beggars, the secular Christ, the San Ernesto de la Higuera revered by the Bolivian peasants"—Che Guevara.[7]

The Other Side of Myths

The historic Túpac Amaru was a lineal descendant of the Incas, emperors of pre-Columbian Peru. When he revolted in 1780, he exchanged his Hispanized name, José Gabriel Condorcanqui, for that of an Inca executed in 1569 by Francisco de Toledo, the viceroy who between that year and 1582 solidified Spanish domination in Peruvian territory.

Vanquished and imprisoned, the second Túpac Amaru was cruelly tortured and put to death, and thus entered history as the martyr and forerunner of Latin-American independence.

This is a typical example of the inaccuracies and myths of Latin America. It was in the name of Charles III, King of Spain from 1759 to 1788, that Túpac Amaru rose up against the excesses of the Peruvian Creoles. In executing him, those Creoles were concerned primarily with defending their privileges as the descendants of conquistadors. Though they still considered themselves close to Spain, they were much less concerned with the wishes of a sovereign who was far away, and who, moreover, was influenced by the new French thought. Indeed, the Spanish monarch had been worrying the Creoles since 1765 by extending to America his *modern* ideas concerning improvements in imperial administration and controls, which had been borrowed from the French system of representatives of the crown (the *intendants*).

At this time of decline of Spain's Latin-American empire, the American Creoles, the seeds of the power structure in all the future independent republics, were divided between two contradictory emotions. On the one hand they were fascinated by the successful uprising of the North American settlers; they, too, felt antagonistic to the imperial motherland. They would have liked to claim all power and all honors for themselves, rather than accept the tutelage of Spain, as personified by administrators from the metropolis. Yet, in their slave-owning society, they knew they were surrounded by enemies. These included not only the seemingly subdued Indians, who nevertheless occasionally revolted—as they did in Peru in

7. Michel Lowy, *The Marxism of Che Guevara: Philosophy, Economics, and Revolutionary Warfare*, New York and London, Monthly Review Press, 1973, p. 7.

1780, or in Mexico in 1624 and 1692[8]—but also the fierce, untamed blacks and the humiliated, vindictive "darks." In fact, the 1692 Mexico uprising against the Creoles and all they stood for united the black slaves, the "darks," the Indians, and even the "poor whites," called *saramullos* in Mexico.[9]

And as if this were not enough, starting in 1791, the revolution in Haiti offered the Spanish American Creoles a vivid demonstration of what race war could be like in the slave societies of America, once the links with the metropolis had been cut, and with them the habits of authority and submission.

Faced with a somber and hostile mass of slaves, serfs, and inferior free castes, the Creoles ardently identified with Spain, and felt themselves faithful subjects of the King. It is possible, and almost certain, that the executioners of Túpac Amaru were Creoles. And probably it was a Creole who formulated the edict proclaimed in Cuzco after the uprising had been suppressed:

"In view of the rebellion, the Indians are ordered to rid themselves of all articles of native dress and hand them over to their *corregidores* [chief magistrates of the towns]; they are required to hand over all paintings or portraits of their Incas to be destroyed, for they do not deserve the honor of being portrayed and placed on exhibit.

"In view of the rebellion, the comedies and such further public performances as the Indians traditionally hold to commemorate past events are forbidden. The same *corregidores* will be held responsible for enforcing this interdiction in the villages under their authority.

"In view of the rebellion, the use of trumpets or clarions

8. On June 7, 1692, the Indians of Mexico City, suffering from hunger and spurred on by the rumor that an Indian woman had been flogged to death, stormed the Viceroy's palace and burned it, acclaiming the King of Spain while shouting down the Viceroy of Mexico.
9. "There were seven castes in the West Indies: (1) the Spanish born in Spain; (2) the Spanish born in America, called Creoles; (3) the mestizos, half-breeds of a white father and an Indian mother; (4) the mulattoes, born of a white father and a black mother; (5) the zambos, of mixed Negro-Indian blood; (6) the Indians; (7) the blacks. There were further subdivisions, such as black zambos (cross between a black man and a mulatto woman; the quarteroons, a cross of a white father and a mulatto woman; the quinteroons, of a white father and a quarteroon mother, and the *salto atras* ['one jump back'], the issue of a mixed union who is of a color darker than the mother's. In Venezuela, the term *pardo* [dark] was used of all people not of pure race (neither white nor Indian nor black but the issue of a mixed union); at the end of the colonial era, this caste included half the overall population." (José Gil Fortoul, *Historia constitucional de Venezuela*.)

called *potutos* [marine shells emitting a strange and eerie sound], used by the Indians in their ceremonies, is prohibited.

"In view of the rebellion, the natives are ordered henceforth to dress according to Spanish laws, to adopt Spanish customs, and to use the Spanish language, under pain of strict and just punishment."

Yet the same Creoles who in 1781 formulated or endorsed this edict worthy of a foreign invader declared themselves soon after, in 1810, "honorary Indians," and viewed themselves as avengers of the noble savage. The national anthem of independent Peru claims the city of Lima (which is, with Mexico City, the most Spanish of the old Hispano-American cities) to be the heir to the hatred and vengeance of the Incas, legitimate rulers of Peru, and goes on to describe the capital as liberated after three centuries of foreign occupation. The Argentine national anthem, in a similar tenor, has the Incas shaking in their graves as they hear the rumblings of the war of independence and see "their sons" resuscitate the old glories of the fatherland. In Ecuador, José Joaquín Olmedo, Great Colombia's poet laureate as it were, in 1825 conjured up the image of the Inca Huaina Capac mounted on a cloud, lamenting that "three centuries of curses, blood, and slavery have flowed by" till, finally, he now sees the happy dawn of a new day, "the new era once promised the Inca."

Yet the living conditions of the Indians—not the Indians of legend, who were dead and buried, but the living ones—continued unchanged, and grew even worse, perhaps, than before the break with Spain. The Spanish colonial administration was in the hands of Spanish-born officials who had no share in the welfare of the colony and were bound neither by blood nor by long acquaintance with the Creole oligarchy. To these officials —viceroys, *intendants*, or captains general—the caste system in the countries they governed was a basic political fact, and their policy consisted in playing each element against the other through a careful system of mediation. It is clear that these administrators had no interest whatsoever in social justice as we understand the term today, and that the Creoles were greatly favored in the arbitration between the castes. Yet, at the same time, the Spanish monarchs were concerned to a certain extent with justice; the controversy in sixteenth-century Christian Spain revolving around the humanity and rights of the American aborigines had led to the so-called Laws of the Indies, many of which were aimed at protecting the Indians.

In the period that followed, the governments of the several

new republics were composed exclusively of ruthless Creole landowners, or, in the case of countries whose social structure had been overturned by the war, by even more ruthless mulattoes with large landholdings. In both cases, the ruling class was an oligarchy concerned with no interests but its own and with the maintenance of social structures founded on the existing land-tenure systems and peon labor. The frequent governmental changes, termed "Latin-American revolutions," in no way affected the basic situation.

The injustice was to be compounded at the end of the nineteenth century and in the early twentieth, when the ruling class sought to explain the failure of their societies, as compared to North America, by blaming the Indians, the blacks, and miscegenation in general. This explanation preceded, and then for a time coexisted with, that current in present-day Latin-American thought that attributes the frustration and the lag in development entirely to North American imperialism.

2

Latin America and the United States

Foretelling the Future Before the Dice Were Cast

As late as 1700, the Spanish American empire still gave the impression of being incomparably richer (which it was!), much more powerful, and more likely to succeed than the British colonies of North America.[1]

In that year, war between England and the Franco-Spanish alliance seemed imminent. Now, with the benefit of hindsight, we can easily discern, behind the rivalry between the three principal European powers, the inexorable growth of Anglo-Saxon predominance, from the defeat of the Spanish Armada, to the Battle of Trafalgar, the Spanish-American War of 1898, and the Second World War. But this trend was far from evident in 1700, and a colonist who dwelt in the small settlements of Boston and New York in that year, seeking to foretell the future, could reasonably have feared instead the strength-

---

1. Mexico City, Lima, and a score of other Spanish American centers were already important cities at a time when the British were still trying to build up their settlements in North America. Mexico's first printing house dates back to 1548. The Universities of Mexico and Lima were founded in 1551. In 1576, there were in Spanish America no fewer than nine courts of justice, thirty central administrations, twenty-four treasurers general, three mints, twenty-four bishoprics, four archbishoprics, and three hundred and six monasteries, not to mention the impressive structures still standing today, built to house these institutions and to serve as residences for viceroys and other grandees. By way of comparison, Boston was not founded until 1630; at the end of the eighteenth century, neither that city nor Philadelphia nor New York could bear comparison with the viceregal cities of Spanish America. The population of the North American colonies was still largely rural.

ening of the vast French and Spanish holdings in North America, to the detriment of the narrow strip of land that the English had settled, beginning only in 1607, between Canada, Florida, the Appalachians, and the Atlantic Coast.

On the other hand, even the wildest imagination could not have foreseen that these hard-pressed British colonies were about to form an independent federal state, powerful and expansionist, that would buy Louisiana from France, Florida from Spain, and Alaska from Russia; that would expel the Spanish Americans from their enormous holdings in California and elsewhere, and fight their way to the Pacific, where they would win Oregon from England.

The confederation born in 1776 did not seem to represent a threat. No European statesman of any judgment could have believed at the time that so unlikely an undertaking would prove politically viable, develop a stable and workable system of government, and maintain peace or even inner cohesion, let alone support foreign wars.

In fact, European opinion was to hold somewhat later that the United States stood to suffer a costly defeat in its war against Mexico. Clearly, it was felt, the Mexicans must have retained some of the warlike traits that had made the Spanish infantry the terror of sixteenth-century Europe; in the southern states, the black slaves, it was thought, would probably rise against their masters; on the western frontier, the Indians would revolt; on the Pacific coast north of California, the English could be expected to take advantage of the situation and further expand their sovereignty. None of this happened.

Between 1860 and 1865, the United States fell prey to a bloody and costly civil war. The victorious North emerged from this confrontation with impressive military power, but this was soon dismantled. In 1879 the United States Navy was inferior to Chile's; at the time Chile was proving the value of its "European-style" navy by easily winning its War of the Pacific against Peru and Bolivia.

During this period, the United States was mainly a producer of agricultural and mineral raw materials. It participated in world commerce mainly by trading these raw materials for manufactured goods and by encouraging foreign investment, the very same situation that today is alleged to be sufficient cause for Latin America's underdevelopment.

However, by 1898 the United States had launched new naval units in record time and destroyed the Spanish Navy in Cuba and the Philippines. From 1904 to 1914 the United

States completed the Panama Canal, which had been abandoned as hopeless by Ferdinand de Lesseps. In 1917, it was United States intervention that sealed the defeat of the Central European powers in the First World War. Until 1923, no American had won a Nobel Prize in physics or medicine, but since then North Americans, or European residents of the United States, have won one Nobel Prize in physics out of three, one out of five in chemistry, and one out of four in medicine. This scientific primacy, coupled with the country's industrial and financial power, led to building the first atomic reactor, and to landing the first man on the moon.

But what is most striking, and certainly most significant in the context of our time, is the spectacular rise of North American agricultural production. With only six percent of the population engaged in farming, the United States both meets its own food requirements and exports food on a world scale.

My purpose in giving this summary has not been to begin to explain the success of the North Americans or to provide a complete list of their achievements, but to underline a point that Europeans, Asians, or Africans may tend to overlook, which is the profound humiliation this North American success constitutes for the other America, still unable to provide itself, or the outside world, with an acceptable rationale for its own failure, which, compared to the success of these formidable northern neighbors, appears even greater than it actually is.

A Conservative Revolution

The first signs of this prodigious North American development could not but strike some eighteenth-century observers. We know that, at the start, liberal-minded Europeans and Latin Americans felt sympathy with the "home of the liberal and republican revolution"—a feeling perhaps comparable, *mutatis mutandis*, to the kind of favorable prejudice from which the U.S.S.R., "home of the socialist revolution," benefited in the first quarter century of its existence. These observers and analysts prayed for the triumph of the young North American republic, while their conservative opponents hoped to see it fail, or at least regress to a less radical and revolutionary bent.

But those who thought the United States inclined to upset the balance of the world proved mistaken. No doubt Virgil's dictum *"Novus Ordo Seclorum"* appears on the reverse side of the Great Seal of the United States: a new order had made its appearance for the coming centuries, a new golden age. But the North American millenarian kingdom was from the start sensible, rational, pragmatic, moderate in all but its ambition. One might say the new republic was *born conservative*.

From the myth of the New World the North Americans drew the optimism, the faith that they could construct a better society than that of Europe, one in which social equality and equal opportunities would be granted to all; in which all those rights of man would prevail which the liberal mind had proclaimed as *natural:* life, liberty, and the pursuit of happiness. They had the hope—and later they themselves supplied the proof—that the United States could be successful. And not for any reasons of predestination, but because the new republic should be able to grow untrammeled by the customs and privileges that constricted European society, with its oppressive and rigid political, social, and economic structures.

From the birth of the new nation, its government was to be dominated by one idea that stood in opposition to the radicalism of a Samuel Adams, and later to the Jacobin influences of the French Revolution: the idea that the new republic should maintain, develop, and improve the society that preceded the Revolution, not destroy it. Some of the North American revolutionary leaders feared that the people might be carried away by revolutionary rhetoric and come to threaten the colonies' basic institutions. But these fears proved unfounded. The extremist trends manifest in Paris after 1792 awakened far more echoes among certain leaders in North America than among the people. This may have been because of their English political background, but, whatever the reason, from this time onward the people of the United States displayed a definite appreciation of the value of political procedures that have been born of experience and consecrated by custom and tradition, along with a commendable suspicion of and opposition to the idealistic utopian schemes put forward by devotees of the Déesse Raison, founded on the contention that man is naturally good, and corrupted only by society.

What is most pertinent for our purposes is that, since the start of the North American experiment, the strength of the law was viewed *in itself* as such an important asset, such a successful conquest over the arbitrariness to which all government naturally tends, that it was considered altogether wiser to support an imperfect law, or even a bad one, than to demand its abrogation or reform by an autocratic decree or an act of revolutionary violence.

Francisco de Miranda's United States

The first Latin American to visit and study this creative and conservative society was a man of considerable culture, remarkable intelligence, and great curiosity, a careful observer who recorded in his diary all he did and saw.

Francisco de Miranda was born in Caracas, Venezuela, in 1750. He served as an officer in the Spanish troops that had a role in the United States War of Independence. As he also fought in the French Revolution[2] and, appropriately, in the struggle for Latin-American independence, his is the only case on record of a man who actively took part in the three great revolutions that occurred between 1776 and 1824.

Miranda's position in the Spanish Army had become untenable in 1783, no doubt owing to his advocacy of the Spanish American emancipation. On June 1, 1783, he secretly sailed out of Havana, giving up all hope of ever setting foot on Spanish soil again except with sword in hand.[3] One week later, he landed in the United States and set out on a protracted journey from South Carolina to New England. He stayed in the United States until 1784.

Miranda's diary during those years is a document of exceptional interest.[4] The United States' Declaration of Independence had shaken the Spanish American empire,[5] and had served to awaken in the Creole caste the contradictory emotions to which I have referred. By a fortunate coincidence, the

2. Miranda fought at Valmy and became a general in the revolutionary armies. His name is engraved on the Arch of Triumph in Paris. He sat among the Girondins, and just barely managed to escape the vindictiveness of Fouquier-Tinville.
3. He did not return to Spanish soil until 1806, landing in Venezuela at the head of a revolutionary expedition.
4. English translations of Miranda include the following: *The diary of Francisco de Miranda: Tour of the United States, 1783–84,* trans. and ed. William Spence Robertson, New York, The Hispanic Society of New York, 1928; and *The New Democracy in America: Travels of Francisco de Miranda in the United States, 1783–84,* trans. Judson P. Wood, ed. John S. Enzell, Norman, Okla., University of Oklahoma Press, 1963. Translations given here are my own.—TRANS.
5. In 1811, the Venezuelan Congress, having to set a date for the country's declaration of independence, chose the same date as the United States' Independence Day thirty-five years earlier. Only adminstrative difficulties caused its postponement to July 5.

man who was perhaps the best suited to be the Creole witness to those North American events was to travel through the United States and would leave us notebooks full of relevant, detailed observations on practically every aspect of daily life in the young republic.

From his first contact, Miranda noted that North Americans are "extremely robust and corpulent," which he unhesitatingly ascribed to their eating well.[6] At his first American barbecue, Miranda observed that "the very first magistrates and people of note ate and drank with the common folk, passing the plate around, and drinking out of the same glass. A more purely democratic assembly could not be imagined. America incarnates all that our poets and historians imagined about the mores of the free peoples of ancient Greece."

In Charleston, South Carolina, he attended a court session, which was open to the public, according to the English custom, and commented: "I cannot express the satisfaction I felt watching the workings of the admirable system of the British Constitution. God forgive me: but what a contrast to the system now current in Spain!" The government of the State of South Carolina also met with his admiration because it was "altogether democratic, as are all the States," with separate and distinct executive, legislative, and judiciary branches.

He was surprised to disembark in Philadelphia "without ceremony or registration formalities." Pondering on the North Americans' ability to make and build things, he reminisced about Benjamin Franklin, inventor of a "new stove, which produces more heat with one third the coal or wood normally required." He commented on the "famous shaving soap sold under Franklin's name," on the lightning rod, et cetera. Arriving at an inn to spend the night, he remarked that it was "the best I have known . . . for cleanliness, the quality of the food, punctuality, and for plain honest dealing." The town's market was "the best, the cleanest, and the best supplied of

6. Nowadays we no longer recognize this commonplace: underdeveloped nations were suffering from malnutrition well before comparison with more fortunate nations made their underdevelopment evident to the world. The noble savage has always suffered from a lack of protein. At a time when ideas were clearer and plain talk more common than they are today, there was no reason not to point out that the European and Semitic peoples stood apart from all others in their ability to domesticate and raise large herds of cattle. Thus they were able to partake of "a plentiful meat and milk diet, and the salutary effect of this diet on the following generations explains the more rapid development of these two human groups." (Friedrich Engels, *The Origin of the Family, Private Property, and the State*, 1884, in Karl Marx and Friedrich Engels, *Selected Works*, Moscow, Foreign Language Publishing House, 2 vols., vol. 2, pp. 172–73.)

any I have seen." He admired the absolute freedom of religion for which Philadelphia had been famous ever since its founding by William Penn. In general, he declared Philadelphia to be "one of the most pleasant and best-governed cities in the world."

On the Advantages of a Free Government

Miranda was only displaying common sense when he attributed the virtues and the prosperity he observed in North American society, not to any abuse of power over other nations (impossible at any rate for the fledgling government), but simply to "the advantages of a free government over any form of despotism"—something that "very few Frenchmen or Spaniards familiar with the United States are able to discern, not having been penetrated by the wonderful secrets of the British Constitution."

On his way from Philadelphia to New York, he stopped to admire the landscape and the prosperity of New Jersey, "the pleasant appearance and the strength of its inhabitants . . . the degree of development and the activity of the farming community. It would be hard to find a corner or plot on which no house stands . . . and I can say that I have never met a man who seemed ill-dressed, hungry, sick, or unemployed. . . . The land, as we see it, is divided . . . into small plots called *farms*. As a result the land is far better cultivated and the density of houses—houses of simple appearance, it is true—is far greater than in other countries."[7] And yet, "it must be said the soil is extremely poor and sandy; but it is watered and tended by hard-working farmers. This fact, and the fact that the people are governed by an independent government, has led them to riches even in the face of harsh nature."

From New York, Miranda took a tour to West Point. He reached this fortified area and stopped at an inn "without anyone's checking or inquiring about the newly arrived strangers. Surely this is one of the pleasantest aspects of living in a free country. How many formalities would we have to comply with in France, Germany, or elsewhere, before being admitted." He went on to admire the famous chain that had been slung across the Hudson River during the War of Independence to keep out ships, a chain whose links, he says, were "of the usual

7. For example, in slave-holding regions such as Cuba or South Carolina.

shape but on a scale such that I cannot guess how it can be held above the water . . . without the tides' breaking it at flow or ebb. . . . This mechanical device bears witness to the daring and the industry of the people who created it. It is said to be worth seventy thousand pounds, and I have no doubt that it would have cost more to the King of Spain, but I think [the North Americans] must have managed to forge it at a tenth of that price."

On his way back to New York, he was told an anecdote "worth being immortalized." It seems that during the war, near King's Ferry, on the Hudson, "A farmer who owned the land on which Rochambeau's troops were encamped asked for his rent. The French officers paid no attention to this 'absurd claim.' Seeing this, this *republican clodhopper* cut short any further discussion and went off to fetch the Sheriff, asking him to arrest the trespasser. Your Excellency should imagine the arrival of these two poor countrymen—the plaintiff and the Sheriff—unarmed but strong in the support of the Law, and resolved to arrest the French General, M. de Rochambeau, in front of all his troops. . . . The General was duly summoned by the Sheriff and required to pay his due (all of ten or fifteen pesos). So ended the affair." Miranda adds: "How, in such a country, could desert land fail to bloom; how could the shiest and most timorous of men fail to turn honest, just, hard-working, educated, and courageous." He might have added: and how could such men fail, in a short time, to become *powerful?*

Two Nations Compared

From New York Miranda went on to New England. He recorded one of his most meaningful observations in Providence, Rhode Island. He had been taken to see a mine equipped with a kind of pump, a "machine to evacuate water by evaporation, invented and built by a Mr. Joseph Brown. The cylinder must measure some two feet by ten; it is of iron and had been cast by Mr. Brown himself. With the use of this machine, water from three hundred feet below the surface can be pumped out at a rate of a hundred gallons a minute. What a difference in the character of these two nations! In Mexico, or in any of our colonies in Spanish America, there is no such machine, there is nothing to compare to it. Thus our richest gold and silver

mines are readily lost to us. Here such a machine is invented
to draw water from a mine producing only iron. . . ."

In Boston, Miranda marveled at this society that viewed as
permissible all that was not expressly forbidden by law, a society that trusted the truth of all statements unless proven
false. His luggage arrived, and he remarked that the customs
officials let him through without even opening his trunks, "on
my simple assurance that they did not contain any commercial
goods."[8]

Near Salem, Massachusetts, he made observations similar to
those he recorded in New Jersey: "The soil seems poor and is
poor. Farming consists mostly of pasture grazing, corn, and
rye. But such is the industrious spirit with which freedom fills
these people that a small plot of land allows them to feed their
large families, pay heavy taxes, and live well and pleasantly, a
thousand times happier than the slave-owning landlords of
rich mines and fertile lands in Mexico, Peru, Buenos Aires,
Caracas, and all the Spanish American world."

These homely truths, describing the reasons for the United
States' prosperity and subsequent power, and antedating the
onset of that country's relations with Latin America, are ignored nowadays in favor of complicated explanations based on
a causal connection between the wealth of the one half of the
hemisphere and the poverty of the other. Such explanations
attribute the poverty of Latin America to Yankee exploitation
—which is said to be the main cause, perhaps the *only* cause,
of their progress and our want. Anyone who still wishes to read
Miranda's words today must do so in utmost privacy, for no
one refers to his writing publicly any longer. The fact is that
an age that thrives on myths would be bewildered by an explanation as clear, as simple, as obviously true as Miranda's—an
explanation given by one of Spanish America's great men, one
of its great heroes.

8. In Venezuela, and probably still in many other countries that were
once part of the Spanish American empire, there still exists today, even
on the most modern highways, the institution of *alcabala*. This toll tax
on individuals and goods has survived since the Middle Ages. A driver
who is going at a normal and realistic speed of, say, eighty kilometers
per hour is suddenly obliged by a signal to slow down to five kilometers,
then to submit to a hostile gaze by a soldier armed with a machine gun.
These *alcabalas* existed long before the *guerrilleros'* insurrection in the
1960's, housed in permanent buildings erected alongside the highways
specifically for that purpose. The practice naturally survived the *guerrilleros* and still exists in Venezuela today, under a democratic government that is respectful of civil rights but, as we can see, helpless or blind
before this fossil survival of feudalism, absolutism, and mercantilism.

Yankee Imperialism

I am not denying the reality of North American imperialism in Latin America. But this imperialism was the result, not the cause, of North America's strength and our weakness, and our opposition to it should not keep us from understanding its causes: even theft should be understood as compounded of the victim's helplessness and the thief's strengths.

Spanish America had practically achieved independence by 1822. The weakness of the new republics, their vulnerability, and their utter lack of preparation for self-determination were all too clear to contemporary observers, including North Americans.

The United States had followed with sympathy an emancipation struggle so obviously inspired by their own example, one that based its legitimacy on the same principles. Henry Clay was speaking for his country as a whole when he expressed his emotion before "the glorious spectacle of eighteen millions of people struggling to burst their chains and be free."[9] But statesmen in Washington were concerned with the demise of the Spanish empire, which they no longer had reason to fear, and with the appearance of a sizable power vacuum in the hemisphere.

The foreign power that most worried the Americans was understandably Great Britain. The United States had just been at war with England. The British had seized and burned Washington on August 24, 1814. George Canning, who became England's Foreign Secretary in 1822, is still viewed today as a friend by Latin-American historians because of his deep interest in the dissolution of the Spanish empire in America, and because, in 1825, under his influence, England was the first great power to give recognition to the new republics. In private, Canning explained his interest: "Spanish America is free, and if we do not mismanage our affairs sadly, she is English."[10]

The United States Discovers Latin America: The Monroe Doctrine

But in 1823, France invaded Spain on behalf of the Holy Alliance, in order to rid Europe of the liberal constitution imposed

9. Quoted in Samuel Eliot Morison, *The Oxford History of the American People*, New York, Mentor, 1965, p. 411.
10. *Ibid.*, p. 418.

on Ferdinand VII of Spain not long before. The whole world expected France to follow up by landing in Spanish America, on the pretext of restoring the sovereignty of the King of Spain. This convinced the North Americans and the British that they shared the same strategic interests. In October 1823 the British consulted Washington on the possibility of concerted acts, so that the world's foremost naval power and the Western Hemisphere's only power could join forces to bar the way to French expansion. President Monroe and his Secretary of State, John Quincy Adams, assisted by ex-Presidents Jefferson and Madison, cleverly eluded the proposal, but took good note of the fact that Great Britain stood ready to interpose its navy between France and the Latin-American republics. The result was the Monroe Doctrine, inserted as a unilateral declaration of intention in the President's yearly State of the Union address to Congress, on December 2, 1823. The operative clauses are as follows: "The American continents, by the free and independent condition which they have assumed and maintain, are henceforth not to be considered as subjects for future colonization by any European powers. . . . The political system of the allied powers is essentially different . . . from that of America. . . . We should consider any attempt on their part to extend their system to any portion of this hemisphere as dangerous to our peace and safety. . . .

"With the existing colonies or dependencies of any European power we have not interfered and shall not interfere."[11]

Reaction among the Spanish Americans was one of joyous enthusiasm. Francisco Santander, Vice President of Great Colombia, expressed his country's unanimous feeling when he commented in 1824:

"Such a policy [the Monroe Doctrine], in itself heartening for mankind, can give Colombia a powerful ally in case its independence and its liberty are threatened by the allied powers [the Holy Alliance]." Only Bolívar seems to have felt some reservations: "The United States, which seem destined by providence to burden Latin America with trouble in the name of freedom . . ."

Pan-Americanism

By the 1890's, the North Americans had achieved control over all their territory, including that which they had wrested from

11. *Ibid.*, p. 414.

Mexico in 1846. Overflowing with energy and resources, they now looked abroad for new fields of action.

Latin America, in return, had watched with interest the extraordinary progress being made by the United States. With some exceptions, the ruling classes as yet felt no reservations toward the "Yankees"; rather, they were prey to "Nordomania," a blind and excessive admiration for anything North American, which manifested itself in formal imitation of North American federalist constitutional thinking. In 1889, the Latin-American governments had welcomed the North American government's intention of forming a "Pan-American Union," with its seat in Washington, based on the Monroe Doctrine— that is to say, on an assumed community of interests between all the American countries governed along republican lines, with North American power guaranteeing security for all.

The superiority and hegemony of the "great northern democracy" was tacitly, and sometimes even openly, recognized. One of Latin America's foremost poets, the Nicaraguan Rubén Darío, composed a hymn of sorts, "Saluting the Eagle," to this Pan-Americanism, so vastly different from that imagined by Bolívar:

Be welcome, magical Eagle with your vast and powerful wings!
Come and cover the South with your great continental shadow,
In your claws in which rubies shine, bring us a palm of glory
      bearing the colors of limitless hope
And in your beak the olive branch of a long, fertile peace.

Sure of yourself, you have striven over the world's conquests.
Sure of yourself, you have had to bear the antique arrow.
If your open wings forever proffer peace,
Your claws and your beak are ready for necessary wars.

E pluribus unum! Glory, victory, work!
Give us the secrets of the hard-working North
And may our sons, forsaking the Latin heritage
Learn tenacity, vigor, strength of soul from the Yankees.
Tell us, illustrious Eagle, how to become a multitude.

Eagle: behold the Condor. He is your brother of the heights.
The Andes know him and know that, like yourself, he fixes the
      sun in flight.

May this grand Union have no end![12] Says the poet,
May you in fulfillment unite your brotherly efforts.

Eagle, I salute you!

May the Latin American countries receive your magical influx. . . ."

12. In English in the Spanish poem.

The Spanish-American War and the Panama Canal

The Spanish-American War of 1898 was a victory by the United States over Spain, the bane of Spanish American schoolbook history. This war gave Cuba its independence, and replaced the Spanish rule of Puerto Rico—outdated, lazy, and corrupt—with the careful, modern, and efficient administration of the North Americans.

Victory gave the United States the sense of being a great world power. Having seized the Philippines, they set their minds on realizing the project that yellow fever and malaria had forced Ferdinand de Lesseps to abandon: a canal to be cut through the Isthmus of Panama, linking the Atlantic and Pacific oceans. In 1903, Theodore Roosevelt decided to complete the canal at any cost.

At that time, Panama was not an independent republic but a province of Colombia, from which it was, and still is, separated by an impenetrable, malaria-infested tropical jungle. Roosevelt started negotiations with Colombia, but the Colombian Congress rejected the treaty he proposed (a version almost identical to the one that was later accepted by Panama). A few days after this rejection, Panama declared itself an independent republic, and North American warships had no trouble dissuading Colombia from any opposition to the *fait accompli*. Washington recognized the new government, and two weeks later Panama reciprocated by ceding to the United States a strip of land ten miles wide (and not sixteen kilometers: even in this detail Panama had to comply). Over the Canal Zone the United States would have not only the right of control, but also perpetual sovereignty. In exchange, Panama received ten million dollars and an annual rent of two hundred and fifty thousand dollars.

The particulars of this sordid affair have been thoroughly studied and require no further discussion here. Nor shall I go into the details of the impressive North American achievement: yellow fever was entirely, and malaria almost entirely, eliminated; the canal was completed in ten years. The first ship passed through it on August 15, 1914, just two weeks after the First World War began, a war during which the whole world was to benefit from American power.

The canal has proved of immense benefit to the international community. In 1971, for example, 14,617 ships, totaling over 121 million tons, passed through it. No doubt the North Americans benefited most by far. A study of this particular case sheds much light on the nature of imperialism, providing us with some helpful observations on a problem whose discussion is usually complicated by the intrusion of emotional elements. Seldom is modern imperialism discussed in a manner free of political bias. The very considerable and excessive profits of imperialist power are invariably exaggerated, as if there were any need for such exaggeration, while the benefits of the imperialist arrangements to the vassalized state are overlooked; yet those benefits are real enough, even if smaller than they rightfully ought to be.

The taxes levied by the canal authorities have been kept artificially low and thus have benefited maritime trade. Since seventy percent of all transit is by ships originating from, or bound for, a North American port, the United States is the main beneficiary. For a single year, 1970, the indirect savings to the North American economy were set at several hundred million dollars by the United Nations Economic Commission for Latin America. We might add that from 1914 to 1970 the U.S. Navy saved a sum estimated at over eleven billion dollars, thanks to the canal.

Other nonquantifiable advantages have accrued to the United States from their absolute sovereignty over the Canal Zone. The Smithsonian Institution was enabled to set up a research base on an island in Gatun Lake; a military center for the study of antiguerrilla tactics was established within the Zone, providing special training for officers of Latin-American armies.

But the Republic of Panama has equally derived benefits from the canal, which, though justifiably considered too small, deserve to be mentioned. It may be unpalatable, but the truth is that had it not been for the canal, Panama would never have existed as a republic. The canal might very well have been dug in Nicaragua, which was a possibility raised in alternative American studies. Had this happened, Panama would still be what it was in 1903: the most backward, the poorest, the unhealthiest, the most forsaken province of the republic of Colombia. If we Latin Americans were to be consistent in our censure of the United States on the subject of Panama, we would have to start by proposing the return of Panama to Colombia. This, however, is unthinkable, and though Panamanians would be the last to admit it, they are, all things considered, under some obligation to Theodore Roosevelt.

Secondly, it is obvious that the economic advantages Panama derives from the canal are not limited to the yearly payment mentioned above. The figure has since been progressively increased and now amounts to the sum—still absurdly low—of two million dollars a year. Since 1972, Panama has understandably refused to accept this figure and has been demanding a less humiliating treaty. But there are other, very substantial advantages that Panama derives from the canal. In 1971, the balance of trade with the Canal Zone was one hundred and fifty million dollars, in favor of Panama. In summary, it may be said that everything that constitutes present-day Panama, good and bad alike, stems from the radical change that occurred in the Isthmus in 1903, through a process of change that the North Americans initiated and developed for reasons of self-interest, but that has brought enormous improvements and better options for Panama itself.

It is easy, however, to see how Panama has reached its current state of exasperation. The first cause lies in the unacceptable terms of the treaty of 1903, which gives the United States "perpetual" sovereignty over the Canal Zone. Another source of irritation is the conspicuous contrast between the life styles and the standards of living of Panamanians and North Americans. Other Latin-American countries *know* that the annual per-capita income in the United States is over $5,000, but the Panamanians *see* it. That their own average income stands at approximately $700—as compared to the $150 or $200 they would have had without the canal—is no consolation to them. Daily they must witness the insolent wealth of the North Americans in their midst, the conspicuous consumption, which goes far beyond any displayed in the United States. Except for the Panamanians who cross the border to look for work (and find only poorly paid jobs), no one in the Canal Zone knows poverty, and there are no slums like those in the continental United States. The Canal Zone as a whole is a kind of display case, a splendid zoo housing fauna that includes some of the least attractive specimens of North American society.

The "Roosevelt Corollary"

In the viewpoint not only of Panama but of the whole of Latin America as well, the most painful aspect of the canal situation is that it marked the beginning of North American military intervention in the Caribbean, and became, in the half century to follow, the cause of frequent "Yankee" meddling in the area, with or without the help of the Marine Corps.

The Latin Americans

The canal provided the occasion for two pronouncements of Theodore Roosevelt's that Latin Americans still feel as a personal affront: "I took Panama" and "Speak softly, and carry a big stick, you will go far."[13] Teddy Roosevelt's big stick was to become the symbol of the United States' abuse of power in Latin America.

And Roosevelt is not remembered only for these two blunt statements. In his 1904 message to Congress, he formulated the "Roosevelt Corollary" to the Monroe Doctrine:

"Chronic wrongdoing, or an impotence which results in a general loosening of the ties of civilized society . . . may force the United States, however reluctantly, in flagrant cases of such wrongdoing, or impotence, to the exercise of an international police power."[14]

The meaning is clear. The Monroe Doctrine had been formulated in order to prevent European exploitation of the weakness of the Spanish American republics. A number of excuses already, and almost inevitably, existed for the European establishment of bases in the hemisphere; given the power vacuum in the area, these were now even more pressing. At the time of the digging of the canal, the republics bordering on the Caribbean had fallen into a state of vulnerability and chronic disorder unimaginable in 1824, giving serious grounds for European intervention: how could these republics hope to guarantee the life and property of foreign residents, or the repayment of foreign debts? The United States resolved not to allow a repetition of what they had had to witness in Venezuela in 1902, when German, British, and Italian warships cruised off the Venezuelan shore, under the pretext of enforcing the settlement of debts, while the North Americans stood by. They also remembered bitterly their impasse in 1863, when, embroiled in civil war, they were unable to act in Mexico; Juarez's curtailment of the settlement of foreign debts led to the establishment of a shadow empire under the Hapsburg prince Maximilian, under French auspices.

The Roosevelt Corollary was first applied in 1905. Certain European powers, headed by Germany, were threatening to intervene in the Dominican Republic to recover old debts. Washington moved in and had an American commissioner take over the Dominican customs and distribute fifty-five percent of its tariffs in repayment of the foreign debts, with the

13. Quoted in Morison, *Oxford History of American People,* p. 826.
14. *Ibid.,* p. 823.

United States underwriting repayment of the remaining forty-five percent to the Dominican treasury.

The Marines in the Caribbean

From 1905 to 1965, there were no fewer than twenty Marine landings in Caribbean countries; they often resulted in the establishment of dictators reared under North American tutelage. One such intervention, in the Dominican Republic, lasted from 1916 to 1924. When the Marines left, Rafael Leonidas Trujillo Molina, commander of a national guard created and carefully trained by the United States, took power and held it for twenty-eight years, from 1930 to 1938 and again from 1942 to 1962.

The Marines were in Nicaragua almost continuously from 1912 to 1933. The Commander of the Nicaraguan National Guard, in the service of the United States, was Anastasio Somoza. His dictatorship ended with his assassination in 1956, but he left behind such an effective system of control that his family has been able to maintain itself in the presidency through the present day.

These are the best known, or, so to speak, the classic examples. From the time of its decision to complete the canal until the strategic revolution represented by the ICBM (intercontinental ballistic missiles), the Polaris submarines, and their Soviet counterparts—innovations that rendered the canal virtually indefensible—the United States strictly adhered to its policy of not tolerating any situation in the Caribbean that might threaten its control of the seaways leading to the canal. This is the *main* reason for North American intervention in the Caribbean, a fact generally ignored in Latin America, where it is agreed that the main (if not the only) object of Marine landings was the protection of (supposedly) vital North American economic interests. Ignoring the primary cause of United States intervention allows critics of that country to take the next step and pin on these interventions the bulk of responsibility for the developmental lag of the countries involved. No one stops to remember the conditions in the Dominican Republic, Nicaragua, et cetera, *before* these interventions.

The United States has rightly been blamed for having tolerated or openly supported such dictators as Trujillo and

Somoza. But it would be wrong to infer that this style of leadership appealed to Woodrow Wilson or Franklin Roosevelt, whose governments supported it. No less misleading is the extrapolation that there must be a deep affinity between the North American political or economic system and the coercive regimes of the client states. When national security is at stake, nations, whatever their form of government, are not particularly scrupulous in choosing their means of protecting it; the American democracy, in fact, may perhaps show greater concern than other countries because of the nature of its institutions.[15]

The point was clearly stated by Henry Stimson, Ambassador to Nicaragua in 1927 and later Secretary of State and War under Hoover and Franklin Roosevelt, respectively:

". . . there are certain geographical considerations which impose upon us a very special interest as to how certain ones of these nations fulfill the responsibilities which go with sovereignty and independence. I refer to those Central American nations whose territory lies adjacent to and in a naval sense commands the great sea route from our Eastern to our Western States via the Caribbean Sea and the Panama Canal.

"This situation does not arise out of the Monroe Doctrine but from certain broad principles of self-defense which govern the policy of the United States, as well as of all other nations which are in any way dependent upon the sea. These principles in part underlie the Monroe Doctrine, although they were not at all created by it. They bear a very much closer and more tangible relation to what I may call, for lack of a better name, our Isthmian policy than they do to the Monroe Doctrine itself. . . .

"Out of this principle of national self-preservation follows the corollary of our interest in the stability of the independent governments resting along the borders of the Caribbean and the Eastern Pacific. If those independent governments do not adequately fulfill the responsibility of independence; if they fail to safeguard foreign life within their borders; if they repudiate lawful debts to foreign creditors; if they permit the confiscation within their borders of lawful foreign property—then, under the common usages of international life, the foreign nations whose citizens and property are thus endangered

15. The world has witnessed with astonishment how the North American political system allows publicity to be given not only to such documents as the "Pentagon Papers" relating to the Vietnam War, but even to the ultrasecret operations of the CIA. What other world power ever proceeded in this way?

are likely to intervene in Central America for the legitimate protection of such rights. History clearly shows that such intervention often leads to continuing control.

"The failure therefore of one of these republics to maintain the responsibilities which go with independence may lead directly to a situation imperiling the vital interest of the United States in its sea-going route through the Panama Canal. . . .

". . . if we will not permit European nations to protect their customary rights within this zone, we must, to a certain extent, make ourselves responsible for this protection. . . .

It follows that "our policy toward this great sea route through the Canal does not rest upon any attitude of mind which is peculiar to us; it is simply the application of principles and policy which would govern any other nation in a similar situation."[16]

The most recent intervention of the United States Marines in the area was in 1965, in the Dominican Republic. This was motivated by political, not by military, considerations: Washington was concerned with preventing a "second Cuba." The action appears in retrospect as a Pavlovian reflex; in Talleyrand's words, it was worse than a crime; it was a mistake. The Soviet Union has no need of a second client state in the Caribbean. And even if it had been Colonel Caamaño's intention to implant a second "Castroist" regime in Santo Domingo, such an event would have given more headaches to Fidel and the Russians than to the North Americans.

The "Good Neighbor Policy"

Anyone who thinks that the United States' Vietnam involvement was their first confrontation with the moral dilemmas of international power is forgetting history. In the twenties, "Get the Marines out of Nicaragua" was one of the slogans of the conscience-stricken North American liberals. In 1928, hardly one year after the publication of Stimson's book, the Department of State produced a memorandum proclaiming that the Roosevelt Corollary was "unjustified by the terms of the Monroe Doctrine, however much it was justified by the application of the doctrine of self-preservation."[17]

16. *American Policy in Nicaragua*, New York, Scribner, 1927, pp. 104–11. Reprinted by permission.
17. Quoted in George Pendle, *A History of Latin America*, London, Penguin, 1973, pp. 183–84.

The Latin Americans

In 1933, in his inaugural address, Franklin Roosevelt launched the "Good Neighbor Policy," by which the United States undertook to "respect the rights of others."[18] Such a declaration at such a time clearly showed that the American public was disgusted with the practical consequences of the Corollary. It also showed that the Americans had not quite forgotten Jefferson's formulation of the convictions of the founding fathers:

"We surely cannot deny to any nation that the right whereon our own government is founded—that every one may govern itself according to whatever form it pleases, and change these forms at its own will; and that it may transact its business with foreign nations through whatever organ it thinks proper, whether King, convention, assembly, committee, president, or anything else it may choose. The will of the nation is the only thing essential to be regarded."[19]

Woodrow Wilson evolved a puritan version of the Roosevelt Corollary—a way of thinking with which Europeans were to become more familiar at the Conference of Versailles—when he argued that it would be immoral to recognize governments come to power by unconstitutional means. In 1931, Secretary of State Henry Stimson, whose analysis of the Corollary I have quoted, rejected such an interpretation while justifying the recognition of regimes such as Trujillo's or Somoza's: "The present administration has refused to follow the policy of Mr. Wilson and has followed [the policy of Jefferson]. As soon as it was reported to us, through our diplomatic representatives, that the new governments in Bolivia, Peru, Argentina, Brazil, and Panama were in control of the administrative machinery of the State, with the apparent acquiescence of their people, and that they were willing and apparently able to discharge their international and conventional obligations, they were recognized by our government."[20]

But how does the "will of a nation" adequately manifest itself? From the philosophical viewpoint here is one subject on which men never have agreed, and never will agree. The simplest answer, implicit in Stimson's views and absent from Jefferson's optimistic idealism, consists in admitting that the "national will" is manifest in any government that reaches power, and succeeds in maintaining itself and in controlling the state. This supposes that nations necessarily give them-

18. Quoted in Pendle, p. 184.
19. Quoted in Pendle.
20. Quoted in Pendle, p. 185.

selves the government they deserve, if not the government they want. The trouble with this reasoning is that nations do not exist in a vacuum, but are caught up in the web of power relations spun between the existing power centers; thus the rise or ruin of a government, the stability or destruction of a tyrant, of a demagogue, or of a democratic ruler, may depend on causes far more subtle than outright armed intervention.

"Destabilization"

In Latin America, and especially in the Caribbean, Washington continues to count on the Latin Americans themselves to interfere indirectly and discreetly with regimes that do not meet with their approval. There are many obvious reasons why the warmest traditional partisans of North American nonintervention in Latin America are invariably the established governments, of whatever side. Indeed, *governments* are remarkably unanimous in this respect. But in each Latin-American country, opponents of the government (or potential opponents within government ranks) must invariably be reckoned with; they are ready to risk anything to get to the top, or to overthrow the current administration. And these elements are ready to accept or invite the intervention, the help, or at least the active neutrality of the United States.

Even the legendary Antonio López de Santa Anna, hero of Mexico and intermittently its President during the early years of the nation's independence, took advantage of his country's difficulties and accepted the complicity of the United States Army to return to power. This was in 1847, when Commander Winfield Scott had surrounded Mexico City but allowed Santa Anna to cross North American lines, to help overthrow the beleaguered Mexican government that so far had stood firm against United States demands for capitulation.

In this case, of course, the fact that American troops were directly involved makes the story particularly shocking. But many more documented examples come to mind the details of which were less blatant, but the ultimate result identical. Throughout, the Latin Americans tacitly accepted—or connived with—the kind of U.S. intervention that has become euphemistically known as "destabilization," discreet or indiscreet—action on the part of U.S. embassies, military missions, or the CIA (or those agencies that preceded it, which were equally "operational" organizations). Leaders as diverse as

Allende in Chile, Perón in Argentina, Trujillo in the Dominican Republic, Goulart in Brazil, Batista in Cuba, Arbenz in Guatemala, and Cipriano Castro in Venezuela, all fell victim to this kind of interference. And the list of Latin-American leaders and regimes that benefited from such meddling is equally disparate: Pinochet in Chile, the Argentine governments between 1956 and 1972, Juan Bosch in the Dominican Republic (himself subsequently "destabilized"), Joaquín Balaguer (Trujillo's ranking civilian supporter, rehabilitated thanks to Bosch's ineptness and his own shrewdness, three times elected President since 1966), the agents of the 1964 Brazilian military "revolution," Fidel Castro, Colonel Castillo Armas (a CIA puppet installed in Guatemala in 1954 to replace President Arbenz, who was suspected of being pro-Communist), Juan Vicente Gómez (Vice President under Cipriano Castro, and subsequently Venezuela's dictator from 1908 to 1935), and others.

The Principle of Nonintervention and Its Ambiguities

The sheer diversity of these cases points up one dilemma for both North and Latin Americans: however Washington reacts to a Latin-American crisis, its position will be a factor in determining the future course of events, even if it decides to stay strictly neutral. But Latin-American reaction to U.S. intervention has been somewhat unpredictable. When Trujillo was murdered, democrats throughout the hemisphere rejoiced; no one showed much concern over the fact that the CIA was almost certainly involved. Neither has the United States ever been thanked (or, for that matter, criticized) for having dropped Batista after he fell into disgrace. But a general outcry arose when Goulart met with the same fate, or when Allende was "destabilized"—it was forgotten how far he had gone in the liquidation of Chilean democracy, in opposition to the majority of his countrymen.

How are we to explain these ambiguities? It is not enough to rid ourselves of the bias inherent in the Marxist hypothesis on the evolution of history, its direction and purpose. The pattern of Latin-American reactions to North American initiative remains no less difficult to understand.

In 1948, the Latin-American states, exasperated by the practical consequences of the Roosevelt Corollary, obtained the

United States' formal agreement with the principle of non-intervention. This principle, incorporated into the Charter of the Organization of American States signed in Bogota at the Ninth Inter-American Conference, declared *inviolable* the territory of each member nation, and outlawed its occupation or any other use of force by any other nation, directly or indirectly, for any reason whatever.[21] In spite of this, during the Dominican crisis of 1964, two-thirds of the Latin-American nations sided with the United States and gave a sufficiently flexible interpretation to the principle of nonintervention to justify and authorize intervention when a country of the hemisphere was threatened by "internal aggression" (that is, stood in danger of falling under Communist domination).

It would be too easy to attribute this resolution, voted by the OAS, to pressure from the United States. Nor should the United States be held responsible for the doctrine of "ideological frontiers," which Brazil proposed around the same time to legitimize its possible military action against pro-Castro forces in Uruguay or Bolivia. The fact is that no power anywhere in the world, when beset by grave difficulties or on the verge of irretrievable breakdown, would turn down the proffered support of a friendly nation. The Hungarian and Czechoslovakian Communists and their Russian allies can bear witness to this.

Imperialism and Underdevelopment

One common outlook prevails in Latin America today, conditioned by Christianity, liberalism, and Marxism; it leads us all to strive for a freer, more equitable society, and we despair because we are still unable to solve the same old problems of stability and institutionalization. The nations of Latin America also share the expectation of rapid economic development

21. "Chapter III, *Article 15:* No State or group of States has the right to intervene, directly or indirectly, for any reason whatever, in the internal or external affairs of any other State. The foregoing principle prohibits not only armed force but also any other form of interference or attempted threat against the personality of the State or against its political, economic and cultural elements. *Article 16:* No State may use or encourage the use of coercive measures of an economic or political character in order to force the sovereign will of another State and obtain from it advantages of any kind. *Article 17:* The territory of a State is inviolable; it may not be the object, even temporarily, of military occupation or of other measures of force taken by another State, directly or indirectly, *on any grounds whatever.* No territorial acquisitions or special advantages obtained either by force or by other means of coercion shall be recognized." (Charter of the Organization of American States.)

common to all countries today; but their expectations have met with frustration, and for this frustration, they blame the United States.

No Latin American who pins the blame for his country's ills on North American imperialism need fear rebuttal. There is an almost general belief in Latin America today that the United States has siphoned off the wealth that could have led to the Southern Hemisphere's development. *They* are rich because *we* are poor; *we* are poor because *they* are rich. The argument is that, but for North American development, there would have been no Latin-American underdevelopment; that but for Latin-American underdevelopment, there would have been no North American development.

We should be wary of this "anti-imperialist" argument for the very reason that its acceptance is so widespread. These may be "revolutionary" slogans, but they are heard or read not only in the passwords of *guerrilleros,* the underground press, or the graffiti on city walls. They are also reflected in the pronouncements of the military who govern Peru, in the speeches of the autocratic President of Mexico, the oligarchic President of Colombia, the social-democratic President of Venezuela, the great dictator of Cuba, or the minor dictator of Panama. Arguments of this sort have become the official truth. I fear that by echoing this line of thought, we Latin Americans are starting on a new cycle in our self-delusion over the causes of our frustration. We are once again refusing to admit that the reasons for North American success and Latin-American failure are to be found in the qualities of North Americans and in the defects of Latin Americans.

A sincere, rational, scientific examination of North American influence on Latin America's destiny would have to dispense with prejudging the issue and keeping open the possibility that the United States' overall contribution may have been positive. On the debit side we would have to list all the harm derived from "Yankee" actions, and indeed from the United States' very existence as an overpowering neighbor. But on the credit side we would have to enumerate the positive contributions that neighbor has made to the global destiny of Latin America. If this were done candidly, I wonder whether we might not find that through some innate deficiencies in our own Latin-American society—deficiencies that are intrinsically our own and that antedate relations with the United States— we have failed to take advantage of all the United States had to offer.

Latin America and the United States

We owe to the United States the political and social doctrines and aspirations on which we pride ourselves. It has been noted with surprise that, for all its failures, Latin America has remained faithful to the ideals and principles of democracy; so much so that even the most tyrannical regimes make a point of retaining exemplary constitutions, at least formally, and that the imperatives of democracy have survived all upheavals. The reason lies in our unspoken attachment to the political idea of North America as a model, as the incarnation of the *American utopia*. This is literally true; the 1853 Constitution of Argentina, which is that country's pride, is so closely modeled on the United States Constitution that Argentine jurists, faced with problems of constitutional interpretation, have been known to refer to North American jurisprudence for precedents. As for our criticism of the darker aspects of North American society, such as racial discrimination, the excesses of consumerism, the disquieting power of the "military-industrial complex," what could that criticism draw on if not on the North Americans' criticism of themselves? And while we are busy echoing that North American self-criticism, are we not overlooking our own faults?

In recent years it has been primarily the North Americans who have provided the model and stimulus for our modernization and development.

And there is no doubt that, but for the existence of this great democratic power to the north, acting as guardian of the hemisphere—for reasons of its own, no doubt, but that is another matter—Latin America, like Asia and Africa, would have fallen prey to European colonialism in the nineteenth century, and later to the even harsher forms of imperialism we are witnessing today.

All this is forgotten, however, when it comes to formulating the causes of Latin America's economic and cultural lag, which is attributed unanimously to North America's influence.

We tend to forget that until the First World War, the main foreign economic and cultural presence in Latin America was by no means North American, but Spanish and, in the nineteenth century, British and French. These European countries were the principal trading partners of Latin America; their manufactured products, technology, and culture dominated us. But Europe's superior development does not trouble Latin Americans: Spain, it goes without saying, is ignored, and we do not feel that we are in competition with England, France, or Germany. Rather, by some trick of compensation within Latin-

American thought, we proudly see ourselves as heirs to the culture of Athens and Rome, as the American *extension* of Greco-Roman culture. The national superiority of the North Americans, however, offends us; we can reconcile ourselves to it only by attributing their advantages over us entirely to their exploitation of our Latin world.

A somewhat more sophisticated version of this thesis holds Spanish, British, French, and North American imperialism to be one single historical phenomenon, with each imperialist power in turn playing the villain's role on the South American scene. Thus, starting in 1492, a single story with a linear plot has unfolded itself. All this fits in with the myth of the noble savage and highhandedly ignores the sorry state that characterized Third World countries long before their insertion into Western culture.

Rereading Marx

Marx is the teacher and guide of those philosophers, sociologists, and economists who staunchly refuse to face the fact I have just stated. Yet Marx had some acute ideas on the subject. He did not write much about Latin America, which was of little interest to him, but he has left us analyses of what is now called the Third World that apply exactly to our subcontinent. Thus in 1853 he argued that the British presence and domination in India—which surely was not one of the more backward of non-Western countries—had a decisively positive influence on traditional Hindu society. It unsettled the patriarchal system and the patterns of village organization, as well as an economic system based on manual crafts, and it thus led to problems, controversies, and tensions that threw this society off balance to an unprecedented degree. Should this be interpreted as a "fall" from grace and beatitude that would otherwise still be intact? Not at all. Marx stressed that rural life in India was far less idyllic than was generally believed, for "we must not forget that these idyllic village communities, inoffensive though they may appear, had always been the solid foundation of Oriental despotism, that they restrained the human mind within the smallest possible compass, making it the unresisting tool of superstition, enslaving it beneath traditional rules, depriving it of all grandeur and historical energies. We must not forget the barbarian egotism which, concentrating on some miserable patch of land, had quietly witnessed the ruin of empires, the perpetration of unspeakable cruelties, the massacre of the population of large towns, with no other consideration bestowed upon them than on natural events, itself the helpless prey of any aggressor who deigned to notice it at all. We must not forget that this undignified, stagnatory, and vegetative life, that this passive sort of existence evoked on the other part, in contradistinction, wild, aimless, unbounded forces of destruction and rendered murder itself a religious rite in Hindustan. We must not forget that these little communities were contaminated by distinctions of caste, and by slavery, that they subjugated man to external circumstances instead of elevating man into the sovereign of circumstances, that they transformed a self-developing social state into never-changing natural destiny, and thus brought about a brutalizing worship of nature. . . . Arabs, Turks, Tartars, Moguls, who had successively overrun India, soon became Hindooized, the barbarian conquerors being, by the eternal law of history, conquered themselves by the superior civilization of their subjects. The British were the first conquerors superior, and therefore, inaccessible to Hindoo civilization."[22]

Marx went on to enumerate the several ways in which a *superior* culture, Western culture, could not help provoking a whole series of desirable transformations in India, thus launching progress of every kind in a region of the earth that was obviously backward and quite inferior to what it would doubtlessly become once it had been "annexed to the Western world" (Marx's words).

Marx stated that the following benefits had accrued to India, or were soon to accrue to India, thanks to the impact of the West: political unity; the recruitment and training of a native army; printing and freedom of expression, "introduced for the first time into Asiatic society"; the possibility of simple citizens' acquiring land (Marx viewed the princes' monopoly over land ownership as the worst blight in Asian society); Western-style education, whose consequences, already perceptible in 1853, were leading to the development of "a fresh class . . . endowed with the requirements for government and imbued

22. This and the following Marx quotes are from "The British Rule in India" and "The Future Results of British Dominion in India," two articles that Marx wrote in English for the New York *Daily Tribune* and that were printed in that newspaper's June 25 and August 8, 1853, issues, respectively. They are included in Karl Marx and Friedrich Engels, *Selected Works*, vol. 1, pp. 312–24.

with European science"; the telegraph; steam, "which has brought India into regular and rapid communication with Europe, has connected its chief ports with those of the whole south-eastern ocean, and has revindicated it from the isolated position which was the prime law of its stagnation"; irrigation; and finally a railroad network, which was to provide the springboard for modern industrial development, since "you cannot maintain a net of railways over an immense country without introducing all those industrial processes necessary to meet the immediate and current wants of railway locomotion, and out of which there must grow the application of machinery to those branches of industry not immediately connected with railways."

Let us transpose Marx's reasoning by analogy to Latin America—not to pre-Columbian America, the home of the noble savage (to which it would strictly apply), but to Spanish America of, say, the 1830's, prior to any North American economic influence. We will then find a succession of oligarchical republics—wretched, backward, disoriented, and oppressed by tyrants or civil wars. That these nations made progress during the period of Spanish control is unquestionable, for how else could they have produced a Bolívar, a Miranda, an Andrés Bello, a Sucre, a San Martín? Neither Marx nor anyone else could have doubted that this progress would be speeded up by the development of economic and cultural relations with Europe and the United States, as in fact proved to be the case.

The thesis that the Latin-American countries owe their social and economic backwardness and their political instability (hence their *underdevelopment*) to the negative effects of imperialism, especially North American imperialism, is clearly in contradiction with the facts. For example, the present rate of economic growth in Latin America is far superior to that in the advanced capitalist countries in the nineteenth century. The latter rate was approximately 2 percent a year, whereas that of Latin America from 1935 to 1953 was 4.2 percent annually, rising to 4.9 percent from 1945 to 1955.[23] With the new oil revenues of Venezuela, Ecuador, and Mexico, the rate of economic growth in Latin America has made another leap. The figure may be considered too low if it is compared to the present prosperity of the advanced industrial societies; and the problem is further complicated by an unequal distribution of

23. These figures have been provided by the United Nations Economic Commission for Latin America (ECLA).

the gains, by misadministration of available resources, and by the population explosion, which leaves considerable segments of the population in a marginal state and renders futile the overall GNP growth. But this does not allow us to shift the blame for our own inability to make proper use of our resources and opportunities to our relations with the United States and other advanced countries.

The Case of Puerto Rico

From the nineteenth century to 1914, Argentina, Chile, and Uruguay had closer contacts with Europe than any other South American countries, and they are still clearly the most advanced today. The same is true of Mexico, whose development has been very satisfactory, relatively speaking, doubtless because it is so near to the United States and because its economy is complementary to that of its northern neighbor. Similarly, Venezuela, but for the discovery and exploitation of its oil resources by the North Americans, the British, and the Dutch, would today still be on the level of development of Honduras. Instead, its economic, political, and social development has been remarkable. Venezuela was the promoter of OPEC (Organization of Petroleum Exporting Countries), and today it is hoping to use its generous supply of petrodollars to enable other Latin-American countries to secure higher prices for their raw materials on the world market, by withholding sales when conditions are unfavorable.

Puerto Rico is a special case. The island's economy is closely linked to that of the United States; it has been administered by the United States since 1898, first directly and then under a form of limited government autonomy in which Washington retains control of such delicate sectors as defense and foreign relations.

In 1898, Puerto Rico was at the same economic level as its neighbors, or perhaps even at a lower level; it has benefited from no providential boon of natural resources such as oil, copper, tin, or bauxite, yet the patent fact remains that its development has been quite extraordinary since that date, on a pattern distinct from that of any other country in the region. Its per-capita income now stands around $2,000, as compared to $100 for Haiti, and less than $400 for El Salvador, Guatemala, Honduras, and the Dominican Republic. Though these statistics speak for themselves, it is in Puerto Rico that we find the most extreme form of the bitterness and resentment that Latin Americans in general feel toward their northern neighbors.

To be a "revolutionary" in Puerto Rico means to dream of seeing the island turned into a second Cuba. It is considered proper for a Puerto Rican to sport the most ardent Hispanic nationalism, and to set himself up as the defender of all aspects of Spanish culture against the encroachments of the Yankee barbarians. I recall one Puerto Rican intellectual, a connoisseur of Spanish poetry, comfortably earning his living in San Juan in a job well suited to his culture and temperament. He owed all this to the peace imposed by North America, and yet he spoke as an arch-nationalist and a violent Yankee-baiter; and I could not help thinking how his peers in other Caribbean countries had been destroyed or driven to exile by tyrants ranging from Trujillo to Fidel Castro.

It is clear that Puerto Rico despises its situation and suffers from an acute case of the Latin-American complex. We can examine it as an extreme example and draw inferences applicable to the other Latin-American countries, in an effort to determine whether the United States has helped or hindered Latin America's development. One could argue that the question allows two contradictory, but equally plausible, replies. If we are concerned with political and social ideals and aims, and with the impetus given to their development, it is obvious that Latin Americans have benefited from the example of the United States, whatever may have been Washington's misuse of power, its clumsiness and exactions.

But there is another way of looking at the question. The most basic need of any society is probably the ability to live with itself, and to accept its position with respect to the rest of the world. In order to understand its own position, a society must face reality and must be able to act effectively on the basis of what it sees.

If the question is regarded from this angle, it becomes clear that we Latin Americans cannot refrain from endless unfavorable comparisons with our more successful northern neighbor unless we turn our backs on our inescapable coexistence with them. The comparison exasperates us, leads us to hide our head in the sand, to delude ourselves, and to invite others to delude us. We are ready to swallow any lie from outside if it helps soothe our humiliation.

Unrequited Love

The democratic prestige of our "good neighbor" Franklin D. Roosevelt, paired with the special world situation during the period of the rise of Nazism, assuaged our anti–North Americanism for some twenty years. Or, more exactly, this period served to strengthen the *love* element in the love-hate complex that characterizes our feelings toward the United States.

From the summer of 1941 onward, even the Communist parties in Latin America (which never had a large membership but did play a significant role, as training ground for political leaders later to become active outside the party, and as a pole of attraction for artists and intellectuals) refrained from criticizing the United States, then viewed as the Soviet Union's noble ally in its struggle in behalf of humanity against the Nazi-Fascist Axis.

But this love remained unrequited. After 1945, the North American administrations were obsessed with the cold war; they lost interest in the Latin-American countries, after having drawn them into a military alliance that made them pawns in the world-wide anti-Soviet strategy.[24]

George Kennan, the influential American diplomat, argued in 1950 that Washington's strategic thinking and foreign policy should concentrate on those regions of the world that might actually present a threat to American territory in case of war. He could find only five such: the Soviet Union, Western Europe, Great Britain, Japan, and China.

The United States had recently experienced the euphoria of victory. Now it noted with some irritation and much concern that it had not solved all its problems simply by eliminating Hitlerism. It did not for a moment believe that the challenge of Communism could alter the traditional, "folklore" conception of Latin America, a stereotype embodied by Carmen Miranda and Xavier Cugat and by a "Pan-American" Walt Disney film, *¡Saludos, amigos!,* in which Donald Duck stood for the United States and a parrot wearing a Mexican sombrero for Latin America.

Between 1945 and 1952, the United States invested 45 billion dollars in the Marshall Plan and other European aid programs, plus 7.3 billion in aid to Greece and Turkey. For the

24. This refers to the Inter-American Reciprocal Assistance Treaty, signed in Rio in 1947 by all the countries that were to sign the Charter of the Organization of American States (OAS) in the following year.

same period, all of Latin America received 6.8 billion, hardly more than what was given to Chiang Kai-shek's Formosa. Then, in 1953, John Foster Dulles took over the leadership of American diplomacy. His paranoia led him to suspect—quite rightly—that Stalin could find the soft underbelly of the Western Hemisphere in Latin America. In 1954, at the Tenth Inter-American Conference (held in Caracas), in the presence of the foreign ministers of all the OAS countries, he proposed the following resolution in genuinely imperial terms: "That the domination or control of the political institutions of an American state by the international Communist movement (extending to this Hemisphere the political system of an extracontinental power) would constitute a threat to the sovereignty and independence of the American States, endangering the peace and calling for the adoption of appropriate action in accordance with existing treaties."[25]

This was not a purely formal proposition, for Washington at the time was convinced that Jacobo Arbenz, the President of Guatemala, was tending to favor, or at least tolerate, Communist activists within his government's executive branch.[26]

Latin Americans looked upon the Dulles resolution as a step back from the principle of nonintervention that had been unambiguously proclaimed and explicitly and solemnly incorporated into the OAS Charter less than six years earlier. They accepted his resolution only after the words "calling for the adoption of appropriate action" were replaced by "would call for a Meeting of Consultation to consider the adoption of appropriate action."[27] Dulles did not hide his displeasure when the resolution was passed in this form; he left the conference, delegating his post to an undersecretary for the remaining sessions.

That same year, the CIA helped Colonel Castillo Armas "destabilize" Arbenz. Armas worked from a base in Honduras, which had been established for this purpose by special treaty with the United States. Significantly, Arbenz sought refuge in Czechoslovakia.

During this period, a phalanx of military dictators assured the stability and anti-Communism of the Caribbean and other

25. Organization of American States, "Report of the Pan-American Union of the Conference," *Annals*, Tenth Inter-American Conference, Washington, D.C., vol. 6, special number, 1964, pp. 10–11.
26. In Guatamala at that time, possibly only by coincidence, was Dr. Ernesto Guevara, who, as we know, was not discouraged by Arbenz's overthrow shortly thereafter.
27. OAS *Annals, ibid.*, p. 114.

areas of Latin America. But in 1958, Vice President Nixon's trip to several Latin-American countries revealed the catastrophic state of the subcontinent's feelings toward the United States. He was everywhere met with insults and stonings and was almost killed in Venezuela, which had recently thrown off a ten-year military dictatorship. Nixon's car was blocked by demonstrators, and came close to being overturned and set afire. He and his wife had been spat upon on landing at the airport.

And on January 1, 1959, Fidel Castro made his triumphant entry into Havana.

Castro the Purifier

The widespread reaction against Fidel for his misuse of dictatorial powers has been amply documented, for there have been many observers of the Cuban scene who were friendly to his successful revolution but could not endorse his later, unconditional pro-Soviet stance. Still, even these critics agree that subsequent objections can never erase the elation Latin Americans felt when they first saw Fidel challenge North American imperial power.

From 1898 to 1958 Cuba had been very much like a North American dependency, almost on a par with Puerto Rico. The country had thus become fairly prosperous, and found itself in 1958 with a per-capita income that was topped in Latin America only by Argentina's, Venezuela's, and Puerto Rico's. The sugar industry was its main (and too nearly exclusive!) source of wealth, but only Argentina, Mexico, and Brazil boasted higher total industrial production. The large middle class was socially active, liberal, and thriving. One member of the labor force out of five could be counted as a skilled worker, and the illiteracy rate was among the lowest in Latin America. In absolute terms, the island had the third highest number of doctors in the subcontinent, the highest number of TV sets, and the highest level of movie attendance.

But for all this, Cuba suffered more than any other country in its pride and its national dignity. Unlike Puerto Rico, Cuba was entirely self-governing, so that Cubans could accede to the highest posts in their own society. But in every Cuban (as in every Latin American) festered the humiliation of being—and of not being—*American*. For the name has been pre-empted by

North Americans; even we call them "Americans," while we have to specify that we are *Latin* Americans.

Further, "Americans" were far more numerous and far more visible in Cuba than anywhere else south of the border.

The usual Latin-American schizophrenia with regard to the United States reached a high point among the Cuban ruling elite. This class had been educated in the North American value system; its sons attended "American" colleges, as their fathers had done. Today most are in exile, and almost all of them have settled in the United States.

Fidel Castro grew up as a member of this class. But he is a man of exceptional strength of character, one of the most remarkable men of power of our time.[28] To conquer power and keep it, he has been willing to risk not only his own life (which many Latin Americans have done), but also the lives of any number of other men. He also has had the gifts—the imagination and the breadth of vision—required to conceive and implement a project no other Latin American had thought of. His strategy was simple and bold: he played the Soviet Union off against the United States, and eventually succeeded in personally confronting "America," in breaking off Cuba's dependence on that country. He thus fulfilled the ambition that secretly or openly thrives in the heart of every Latin American: to find revenge for the multiple, tangible humiliations his people have met with individually or collectively from the Yankees, and for the great, all-embracing humiliation inherent in comparing North American success with Latin-American failure.

This is why, in his early days, Fidel Castro was a new sort of hero to Latin Americans, different from Bolívar and endowed with an even wider appeal; this is why he continues to enjoy a far greater prestige than he deserves, and than would seem possible under the present circumstances. When Castro was triumphant at the Bay of Pigs, every Latin American fancied himself a participant, fighting the North Americans alongside Fidel and beating them. The truth is that it was not over North Americans that Fidel triumphed at the Bay of Pigs, but over a handful of other Latin Americans who had been fooled, ill-armed, and then abandoned by the North Americans in their defeat. One more source of confusion had been added to the many from which Latin America has yet to free itself.

28. The admiration shown for Fidel Castro by many Latin-American, European, and North American intellectuals stems partly from the fascination they feel for the "strong man," the man of power. Stalin and Mao benefited from the same sort of adulation.

The Alliance for Progress

When John Kennedy became President of the United States in January 1961, the Cuban Revolution was already a page of history that fascinated all of Latin America. Fidel had not yet declared himself a Marxist-Leninist; this he was not to do until the end of the year. He had, however, already welcomed Mikoyan in Havana, and the U.S.S.R. had agreed to buttress the Cuban economy against North American hostility and reprisals.

Kennedy made the mistake of giving the go-ahead to the ill-conceived CIA plan for a landing at the Bay of Pigs by anti-Castroist exiles, which, it was naïvely hoped, would lead to a general counterrevolutionary uprising in Cuba. At the same time, however, Kennedy had been convinced by the Cuban situation that the United States urgently needed to contribute systematically to the political, social, and economic progress of Latin America. On March 13, 1961, he launched an "Alliance for Progress" for the hemisphere.

The Alliance was conceived as a plan to coordinate massive North American aid, both financial and technical, with complementary contributions from the Latin-American countries themselves. It was to set itself very ambitious aims for the next decade, including a yearly increase of at least 2.5 percent in real per-capita income; better utilization of natural and human resources; agrarian reform; an increase in agricultural production; improvements in transportation, and in the storage and marketing of agricultural goods and livestock; the elimination or drastic reduction of illiteracy, with a minimum of six years of primary education for all Latin-American children; improvements in public health and related services such as housing, water supply, and public sewage systems. It was hoped that these improvements would raise the average life expectancy by five years and reduce infant mortality by half.

To finance their share of this ambitious project, the Latin-American countries were being asked to institute fiscal reforms that would tax the rich more heavily.

Before his final break with the United States, when he was still invoking that country's obligations toward Latin America, Fidel Castro voiced the idea that the North American contribution to the subcontinent's development should not fall below thirty billion dollars over ten years. Kennedy's offer came to one-third of this. Then the Alliance was to be further compromised by the Bay of Pigs landing in April 1961, just before the date set for the program's official launching. Che Guevara, who attended the preparatory conference in Punta del Este, Uruguay, mocked the North Americans and their Latin-American "vassals," and told Secretary of State Dean Rusk that the aid in question was but a pittance doled out to Latin America; it represented only a fraction of what imperialism had extorted from the Southern Hemisphere, and was motivated solely by the fear of a virulent spread of the Cuban Revolution. There was some truth in this charge.

After Kennedy's death, the Alliance, which had already fallen behind schedule, lost its drive and foundered. It was finally buried by Nixon, who rejected the idea of multilateral aid to Latin America in the following terms: "No aid: trade and private investment . . ." He formalized the practice of bilateral aid on a preferential basis to countries that were viewed as of special importance, such as Brazil.

In 1969, a North American study on the impact of the Alliance concluded that its ambitious objectives for the decade 1961–1970 could not have been met in any case.

It has been said often, and in many quarters, that the Alliance for Progress was a failure, but little thought has been given to the causes for this failure, and the positive results have been minimized.

Clearly the Alliance had set itself impossible goals, on the basis of certain hypotheses formulated by the United Nations Economic Commission for Latin America, or by other agencies of the UN, on the causes of underdevelopment and on development strategies. In his *Asian Drama: An Inquiry into the Poverty of Nations* (1968) and *The Challenge of World Poverty* (1970), Gunnar Myrdal questions these hypotheses, arguing that the views propounded by the UN economic organizations, which attribute the poverty of Third World nations primarily to factors external to them, are simplistic or downright erroneous, since they overlook the shortcomings and limitations inherent in those societies themselves. The Alliance took as its point of departure diagnoses formulated for the UN Economic Commission for Latin America largely by Chilean economists who later were to help Allende define his economic policies. It is therefore not surprising that the results proved disappointing: they failed to take into account the cultural impediments to development inherent in the ancestral customs and traditions of the Latin-American societies.

Habitual reference to the "technical" hypotheses and measures recommended by the "international experts" has led us to lose track of one important element: the very real success scored by the Alliance. Or, rather, by the joint impact of the Cuban Revolution and the theories, aims, and programs of the Alliance. Established ancestral habits were shaken, the self-satisfaction and inertia of Latin-American leaders disturbed, and hope was held out to the people. Today, Latin America as a whole, including such formerly staunch conservative sectors as the Church and the army, rejects immobilism, and has started thinking along dynamic lines. The idea of economic planning has been everywhere accepted. And the conviction has become general at all levels that the links that bind Latin America to the North American economy are excessive and must be lessened.[29]

One political consequence of the Alliance that Washington had not foreseen is a general Latin-American opposition to the United States' hegemony. But I must point out a second consequence, which had not been foreseen by such democratic leaders as the Venezuelan Social Democratic President Rómulo Betancourt or the Colombian Liberal Democratic President Alberto Lleras Camargo (both of whom were first understood and appreciated in the United States because of Kennedy and the Alliance). This was the development in Latin America of leaders of a new stripe who are, on the one hand, anti-Communist and development-minded, but, on the other, reject categorically a necessary interdependence of democratic reforms and development policies, as explicitly stated in the preamble to the Alliance. Such leaders, who are as different from the hard-headed traditionalist anti-Communists as they are from the democratic anti-Communists, have become common throughout the continent.

It is disquieting to see that this view, which separates social progress and the furthering of democracy from economic de-

29. Until the First World War, the level of North American investments was below that of the British. Most of the North American investments had been made in Mexico during the Porfirio Díaz regime. Of course, there was also the immense investment—more strategic than economic—in the Panama Canal. After this period, North American investments grew at an accelerated pace. During the sixties, they reached ten billion dollars—a figure that may be insignificant in terms of the overall North American economy, but is enormous in Latin-American terms. At the end of the decade of the Alliance for Progress, the corporations called "multinational," which in fact originated in the United States, were responsible for one-third of all Latin-American exports, producing one-fifth of the fiscal revenue and one-tenth of the GNP (these figures include Brazil). For some countries, *practically all exports* go through international corporations. This makes the host countries all the more vulnerable to foreign pressures.

velopment, gained favor in certain power groups in the United States, even when the Alliance still officially dictated policy. Figures for the years 1961–1970 show that the greater part of United States aid to Latin America went to the Brazilian military government, which was in favor of economic growth and modernization, but at the same time clearly repressive and antidemocratic.

The Ubiquitous CIA

The failure and the tragic end of the Allende government[30] contributed substantially to the fund of self-delusions on which the conscience of Latin America feeds.

The view that the Chilean Popular Unity Movement owes its failure entirely to Washington and the machinations of the CIA now seems to have gained control over Latin-American thinking. The CIA emerges unfailingly as the ubiquitous villain, responsible for all that goes wrong south of the border. What is new in the situation is that the governments themselves now make use of the CIA as an ever-handy whipping boy, always available, as was "international Communism" in earlier days, as a cover-up for the Latin Americans' own abuses and ineptness.

It is undeniable that the CIA is a force as real as the international Communist movement subordinate to Moscow, and, like the Communist movement, it has committed reprehensible acts in the interest of a foreign power. The trouble is that certain Latin-American governments have taken advantage of this situation to attribute to CIA initiative and dollars whatever goes wrong in their countries. Even the most legitimately native and spontaneous actions are thus explained away; any opponent of a given regime is immediately described as a CIA agent, and thus automatically discredited and made ripe for political (and physical) liquidation in the name of the fatherland's most sacred interests. The "progressive" international conscience then stands by unconcerned, though it is always ready to denounce comparable abuses of power when they are committed in the name of anti-Communism.

An example. In March 1975, Echeverría, the President of Mexico, decided to visit the Autonomous University of Mexico. The students had not quite forgotten that he had been Minister of the Interior in 1968, when several hundred dissenting stu-

30. To be examined in detail in Chapter 9, "The Forms of Political Power in Latin America."

dents demonstrating in the Square of the Three Cultures were surrounded and massacred by the police and the army. Nor had they forgotten that under Echeverría's presidency, the "falcons"—groups of policemen in plainclothes and armed with pistols—had hunted down students who demonstrated in memory of the victims of the earlier massacre.

Far from welcoming the President, the Mexican students therefore stoned him, and they succeeded in hitting him in the head. Echeverría responded by shaking his fist at the students and shouting at them the darkest accusation in the repertoire of Latin-American politicians today: "Youngsters manipulated by the CIA!" The inference, duly drawn by some of Echeverría's intellectual collaborators, was that the hundreds of students killed on the Square of the Three Cultures were CIA agents or tools as well.

An unmistakable sign of the success of this process of mystification is that the incident on the Square of the Three Cultures is hardly remembered, even though many foreign correspondents were on hand to cover the coming opening of the Olympic games. They personally witnessed the massacre and testified that the dead numbered not twenty or thirty, as the government claimed, but in the hundreds. The well-known Italian reporter Oriana Fallaci was shot and almost killed while standing at what she considered a safe distance from the trouble, on a high balcony overlooking the square. The soldiers and police had apparently been ordered to teach the people a lesson, and to shoot anything that moved. Why not? Was not the pernicious CIA involved in this shameful demonstration against the virtuous, revolutionary Mexican government?

The CIA was also blamed when, early in 1975, Peruvian demonstrators burned down the Military Club in Lima as well as the office of one of the newspapers that, confiscated a year earlier by the military government, had since been in the service of the so-called Peruvian revolution. Similarly, the CIA label has been placed on the Peruvian Trotskyists, who are skeptical about the outcome of the military dictatorship and, in any case, know that they are in danger of extermination as rivals of certain collaborating Marxist groups. The journalists and simple citizens who opposed the confiscation of newspapers or later demonstrated against this measure? All CIA agents.

Anyone can play this game. Recently Gabriel García Márquez, the author of *A Hundred Years of Solitude,* who resigned from the Communist party to endorse a less dogmatic version of Marxism, was branded a CIA agent—probably by party members.

One is reminded of the Moscow, Prague, or Budapest trials, in which "socialist" governments liquidated all dissidents, imprisoned, tortured, and shot or hanged their opponents and some of their own members lately fallen from grace, all on the pretext of fighting foreign espionage. Is this what Latin America is coming to? To some extent it is already there. This is exactly what the revolutionary Cuban government has been doing. Cubans attach the CIA label to such men as the American sociologist Oscar Lewis, the French writer K. S. Karol, the French agricultural expert René Dumont.

The "New Dialogue" and Its Alternatives

In the past few years, the United States' policy has been the Kissinger policy; as a corollary, there has been an almost total lack of interest in Latin America as a whole. Kissinger added one danger area to those listed by Kennan in 1950, the Middle East, not only because the Arab-Israeli conflict gave Russia an opportunity to fulfill its old dream of acquiring a foothold on the Mediterranean and the Persian Gulf, but also because the Middle East controls the world's largest known oil supplies—with all this implies in the present world situation.

As Secretary of State, Kissinger held frequent meetings with the Egyptian President, the King of Saudi Arabia, the Shah of Iran, the Israeli leaders, and even the President of Syria; Latin America saw him only twice during his secretaryship.

Kissinger's first visit took place in Mexico (with a stopover in Panama) in February 1974. His purpose was to meet the ministers of foreign affairs of the member states of the OAS and to propose a "new dialogue." In contrast to John Foster Dulles's disdainful arrogance, Kissinger spoke with a certain down-to-earth frankness; he pointed out to his counterparts the customary ambiguity in Latin-American statements on their relations with the United States. At times, he intimated, Latin America gave the impression of viewing its and the United States' basic interests as mutually contradictory. If this were truly the case, he implied, what would be the point of trying to define areas of common interest? Kissinger immediately gave assurance that the United States was persuaded that such areas of agreement did exist, and was ready to explore them. Were the Latin Americans willing to do as much?

Latin America and the United States

In March 1975, more than a year after his Latin-American trip, Kissinger made a speech in Houston in which he stated that the countries of the hemisphere were "more than ever" interdependent. But he added: "Latin America has developed important trading relationships with other industrial nations and has come to share certain political perspectives with the Third World."[31] This is a reference to the Third World's conviction, now shared by Latin America, that the advanced capitalist countries owe their wealth, and the Third World countries their poverty, to colonialism and dependence (imperialism); and that the Third World must seek, through negotiations, to effect economic readjustment on a global basis, in its favor and at the expense of the high standard of living in the West. This is to be accomplished by raising the price of Third World raw materials and by opening up the domestic markets of the capitalist countries on a tariff-free basis to manufactured and semimanufactured products from the Third World.

Another solution is put forward as necessary and inevitable by certain Third World groups, and is clearly endorsed by the socialist bloc. This solution is predicated on the assumption that the Third World's political, economic, and cultural relations with the advanced Western countries can be equated with their *dependence*, and therefore recommends the drastic severing of all ties with the West. As with Cuba, incorporation into the Soviet bloc would follow.

Kissinger was referring to the first hypothesis, negotiation, when he stressed: ". . . the global dialogue between the developed and less developed nations requires answers that will be difficult to find anywhere if we do not find them in the Western Hemisphere. . . . The United States is concerned by the growing tendency of some Latin American countries to participate in tactics of confrontation between the developing and developed worlds. . . . The temptation to blame disappointments on the intrigues and excesses of foreigners is as old as nations themselves. Latin America is perennially tempted to define its independence and unity through opposition to the United States. . . . We do not expect agreement with all our views, but neither can we accept a new version of paternalism, in which those with obligations have no rights,

31. "The United States and Latin America: The New Opportunity," speech delivered at the Combined Service Club, Houston, Texas, March 1, 1975, published in *Vital Speeches of the Day*, New York, vol. 41, no. 12, April 1, 1975, p. 354.

and those who claim rights accept no obligations. The choice for the United States is not between domination and indifference. The choice for Latin America is not between submission and confrontation. . . . After decades of oscillating between moods of euphoria and disillusionment, between charges of hegemony and neglect, it is time for the United States and Latin America to learn to work together, calmly and without confrontation, on the challenges to our common civilization."[32]

Some respected voices are still raised in Latin America today in defense of a community of interests with the United States, and of special links that are worth preserving and cultivating. Perhaps the most articulate defender of this viewpoint is Carlos Andrés Pérez, the President of Venezuela. He speaks with the authority of the financial power and moral prestige that Venezuela derives from being an oil-producing country, and a member of OPEC, and as the spokesman for the political views of the Third World to which Kissinger alluded.

Carlos André Pérez expressed his position in the following terms: "Our experience of history teaches us that no world problems have ever been solved by confrontation. Today, we are witnessing the crumbling of the order imposed by the victors of the Second World War, an order that they have maintained with difficulty for thirty years. More than half this period will have seen the appearance and proliferation of contradictions within the order imposed by the strong on the weak. The countries of Latin America and the countries of the Third World in general must not try to score ephemeral victories, but must try to win and secure permanent gains for universal solidarity and for the good of mankind. This is why petroleum will never be a weapon for Venezuela; it is an instrument. I think that OPEC is the forerunner of the Third World and that petroleum is going to lead to a dialogue between the industrialized and the developing countries. We feel no strategic hatred toward the United States."[33] We recognize that the United States is a geopolitical reality. . . . It is in our interest to establish relations with the North Americans and to make sure that they understand the great responsibility they have toward the whole world and particularly toward Latin America."[34]

---

32. *Ibid.*, pp. 354–58.
33. Here Pérez is alluding to the contention that anything that weakens the United States and strengthens the U.S.S.R. or China is, of itself, beneficial to mankind.
34. Press conference, Mexico, March 22, 1975.

Latin America and the United States

Although a certain measure of agreement seems to exist between Kissinger's and Carlos Andrés Pérez's viewpoints, I cannot help being pessimistic. Pérez is far more reasonable and courageous than most Latin-American leaders—not surprisingly, since Venezuela's oil wealth has transformed the country these last fifty years in such a way that it may be the most likely of all Latin-American republics to allow far-reaching democratic leadership to develop and maintain itself. The basic problem, however, as I have repeatedly stressed, is not at the level of leadership, but at the level of the collective unconscious: Latin-American societies suffer from a psychological need to compensate for their feelings of inferiority and humiliation with regard to the United States.

The United States, for its part, suffered an initial overreaction in the 1960's when confronted with the explosion, triggered by the Cuban Revolution, of Latin America's undeniably true feelings—a mixture of admiration and envy, of love and hate, toward the overbearingly successful North Americans. But it now appears that the United States has discarded what might be called the "Monroe Syndrome," the belief that it must maintain a paternalistic attention to the hemisphere as a whole, that even a small, localized fissure in the hemisphere's imperviousness to extracontinental influence would lead to grave strategic losses, and consequent real dangers, to the United States. It would seem that since ICBM's and nuclear-submarine-based missiles revolutionized strategic calculations, Latin America no longer appears, in Washington's view, to be a sister region, albeit a poor relation, requiring close and special attention, to be cajoled or threatened, helped or checked, on a global, multilateral scale. Instead of the "hemisphere" of Pan-American rhetoric, North American strategic calculations would now consider Latin America as a mosaic of countries, holding varying degrees of interest (or lack of interest) for the United States. The United States therefore could and indeed ought to maintain selective, bilateral relations with individual Latin-American countries, reflecting in each case United States strategic requirements, and closely related to the willingness of each Latin-American country to maintain friendly political and economic relations with the United States.

Lest this policy be considered merely as Kissinger's realpolitik, and as such likely to be discarded by a Jimmy Carter ready to follow in the footsteps of Franklin Roosevelt and John Kennedy, let me quote from one of the new, presumably post-Kissinger North American voices: Abraham Lowenthal, special consultant on the staff of the Linowitz Commission, which is the primary source of Latin-American policy ideas for the new Democratic administration. Writing in the October 1976 issue of *Foreign Affairs,* Lowenthal found Kissinger naïve or ill-advised when in Tlateloclo he put forward the idea of a "new dialogue" between North and South America on the basis of "hemispheric community." "The first step toward an improved [United States] Latin American policy would be to realize that for most purposes we probably should not have a distinct Latin American policy at all. . . . We should no longer assume that common interests automatically bind the United States and Latin America. . . . The challenge of U.S. policy in the Americas is to nurture common interests where they exist or are latent. . . . In practice this means analyzing how the interests and objectives of the various states of Latin America and the Caribbean differ among themselves, and how they relate to our own interests."[35]

Something of a revolution must have taken place if a spokesman of the North American liberal establishment can thus turn the page that began with Henry Clay and included the grand vision of the Alliance. Perhaps it was inevitable that it should happen. Perhaps this cool ruthlessness has been the permanent core of United States policy toward Latin America, and the Clays and Kennedys were eccentrics, out of touch with their compatriots' true feelings about the whole matter.

The sensible course for each Latin-American country should be to take note of this new North American recognition that the special relationship between North and South America, while substantial and in a way indestructible, is not one of natural harmony or of necessary conformity; to acknowledge that recognition ourselves; and from this fresh perspective to adjust our policy toward the United States on the basis that we have a much broader range of options than either outright submission to Washington, as in the past, or a self-destructive revolutionary break from North American influence, like Cuba's. Brazil, Mexico, and Venezuela have shown, in different ways, that it is possible to define new ways of being Latin American without either submitting to or confronting the United States.

However, because of Latin-American society's psychological need to compensate for its feelings and past experiences of

35. Abraham F. Lowenthal, "The United States and Latin America: Ending the Hegemonic Presumptions," *Foreign Affairs,* vol. 55, No. 1, October 1976, pp. 210, 212.

inferiority and humiliation caused by the United States, it may be excessive to hope that all Latin-American countries will be able to bury that resentment and forget those frustrations, or even to limit themselves to externalizing them in rhetoric, like the Mexicans.

So-called Third World countries really have only one thing in common: the traumatic experience of systematic humiliation of their people by white European or North American foreigners. This shock has been so deep that xenophobic nationalism may be the single most urgent motivation of those countries in their search for a new political equilibrium.

That is why, following Cuba, other Latin-American countries may seek salvation in anti–North American revolution, hoping to find in such a complete break a resolution of their unhappy love-hate relationship with the United States.

3

Independence: Its Heroes and Traitors

The Constitutional Lie

We Latin Americans want first of all to see ourselves as the victims of Spanish conquest and colonization, so that the independent republics born from 1810 onward should in no way be considered Spanish or indebted to Spain. Secondly, we want to view these republics as equal, or even superior, to the United States—not just in terms of international law, but *intrinsically* equal or superior.

Both these claims are quite unfounded. They lead to interpretations that disregard the facts, to ways of thinking that can only be ineffectual and that will bring frustration, bitterness, and failure in their wake. Further, these claims do not fit in with the theories on which they were founded or which they were intended to explain.

We Latin Americans may even go to the extreme of attempting to base our claim of superiority over the North Americans on our success in the art of self-delusion. In his otherwise admirable *The Labyrinth of Solitude*, Octavio Paz concludes that "we tell lies for the mere pleasure of it." He is speaking about Mexico, but the same can be said of all Latin America: "Lying plays a decisive role in our daily lives, our politics, our love affairs and our friendships, and since we attempt to deceive ourselves as well as others, our lies are brilliant and fertile, not like the gross inventions of other peoples. . . . The Mexican tells lies because he delights in fantasy, because he is desperate, or because he wants to rise above the sordid facts of his life; the North American does not tell lies, but he substitutes social truth for the real truth. . . ."

Elsewhere in the same book, Paz said that from the day of independence, and obviously following an inclination already anchored in the heart of colonial Spanish American societies, "the political lie established itself almost constitutionally. The moral damage it has caused is incalculable; it has affected profound areas of our existence. We move about in this lie with complete naturalness . . . hence the struggle against the official, constitutional lie must be the first step in any serious attempt at reform."[1]

The tragedy of this "constitutional lie" is that, broadly speaking, almost nothing of what Latin Americans have said or done has been based on a scientific search for truth. In our most far-sighted beliefs, in our most serious actions, there is, invariably and inevitably, a measure of distortion, some compromise with our need to see Latin America come out well in comparison with the rest of the world—and particularly in comparison with the United States.

Carried to its conclusion, this innate trait of our culture leads us to glorify the greatest deceivers as heroes and to label as contemptible traitors the very men who try to tell us the truth.

Tocqueville's Diagnosis

From the start, the 1810 independence movement was marked by an ambiguity that did not come to be recognized until much later, and then only imperfectly.

The ambitions of the rich (or merely educated) Creoles were suddenly stimulated by events taking place in Europe: Napoleon had overthrown the Spanish Bourbons and had his brother Joseph crowned in Madrid.

The majority of Creoles were prudent conservatives, fearful of social disruptions. Only a few were genuinely fired by the North American republican ideas or by the Jacobin ideas of France. But all—without exception—were actuated by an ambition that today we would call nationalistic, eager to occupy

1. New York, Grove Press, 1961, pp. 23, 40. Copyright © 1961 by Grove Press, Inc. This and all subsequent quotes from *The Labyrinth of Solitude* reprinted by permission of Grove Press, Inc.

the key posts in Spanish American society, and to replace officials sent over from the metropolis.

Far more numerous were the poor whites and the mass of Indians, blacks, and half-breeds whose attachment to the King and to the exhortations of the Church promised little support for the cause of independence.

At the start, the contest consisted mainly in an attempt by the Creoles to replace the higher echelons of the Spanish administration through a series of coups d'état, launched on the pretext of defending the legitimate Spanish ruler against the usurper of imperial power, Bonaparte. But soon the power struggle among the upper strata of society degenerated into a pitiless civil war, during which the nationalist or "patriot" faction, as it called itself, came to see its role as that of avengers of the misdeeds related in the so-called Black Legend, a centuries-old accumulation of stories picturing the conquest, colonization, and Catholic evangelization of Latin America in exclusively gruesome terms. The patriots made use of this legend in its crudest form, tailored to fit the needs of domestic or foreign propaganda.

The original source for the Black Legend was Fray Bartolomé de Las Casas's *Very Brief Relation of the Destruction of the Indies* (1552). Las Casas wrote with passion, as a witness to and repentant participant in the cruelty and cupidity of the conquistadors and Spanish colonizers. The descendants of these same conquistadors and colonizers, inheritors of their privileges, ended up convincing themselves in the heat of battle that they were the descendants of the Indians who had been murdered or condemned to slavery, while the actual descendants of these slaves were slaves still, and were long to remain in that condition. Moreover, these descendants of the conquistadors convinced themselves that theirs was a war of liberation, pitting them against an invader and a foreign army of occupation, and they went so far as to claim that the generation of 1810 had fulfilled the mission of avenging Cuauhtémoc and Atahualpa.

Thus, what had started as a game between political dilettantes ended in an explosion of hatred toward all that was Spanish; the violent anger of sons who had been kept down too long by their historic Spanish father and now demanded his ritual sacrifice.

Very few native Spaniards took part in the fighting, but a hundred years went by before anyone dared say what everyone had known all along—that these confrontations were nothing but civil wars between Spanish Americans.[2]

In certain regions, the rich Creoles lost control of the situation, so that the war and the social convulsions that followed (and lasted for a good part of the nineteenth century) left a wake of blood and destruction. The societies that emerged from this series of trials were more open, more tolerant, better able to foster social mobility—more *American*, in the good sense of the word.

In other regions, the war destroyed the imperial Spanish sovereignty without social upheaval; Creole oligarchies succeeded[3] in simply replacing the proconsuls from abroad, and in instituting a traditional and hereditary form of power that in some cases has survived to the present day. A new governing class resulted: in 1974, all three candidates for the presidency of Colombia were children of former Presidents, a situation that seemed perfectly normal to the political establishment.

But in either case, the new republics were born traumatized, divided, weak, irrational, unstable, beset by convulsions and confusion—in sharp contrast to the United States, with its vigor, lucidity, unity, and political health. The United States had, moreover, the advantage of an extra half-century in the practice of independence.

As early as 1833, Alexis de Tocqueville, with his considerable perspicacity as a social and political observer, had no difficulty drawing the relevant conclusions from the coexistence within the Western Hemisphere of two such different entities: "It is unquestionable that the North Americans will one day be called upon to supply the wants of the South Americans. Nature has placed them in contiguity and has furnished the former with every means of knowing and appreciating those demands, of establishing permanent relations with those states and gradually filling their markets. The merchant of the United States could only forfeit these natural advantages if he were very inferior to the European merchant; but he is superior to him in several respects."[4]

2. The first to point this out was the Venezuelan Laureano Vallenilla Lanz, during a lecture given in Caracas in 1911, which he followed up with an article, "Fue una guerra civil" (It was a civil war), in his book *Cesarismo democrático* (1920).
3. Sometimes against their will, as in Peru, which San Martín had to invade from the south, and Bolívar from the north, before the Peruvian Creoles resigned themselves to becoming independent.
4. *Democracy in America*, New York, Vintage Books, 1945, vol. 1, p. 445.

Tocqueville adds: "The Americans of the United States already exercise a great moral influence upon all the nations of the New World. They are the source of intelligence, and all those who inhabit the same continent are already accustomed to consider them as the most enlightened, the most powerful, and the most wealthy members of the great American family. . . . The American Union will perform the same part in the other hemisphere, and every community which is founded or which prospers in the New World is founded and prospers to the advantage of the Anglo-Americans."

The situation could not have been better described. Tocqueville noted the trends and traced them to their logical conclusions: the primordial ideological influence of the North Americans, their coming political and economic domination, and their primacy in the continent's history for the decades to come.

Bolívar's Diagnosis

In 1824, Bolívar proposed a congress of the new Latin American republics, calling it "amphictyonic" to invoke the confederation that bound the city-states of ancient Greece. The Liberator was deeply convinced that the various countries of Spanish America should unite to form one great nation, or at least a confederation of large states, rather than leave the continent helpless before the North Americans—as Tocqueville was going to find it some years later.

Bolívar had no great illusions about the chances for Spanish American unity, at least in the immediate future. He lived to see Colombia—the largest state that he personally sought to create, containing Venezuela, New Granada, and Ecuador—fall apart, with the leaders of each of these regions just waiting for Bolívar's death or resignation before seceding from the union. Furthermore, Bolívar, a man not given to feelings of inferiority, had no need to compensate for small-minded actions with heroic words; he understood what was going on, and clearly said so. In his famous "Letter from Jamaica" (1815), he says that, in an independent Spanish America, "a great monarchy would not be easy to maintain, a great republic impossible. It is a grandiose idea, to aim at fashioning all this New World into one single nation, with a single link binding all these different parts into one whole. Since this New World shares a common origin, a common language, set of customs, and religion, it would clearly benefit from a single government federating all the different states that might develop. *But this is not possible because [the regions of Spanish] America are divided by differences in climate and geographic location, by contending interests and dissimilarity of character.*"

As to successfully adapting the North American system of government, Bolívar again displays inexorable lucidity. "It is a pity that the laws and customs of the [North] Americans cannot be applied toward the happiness of [Great] Colombia. You know it to be impossible, as impossible as, and even more so than, it would be for Spain to fashion itself after England."[5] And again: "I think it would be better [for Spanish America] to adopt the Koran [as a political code] than the form of government of the United States, even if the latter is the best in the world. What else is there to say; it is enough to consider to what a pass Buenos Aires, Chile, Mexico, and Guatemala have come, and to recall our first years.[6] These examples by themselves tell us more than all the literature on this subject. . . ."[7]

Bolívar passed in review all the powers likely to exert an effective influence on the destiny of Spanish America. It seemed possible to him that Spain might attempt to reconquer the lost colonies, at the instigation and with the help of the Holy Alliance. He saw only England as a potential source of assistance and protection against this threat and the threat represented by the United States. In March 1825, he wrote to Santander, Vice President of Great Colombia: "We will save [Spanish] America if we reach an agreement with England *on political and military matters.* This simple sentence should tell you more than two big volumes." And to Santander again, in June of the same year: "A thousand times I have been on the verge of writing you about a difficult business, which is the following. Our America cannot survive if England does not take it under its protection; I wonder, therefore, whether we should not invite it to sign an offensive and defensive alliance with us. The alliance would have only one shortcoming: to bind us to the vicissitudes of British politics. But this difficulty is only a possibility, and probably a distant one. I submit this thought to you. To be living is the first good, the way we live is

5. Letter to Belford Hinton Wilson, August 3, 1829.
6. Before Bolívar was granted full powers as virtual dictator in Columbia.
7. Letter to Daniel Florencio O'Leary, September 13, 1829.

a secondary consideration; if we bind ourselves to Great Britain, we will live, and if we don't we will be irremediably lost. We must therefore prefer the first alternative. In due course, we will grow, we will become stronger, and by the time the relationship with our ally becomes a threat to us, we will have developed into real nations. Then, our own strength and such relations as we will have built up with other *European*[8] powers will allow us to keep at a distance from our tutors and allies.[9] Therefore, my dear General, if you are of the same mind, consult the Congress or the Government Council which you have created within your Ministry to settle difficult questions. If these gentlemen agree with my reasoning, it would be important for us to sound out the British government on this question and to consult the Panama Congress.[10] For myself, *I do not intend to give up this project, even if it finds no supporters.* Naturally, our good friends from [North] America will be the principal critics, in the name of independence and freedom, but in fact for reasons of self-interest and because they themselves have no such fears as ours at home. I warmly recommend this purpose to you, never lose sight of it, *however unsound it may appear to you.* We may someday turn to it when all is lost. . . ."

No other Latin-American chief of state until Fidel Castro had so clear a vision of world politics as it is really played, coldly and ruthlessly, among the great powers. Naturally, no one would listen—in this matter as in many others, Bolívar was preaching in the desert. The Western Hemisphere was to be abandoned to North American hegemony under cover of the Monroe Doctrine.

One example. In 1844, Mexico ought to have realized that it could not hope to retain Texas. It could still have arranged for the contested area to be made into a buffer state separating Mexico from the United States, and the borders of this new state would have been guaranteed by France and England, whose own interests happened in this case to coincide with Mexico's. But no one in Mexico understood the situation or dared propose this solution. Not much earlier, Bolívar, as we have seen, had had the courage to state Spanish America's need to place itself under British protection, and his willingness to put this

---

8. These italics, and all subsequent italics in this quotation, are mine.
9. It is interesting to note that Bolívar's reasoning presages Fidel Castro's in 1960, with the United States taking the role of the Holy Alliance and the Soviet Union that of England.
10. This refers to the "amphictyonic" Panama Congress, convocation for which had been issued the previous December.

before the amphictyonic Panama Congress. But no one after the Liberator had similar courage; and had there been anyone, it is clear that he would have met with a campaign of censure and vilification. The fact is that Mexico preferred illusory sovereignty over Texas to the very real alternative of a buffer state whose existence could have changed history in the hemisphere.

The Fragmentation of Spanish America

The various leaders left behind by the retreating tide of war did not dream of trying to integrate Spanish America into a single great confederation or, failing this, into two or three great blocks comparable to Bolívar's Great Colombia and strong enough to inspire some respect; instead, their only ambition was to carve out personal fiefs. None of them perceived a problem in the United States' power, or felt it necessary to find a way for Latin America to become a counterweight to the growing strength of its powerful northern neighbor.

Since Bolívar himself had been unable to realize his limited objective of maintaining the unity of Great Colombia, it was quite evident that even if some of his successors had shared his ideas and his strategic vision (which they did not), they would have had even less hope than he to establish a rule based on his program and ideals. Only for a fleeting historical moment had Bolívar's intelligence and will imposed on the foreign offices of the great powers the impression that Great Colombia was a power to be reckoned with, an active agent in the destiny of the Western Hemisphere. Great Britain, the United States, and Holland had taken seriously the amphictyonic Panama Congress, which opened on June 22, 1826, and had sent observers. At that congress, the Spanish American nations that were represented (Great Colombia, Peru, Mexico, and the nations of Central America) agreed to create a permanent confederation to defend their sovereignty and independence against foreign interference.

Nothing, however, came of this agreement, for the former Spanish colonies in the Americas proved incapable of implementing a project that the British colonies had successfully carried out in 1776.

Rather, the first *caudillos* appeared—second-rate military leaders who, in the upheavals of war, had risen to power from the class of mestizos. These warlords also included a few Creoles, such as the cunning Santander. These men were to complete the process of fragmenting Spanish America, "some of them . . . succeeded in taking over the state as if it were medieval booty."[11] Each of these men is now looked upon as a "national hero," and has his statues and his personal cult in the country to whose ruin he contributed.

From Rosas to Perón

Thus we see Spanish America spending the balance of the nineteenth century in internecine strife, civil wars, and coups d'état. Theoretically, these confrontations were motivated by ideological considerations, including the false distinction between Centralism and Federalism, and the overblown dichotomy between conservatives and liberals. In reality, however, they were no more than power struggles for the same unchanging prizes: control over government and the public treasury, the only reward understood in politically backward societies.

Antonio Leocadio Guzmán, the main exponent of Federalism in Venezuela, aptly summarized the meaninglessness of the political controversy between Centralism and Federalism. When his cause triumphed, he commented: "Had our opponents pre-empted the name of Federalists, we would have taken that of Centralists."

Even today, there are historians and political figures who will argue that each of these factions had something positive to contribute: the Centralists, national integration and the search for a modern state; the Federalists, the promotion of local government, social equality, et cetera. But they overlook the main historical facts; either they are biased, speaking as followers—for there still are followers—of the old contenders, or else they are trying to appeal to the mythology advanced by the schoolbooks in the interest of today's political propaganda.

Consider the example of Argentina, whose bloodthirsty "Federalist" tyrant Juan Manuel de Rosas (who ruled from 1835 to 1852) has been hailed in our century as forerunner by a variety of self-appointed "Rosists": first by the traditional nationalists, then by the fascists and the leftist nationalists, and finally by today's Marxists. They praise Rosas for his nativism and primitivism, either because they truly consider these traits praiseworthy, or because they are catering to to-

11. Octavio Paz, *The Labyrinth of Solitude*, p. 121.

day's xenophobic fashions, in particular those of the noble savage and the virtuous revolutionary. In fact, once he had conquered Buenos Aires, Rosas proved the most "centralizing" of all government heads in Argentine history. His so-called Federalism disguised his principal purpose of carving out a private fief for himself preparatory to subduing or eliminating the other feudal barons—true to the ways of other Spanish-American leaders.

However, this truth interests no one and has been relegated to the background. Today, some Argentines glorify Rosas in order to discredit his historic opponents, the men who attempted, with some success, to transform Argentina into a liberal society, governed by reason, rather than by the obscurantist passion bred of an inferiority complex. The purpose of Rosas's admirers is to rout today's heirs to a civilizing tradition that is one of the main threads of our continent's history.

Here is the comment of an Argentine intellectual of considerable stature, who in 1971 despaired over the political chaos against which his country was struggling, and had come to wish for the return of Perón: "Rosas's tyranny was one of the saddest and most humiliating periods of our history. After twenty years of cruel despotism, during which all life and property were at the mercy of the tyrant and his minions, the Argentine people were allowed to breathe again. Once again, they dared talk freely, schools reopened, books and newspapers started appearing again, civic institutions multiplied; the citizenry, which had seen its rights drowned in blood in two decades of arbitrary rule, found its rights and dignities restored; above all, doors were opened to the outside world, allowing the Argentine people to communicate once again with the civilized countries. . . . But the irrational never wholly dies in man. The masses' 'other self,' which at any moment can transform Beethoven's fatherland into Hitler's Reich, is always [in Argentina] struggling to raise its head. This other self is angered by progress and humiliated by civilization. . . . It has never ceased its struggle to reconquer its lost primacy and to take its revenge. Disguised as the peaceful lover of local folklore, it struggles for recognition by simulating love of tradition. Many have given their support to this cause, which they thought good and useful, little knowing that they were helping bring back the dark age of history. Peronism was born with the help of reason and appeared as a remedy to manifest errors and injustices. But it was soon devoured by the negative aspects of irrationalism. Perón was attracted by the

irrational, and tried to renege the [civilizing] Argentine projects in favor of a plan conceived along entirely opposite lines.
No question of Europe, of course: why Europe? We are Americans, and somehow 'Indians.' Let us revert as far as possible to
the cultures as they existed before the arrival and triumph of
the Spanish, Greco-Roman, European culture. Let us reject as
an evil shadow the memory of those who made possible the
Argentina of the railways, ports, roads, and factories; who
made the country one of the granaries of the world and one of
its principal cattle breeders; who transformed Argentina into a
kind of El Dorado and a haven for all the needy and persecuted of Europe. All this was the work of Rivadavia, of Sarmiento, of Mitre, of Alberdi, of other great men hated today
while Rosas, Facundo Quiroga and their like are praised to the
skies. . . . Thus we have seen a Peronist provincial governor
proclaiming: 'In this province, the names of traitors such as
Rivadavia, Sarmiento, Mitre, must not be heard again.' "[12]

Perón evidently succeeded in bringing Argentina back to
nativist obscurantism. Having ruined the country politically
and economically in his ten years of government, he spent the
following seventeen years of exile exerting himself to prevent
Argentina's recovery from its first Peronist bout; he managed
to make the country ungovernable, and it remained so even
after his return, despite the fact that he was granted almost
absolute powers. When he learned he was ill and dying, Perón
crowned his "achievement" by committing the final indignity:
imposing as his successors his wife, a former showgirl, and his
"private secretary," a former police sergeant, self-appointed
astrologer, and the author of a book recounting his personal
conversations with the Archangel Gabriel.

Truth or Lies

One has to admit that the traditional Latin-American quarrels
between conservatives and liberals are not entirely without
foundation. Among the liberals were men who seriously
wanted to modernize and liberalize Latin-American society.
Whenever their faction won out, it enforced significant reforms, such as the separation of Church and State, the secular-
ization of Church property, the institution of civil marriage,

12. Francisco Luis Bernárdez, "Nuestra Argentina," *El Nacional*, Caracas, March 14, 1976.

record keeping of vital statistics by civil authorities, et cetera. But since Church lands ended up as the property of the liberal warlords and their followers, the question arises whether this self-enrichment was not the prime motive behind "liberalism" in nineteenth-century Latin America, with the ideologists and legislators serving merely as administrative tools.

No progressive bourgeoisie could possibly have resulted from these reforms, which were in fact nothing but empty theoretical formulas imported from abroad, corresponding in no way to the basic economic realities or to the power structure in the countries in which they were introduced.

Actually those who called themselves liberals sometimes deserved that label less than the so-called conservatives. In Venezuela, the terms "liberalism" and "federalism" were usurped by those elements that had been partly or wholly passed over in the redistribution of power following Venezuela's separation from Great Colombia. The men then in power were perhaps among the least objectionable in Venezuela's tormented history; they were finally eliminated during a bloody civil war that lasted from 1859 to 1863. They have since been stigmatized with the name *godos* (Goths)—a term whose connotations are difficult to translate but which, because of the associations it acquired among the Spanish colonial regime and the pro-Spanish party during the wars of independence, is used in political confrontations to mean "reactionary." In many Latin-American countries it is applied to anyone hated or held in contempt.

The following comment by a distinguished contemporary Venezuelan historian is atypically illuminating: "The 'Liberals' and 'Federalists' having controlled propaganda for more than half a century, all Venezuelan historical writing portrays the Conservatives as monsters. And of course, the Liberals presented themselves as the liberators of the people from an iniquitous oligarchy, as the only true repositories and interpreters of the popular will, as the daring innovators aiming to bring genuine democracy to Venezuela. But after a few years it became quite apparent that the 'Liberal Federation' was nothing but eyewash, the all-powerful arm of the ruling group, and intended to strangle any attempt at regional autonomy, any show of collective vitality. Freedom of the press, which had once been the rule, disappeared altogether. An opposition leader need only be labeled *godo* or *reactionary* for his life and property to be at the mercy of the men in power.

The Latin Americans

"Elections were a farce. The Constitution of the Republic was itself violated or modified without any popular consultation, to suit the whims of the Executive.

"The death sentence for political offenses, abolition of which had been welcomed as a major achievement of Liberalism, was again in force, arbitrarily and without prior trial.

"As for the common man and his daily life under 'Liberal Federalism,' suffice it to recall that in the haciendas workers were paid in company vouchers, a practice that made them entirely dependent on the owners and re-established a relationship much like slavery;[13] the 'common people' were subject to military service, to the much-dreaded conscription. The whip and the stocks, all the humiliations and suffering known to the soldiery of that period, were imposed on the powerless and bewildered majority of the population.

"These harsh realities did not keep propagandists from continuing to praise the achievements of the 'Liberal revolution.' The name of the Federation was, and continues to be, associated with God's in the motto used in all official governmental statements.[14] But of the impoverished common man, who lived and died as a serf, hungry, prey to untended diseases, and illiterate, it was said that he had finally conquered his freedom."[15]

The so-called Federalism actually abolished the few liberties and the precarious judicial institutions established during the first years of the Venezuelan republic, and with them the modicum of probity that thus far had distinguished public leadership. These freedoms have reappeared only in our own day, and once again they are tenuous and threatened by new barbarians, who claim to be acting in obedience to new "revolutionary" ideas.

This state of contrast in the nineteenth century, between Centralist or Unitary Conservatives on the one hand, and Liberal Federalists on the other, was, however, in no way representative of the basic cleavage that runs through Latin-American societies and opposes "two ways of being, two tendencies: on one side, demagogy, an insatiable thirst for power, the

13. The workers received their salary in these vouchers, redeemable only at the hacienda's store, where the exorbitant prices had been set by the hacienda itself.
14. Even today every official Venezuelan document bears the motto "God and Federation," and is dated from the year of independence and the year of federation.
15. Augusto Mijares, "Actualidad de un viejo antagonismo," *El Nacional,* Caracas, January 24, 1975.

search for personal success and applause . . . on the other side, reason, the love of free thought and reflection. Nor could either tendency be entirely identified with the political factions in existence then or now. We are in the presence of a dilemma that for all Latin America has the character of an intimate spiritual conflict: do we prefer truth or lies?"[16]

The answer, unfortunately, is all too obvious. We find the truth about ourselves too hard to bear, and that is why we Latin Americans have been so receptive to interpretations of our history or to political notions founded on lies or on half-truths. This is why we end up rejecting men who represent the best part of ourselves, such as Sarmiento or Jorge Luis Borges, and admiring others who represent the worst, such as Juan Manuel de Rosas or Perón. Bolívar is an exception; he has remained a hero respected and acclaimed by all; his military accomplishments have made him an Olympian deity in the Pantheon of Latin-American history, unchallenged, beyond controversy. Everyone lays claim to his image; it is distorted and sanctified in a thousand books of political hagiography and in an even greater number of lay sermons preached from all the political pulpits of Latin America. Actually, Bolívar is little read, and quoted only with circumspection.

16. *Ibid.*, p. 104, footnote 1.

4

Ariel and Caliban

Civilization and Barbarism

Another school of Latin-American thought argues that we Latin Americans are endowed with spiritual and mystical qualities that more than compensate for the vulgar, materialistic success of the United States. This is no doubt less objectionable than exalting the dark forces of barbarism present in our history, and tracing our historic identity to these hidden roots. But both views lead to distortion in the perspectives through which we try to view and justify ourselves. The claim of intrinsic superiority over the United States is all the stranger if we consider that throughout our history, from independence until the belated appearance of Marxism, we have borrowed almost all our political ideas and our laws, not to mention the theory and practice of democracy and freedom, from the United States.

Some have expressed surprise at finding that Latin-American countries, which in practice have been so perverse in matters political, and have succumbed to the worst dictatorships, should have shown so much soundness in the formulation of their constitutions and their laws, and should have remained so scrupulously faithful to democracy in theory. The reason is not hard to identify. We have sought to imitate "the great democracy to the north," to live up to the moral and intellectual enlightenment described by Tocqueville. One of the most harmful consequences of Marxist teaching in recent years is that it has broken down this Latin-American ideal of "formal," representative democracy, cast doubts on the aims, achievements, and principles of the liberal revolution, and made us lose our sense of regret or shame when we stray from those high purposes and ideals.

Latin-American resentment of the United States developed even before it was justified by any substantive grounds. Except for the annexation of Mexican territory from north of the Rio Grande to the Pacific—admittedly an offense of considerable importance—the United States gave us no cause for resentment until the twentieth century.

The resentment, however, can partly be explained by well-founded apprehensiveness. The power of the United States was growing visibly, and, even setting aside the usual jealousy and complexes, the Latin-American nations were understandably concerned and distrustful, although their habit of comparing themselves to their northern neighbor did lead to some healthy feelings of emulation.

The Latin American who best incarnates the pro–North American stance may be the Argentine Domingo Faustino Sarmiento, who, in direct consequence, is still looked upon as a traitor by some Latin Americans. Sarmiento was Ambassador to Washington in the mid-nineteenth century; he was elected to the presidency while away from his country—quite a feat in itself—and brought back a number of progressive ideas drawn directly from what he had seen and liked in the United States. There is no doubt that Sarmiento looked to the United States as a model for his country to emulate in its effort to become a truly American, "New World" nation. This led him to introduce in Argentina policies of popular education, immigration, political democracy, economic development, and even conquest of the "desert" (a euphemism for the territories that at the time were still occupied by primitive Indians), all inspired by North American practices.

Sarmiento's immense prestige stemmed from his steady opposition to the Rosas tyranny, and from the book he wrote to expose Rosas's barbarism. *Facundo* remains a classic, one of the more significant studies of the basic Latin-American dilemmas.[1]

Facundo is in fact the biography of a *caudillo* who was exterminated by Rosas during the period following the wars of independence: a regional tyrant who was the incarnation of barbarism, bent on uprooting such civilizing institutions as

1. *Facundo* was first published in 1845, under the title *Civilización y barbarie*. There is an English translation by Stuart Grummon in *A Sarmiento Anthology*, Princeton, 1948.

had begun to take root. From this example, Sarmiento drew up a sociological thesis on the reasons for Argentina's developmental lag and on the means for overcoming it.

Sarmiento viewed barbarism as the *natural state* of the Spanish American republics, the inevitable outcome of the encounter of aboriginal cultures with the Conquest itself and with Spanish colonization, followed by the war of independence and the civil wars. Before these wars, a measure of civilization had begun to develop in the cities, but little of it remained by 1845. Until the outbreak of revolution in 1810, La Rioja had been a "city of the first rank," and its population contained "a number of capitalists and notables." By 1845, the town had practically been wiped off the map, and its population had fallen below one thousand five hundred, of whom perhaps only one or two were literate. In another city, "for the last ten years, there has been only one priest left, there is not a single school, not anyone dressed European-style." An important agricultural center, whose population was swollen to some forty thousand by the influx of refugees from war-torn zones, did not have a single lawyer among its inhabitants: "All the courts of law are made up of men who have no knowledge of the law and who, moreover, are . . . stupid. There is not a single school . . . not a single physician . . . not three young men able to speak English, or four, French; only one is familiar with mathematics. There is only one young man whose education is worthy of a cultured nation. This is Mr. Rawson. His father is North American, and that explains why he has been to college."

Only thirty-five years earlier, these cities had been able to boast of "books, ideas, civic sense, judges, principles of legality, laws, education—*all the points of contact and solidarity that we shared with the Europeans.* The basis of an organization existed, though no doubt unfinished and backward."

Sarmiento, like Bolívar, was one of the few Latin Americans who have not hesitated to call things by their real names; and that is why the Argentine nationalists and fascists look upon him as a traitor while they sing Rosas's praises. Sarmiento refrained from idealizing the Indian, the gaucho, or folklore. Nor did he imagine the Argentine earth to exude some kind of magic fluid that could cure men of all human frailties. His nationalism did not lead him to view his country's defects as virtues and other countries' qualities as defects. He was convinced of the cultural superiority of Europeans—with the exception of Spaniards—and of North Americans; he saw the "noble savage" of the new continent—whether still in his natural state (an irrepressible nomad roaming the pampas, much like the North American Plains Indians), or denatured and degenerate as the result of Spanish colonization and hybridization—as obviously backward.

Sarmiento insisted that the general Latin-American situation, already unsatisfactory before independence, had since further deteriorated. Given the prevailing circumstances, particularly in the countryside, only cities could become the nurturing grounds from which civilization might someday arise again. Only in the cities were there workshops of a building industry, commercial establishments, educational facilities, administrative offices of organized government: "in brief, all that is characteristic of civilized peoples."

To this he compared the desert that "surrounds the cities, encircles them, oppresses them, reduces them to poor oases of civilization." All that this desert had to offer was a primitive, "completely barbarous and backward" life, comparable to that of the nomads of Central Asia or the Bedouins. It followed that "progress is doomed, for there can be no progress without permanent ownership of the land, or without cities, which develop the industrial faculties of man and allow him further to extend his knowledge."

In the Spanish American hinterland, "society has altogether disappeared, and no kind of government is possible any more. Municipalities no longer exist, the police are helpless, and civil justice is incapable of apprehending outlaws."

Sarmiento then came to the heart of his terrible diagnosis: "I don't know any other place in the modern world that presents an example of so monstrous a society [as that in Argentina and elsewhere in Latin America in the 1845's]. We are witnessing something comparable to the feudalism of the Middle Ages. But here, both the baron and his castle are lacking. There is no way either to inherit or to retain power. As a result, even savage tribes are better organized than our rural society. Moral progress and cultivation of the intelligence, which are normally neglected by primitive tribes, are here not only neglected but made impossible. . . . Civilization is utterly out of reach, barbarism is the norm. . . . [Even] religion is affected by [this] dissolution; the parish is a sham, the pulpit has lost its congregation; the priest abandons his deserted chapel, or grows demoralized from inactivity and loneliness;

vices, simony, barbarism . . . find their way into his cell, and he too ends up by becoming a leader of some political faction. . . ."

Sarmiento saw only one small ray of hope—Buenos Aires, the country's main city, which, in the midst of all troubles, had remained "so rich in elements of European civilization that it will finally end up educating Rosas[2] and getting the better of his bloodthirsty and barbarous instincts."

To Govern a Country Is to People It

In Sarmiento's view, the city was also the magnet that would attract European immigration, which was indispensable to Spanish America if it was to dilute the barbarism inherited from its pre-Columbian past, its colonial society, and its wars; this situation was evident even in Buenos Aires:

"We feel shame and sadness when we compare the German or Scottish settlements south of Buenos Aires with the Creole quarter in the same suburb. In the former, the little houses are painted, their fronts always clean, and decorated with flowers and bushes; furniture is simple but sufficient, dishes are of tin or copper and always shined; the bed has its pretty curtains and the people are busily going about their affairs. Some families have built up sizable fortunes, simply milking their cows and churning butter and cheese. . . .

"The Creole quarter is the very opposite. Dirty, ragged children live among bands of roaming dogs; men lie about the streets with nothing to do; everywhere reign poverty and neglect; furniture consists of a small table and coffers; for housing, there are poor shacks; the general appearance is that of a tribe of savages."

It was when faced with this same reality that Juan Bautista Alberdi formulated his famous slogan: "to govern a country is to people it." Like Sarmiento he has been branded a traitor by the *aficionados* of the "noble savage" and "good revolutionary" ideology, past and present.

Once the "authentic," "indigenous" Rosas had been overthrown, the Argentine administrations that followed in the second half of the nineteenth century were so successful in encouraging immigration that the population of Argentina finally came to include as many foreign-born as native citizens.

2. As we have seen, this tyrant, born in the country, was to Sarmiento the symbol of all that was barbaric in Spanish American society.

This was no doubt a strange situation, but it merely reflected the singularity of the American historical adventure as a whole. It certainly makes more sense to recognize the primary influence of Europe than to argue that the Conquest, Spanish colonization, and later European and North American influences fall outside our history and are *opposed* to Latin-American nature; they obviously are basic, decisive components.[3]

It is fashionable today to condemn the contributions to Argentine history made by Sarmiento, Rivadavia, Alberdi, and Mitre. But those who hate these men and call them traitors are themselves the products of the historic processes to which these statesmen so greatly contributed; they are the cultural inheritors and the lineal descendants of immigrants who would not have come to Argentina but for the very policies they now decry. The barbarous Argentina described by Sarmiento is long forgotten. Its first railway, built in 1857, boasted only ten kilometers of tracks; by 1890 there were nine thousand; in 1900, seventeen thousand; in 1912, thirty-three thousand. The same country whose social life fifty years earlier had been compared to that of Central Asian nomads, or worse, had, by the end of the nineteenth century, been effectively civilized and converted into one of the most productive farming and cattle-breeding areas in the world, thanks to the double action of British capital and Italian immigration. From 1869 to 1914, the area of land under cultivation rose from 0.05 hectare per capita to *almost three hectares per capita* (while population increased tenfold, because of immigration). By way of comparison, for the same year, 1914, France had 0.6 hectare per capita under cultivation, the United States less than two. In 1875, Argentina was still an importer of grains; in 1887,

3. Jorge Luis Borges has this to say on the question: "A ridiculous kind of nationalism exists here [in Argentina]. I was giving a lecture when someone asked me what my favorite tree was. The eucalyptus, I replied, it smells nice and is a handsome tree. And I said the tree had been imported from Australia by Sarmiento. . . . So someone in the audience jumped up and shouted: Imported from Australia! What a disgrace! This implies that any tree that is not a native tree is an evil tree, a bad tree, which is silly. . . . We don't talk Quechua, Mohican, Comanche, Mayan, or any such language. We speak Spanish; the whole country therefore has been imported. . . . I have read some fanciful pamphlets that tried to prove that cows and horses had not been introduced by the Spanish, that there had been cows and horses here before them. . . . On another occasion, someone reminded us that the first roses had been brought in from England by Daniel Dávalos. . . . Naturally, this intelligence was received with a certain sadness. . . . We didn't like to hear that roses had been brought in from England. An absurd country, Argentina . . ." (Quoted by Margarita d'Amico, in *El Nacional*, Caracas, April 6, 1975.)

barely twelve years later, it was exporting 237,000 tons. To-day, Argentina is still an important food-exporter, and its do-mestic meat consumption was still an incredible 70 kilograms per capita in 1974.

Nevertheless, young Argentines, whose very names betray the fact that their ancestors came from every corner of Europe, continue to find their country's situation intolerable, and de-clare it to have been "ruined by imperialism." As right-wing or left-wing Peronists or Montoneros,[4] or members of the "People's Revolutionary Army" (also Marxist), they have no qualms about declaring themselves the heirs and avengers of the pre-Columbian Indians, or about giving to the tyrant Rosas the title of hero and precursor.

A Certain Latin-American "New Left"

This peculiar affliction of Argentina, the most paradoxical case of the Latin-American *malaise*, may be less puzzling if we consider that the frustration, bitterness, and irrationality of those who find themselves unaccountably "not up to par" in-creases—instead of diminishing—with relative success.

In one sense, Argentina suffers more than any other Latin-American country from its inferiority vis-à-vis the United States—precisely because Sarmiento's emulation policy was so successful that by 1900 Argentina could reasonably hope to catch up with the United States someday and to become the "Colossus of the South," an imperialist power comparable or superior in power and influence to the "Colossus of the North."

This explains the importance in Argentina of a phenomenon rare in the rest of Latin America: the rise of a politically significant rightist, anti–North American activism. A move-ment of this kind is characteristic of countries that knew a period of greatness at a time when the United States did not yet exist as a nation, or had little sway. This rightist anti-Americanism has no moral objection whatsoever to the im-perialistic use of national power; nor would it be opposed to an imperialistic hegemony. What it does object to—vehemently— is the fact that currently it should be the North Americans who are world-powerful and imperialistic, and not its own country,

4. The Montoneros are the Argentine counterpart of the Uruguayan Tu-pamaros. The name Montonero was first applied to the bands of irregu-lars who scourged the Latin-American countryside following the war of independence and, in some places, continued to do so even well into the twentieth century.

be it France, England, Germany, Japan, Italy, Spain, et cetera. Rightists, like all the other traditionalists of the world, are horrified by the "corrupting and disintegrating" effect of North American ways on their own societies. They view the United States in this context as the source and breeding ground of a "pop" culture that corrupts the traditional values of family and fatherland.[5] But only people whose countries can claim a past greatness can take such positions: it is hard to imagine a de Gaulle emerging in Luxembourg or Monte Carlo, or a Perón in Ecuador or Guatemala!

In fact, in its origin and its essence, Peronism constituted an extension of this illusion of a "Colossus of the South" and sought to revive it by appealing to European forms of fascism, but the moral and military bankruptcy of Nazi Germany and Fascist Italy made this impossible. The evolution of Peronism following this failure typifies the road that Latin America's anti–North Americanism has traveled since 1945. Anti-Americanism has taken a paradoxical turn. In Latin America, a "man of the left" used to be a man in active opposition to authoritarian governments, actively engaged in struggling for the rights of the individual, and an opponent of the establishment and of institutionalized injustice. He was therefore opposed to the United States, which, he felt, was more interested in seeing Latin America stagnate passively in the *status quo* than in helping it develop. But today, to be of the left, one need only be opposed to the United States. As a result, the label covers men of fascist leanings as well as tyrannical and corrupt establishment figures.

Back to the Noble Savage

This redefinition has been a real and profound consequence of the Cuban Revolution, before which only one Latin-American country, Argentina, had seriously dreamed of defying North American power. In other Latin-American countries, men of the right had never dared voice their dislike of the United States; certainly they could not have built a political career on such a platform. To become part of the power structure in Latin America, one needed to be politically pro–North American, or at least not openly anti–North American. Yet at heart, those furthest to the right have shared, or in some cases held

5. On this, see Jean-François Revel, *Without Marx or Jesus: The New American Revolution Has Begun,* New York, Doubleday, 1971.

more strongly than anyone else, the contradictory emotions with regard to the United States that prevail in Latin America. However, they could not externalize into political action the *hate* component of this double feeling, and so could only vent it in words. Or they had to make do with operetta gestures, as when Juan Vicente Gómez, the "Germanophile" Venezuelan consular dictator,[6] adopted the Prussian uniform for his army, complete with spiked helmet. When, through some miscalculation, they expressed their antagonism somewhat too strongly, they incurred the "destabilization" that we have described in reference to Cipriano Castro in Venezuela, and to Jacobo Arbenz in Guatemala.

This explains why ultra-Catholic, Hispanizing writers anathematized the "blue-eyed Yankee heretics." These men of letters felt themselves to be the spiritual soldiers of the Pope and of the Duke of Alva; they called upon the Latin Americans to remember with pride the victories of Lepanto and Breda, and to lament the misfortunes of the Invincible Armada—not to mention the humiliation of the Spanish-American War.

There is also a literature of evasion, contemptuous of both Americas, and regarding them as equally unworthy of serious attention. Latin America's cultural lag is regarded as simply another aspect of overall American barbarism. In the Prologue to his *Prosas profanas*,[7] Rubén Darío has no qualms about saying: "Is there some African or Indian blood flowing in my veins? Perhaps there is, though my hands resemble those of a marquess. And it is true that in my verse you will find princesses, kings, empires, visions of distant lands or fairylands. Can I help it? I detest the time in which it has been my lot to be born; and I could not speak to a president of the republic in the language in which I could sing to thee—O Heliogabalus— whose palace, all of gold, silk, and marble, forever haunts my dreams.

"If there is real poetry in our America, it is to be found in things refined, in Palenque, in Utatlan, in the legendary Indian, in the subtle and sensual Inca, in the great Montezuma of the golden throne. *The rest I leave to you, O democratic Walt Whitman. . . .*"

Escapist literature found another incarnation in so-called tellurism, the belief that there exist tutelary spirits within the

6. See Chapter 9, pp. 224–27.
7. *Prosas profanas y otros poemas,* 1896. There is an English translation by Charles B. Michael, *Prosas Profanas and Other Poems,* New York, Nicholas L. Brown, 1922.

earth, in the soil, and that these have been dominant in shaping the culture and the actions of the Latin-American peoples who inhabit their lands. These spirits—the Latin *lares*—which reigned before Columbus's landing, were terrorized by the atrocities committed by the conquistadors, and driven off by the exorcisms of the new and incomprehensible foreign faith. But the *lares* returned when emancipation was proclaimed, and later withdrew again before the waves of immigration (foreign, like Borges's eucalyptus) of the second half of the nineteenth century and the early twentieth century. Today, they await a new rebirth, the synthesis that will make Latin America a beacon for all humanity.

The "tellurist" who is least painful to read today is the Argentine Ricardo Rojas (1882–1959). In his *Eurindia* (1924), he writes:

"The Spaniards Hispanized the natives, but the Indies and the Indians Indianized the Spaniards. The conquistadors penetrated the aboriginal empires and destroyed them, but three centuries later, the peoples of America expelled the conquerors. Independence was the vindication of the Indians against the civilization come from abroad."

In claiming that the independence movement started "from the cities most attached to the American land," Rojas contradicted the facts of history. If Caracas and Buenos Aires spearheaded the revolt against Spain, it was owing to their readier access to the ideas of the times, as formulated in the United States and in France. This was pointed out by Sarmiento and has since been confirmed by all serious historians.

Rojas's lyricism then led him to argue that political emancipation "liberated the spirits of the countryside, with its Indians, its gauchos, its caciques." Sarmiento had clearly pointed out that for the Indians, the blacks, the mestizos, and the mulattoes (and even for the poor whites), emancipation, the responsibility of power, "and all those problems that the revolution set out to solve, were foreign to their way of life and to their needs." But the lower strata of Spanish American society soon perceived that their own interest imperatively required them to break away from the King's authority: ". . . for this was the way to rid themselves of all authority." The result was described by Sarmiento in *Facundo:* the Latin-American provinces reverted to barbarism, bringing in turn the fierce authoritarianism of the dictators as the only alternative to anarchy.

The telluric interpretation of simple fact is astounding. So-called barbarians (such as Rosas), it held, were the authentic representatives of the tutelary deities of the place. "Civilizers," such as Sarmiento, were outside agents, opposed to these native genii. I am reminded of Francisco Bernárdez's image of the sinister "other self"[8] (as opposed to the *lares*, the *genii loci*, the tutelary deities) of the Argentine people. Rojas, and many others, *revised* Sarmiento when they were not busy tearing him apart, and in doing so they sowed ideas that were later to be seized by Perón and that remain virulent to this day.

Two reasons account for the appeal of Ricardo Rojas's theories to rightist Argentine nationalists, to Latin-American nationalists in general at the time, and to Latin-American leftists of today. Above all, these magic theories charm away the Latin-American failure to which I have repeatedly referred. The successive historic stages of that failure are viewed, rather, as a process that in due course will lead us to a complete triumph, to "Argentinity" (or, to extend the term somewhat abusively, to "Latin Americanity")—a synthesis that will be superior to anything European, and certainly to anything North American. Thus Argentina will fulfill its exceptional destiny, "alloying in one crucible the Indian, the gaucho, and the Spaniard to culminate in an American with a truly Argentine consciousness, taking the Latin, Germanic, and Slavic elements to their ultimate limits and fusing the old Aryan, Semitic, and Western dreams, *thus squaring the circle of human culture.*"

Secondly, the fable of "the tutelary deities" admirably disposes of the inconvenient fact that everything important and alive in Spanish American culture—and foremost the language—can be traced to Europe or to the United States. According to Rojas, "Race is a spiritual phenomenon, endowed with collective meaning, determined by the soil. . . . Individuals, whatever their origin, function as a historic group." And also, of course, within a given topographical framework, a place. "Territory is not only a political reality, it is a crucible in which cosmic forces act on man and determine his character. . . . Race is the collective consciousness of a people that recognizes itself in a common love of the land."

According to this theory, the son of a recent immigrant is of the same "Argentine race" (or Latin-American race) as the pureblood Indian or the black, and all are Tupamaros, descendants of Túpac Amaru. In logical extension of this reasoning, it would now be incumbent on us to dig deep down to uncover, in subsequent layers, what is truly "indigenous" and "authentic," and has been buried there since 1492. All the rest is

8. See pp. 75–76 of this book.

"cosmopolitanism," "alienation"; it is the acceptance of values and attitudes that endorse and prolong imperialist domination and condemn us to cultural dependence, which is in itself the foundation (and the "cause") of economic dependence. When we learned a European language—which happened to be Spanish—we signed away our freedom and became slaves. When we unlearn that language, we will be free—*again*.

The Cosmic Race

At the other end of Spanish America, in Mexico, a writer almost contemporary with Ricardo Rojas prophesied for Latin America an exceptional destiny somewhat similar to that predicted by Rojas, and also, like Rojas, promised compensation for all our humiliations, all our frustrations, and all our failures.

José Vasconcelos (1881–1957) spoke of the destiny of all Latin America; Rojas spoke only of Argentina, infected with the kind of petulant and chauvinistic sense of superiority that some Argentines profess over the rest of the hemisphere. According to Vasconcelos, Latin America will become a bridge between the white, industrial world and what today is called the Third World. This is a role for which history, geography, and our mestizo nature have combined to prepare us. We are Western but of mixed blood, and we have the occult qualities needed to act as mediators, and even as guides, in the planet's progress toward a future of human brotherhood.

The seduction of Vasconcelos's vision lies in its Latin Americanism and its universalism. Though his lyricism may be excessive, he is less prone to resentment than those who, before or after him, relentlessly harped on North American success as opposed to Latin-American failure. Vasconcelos even goes to the length of puncturing, in one telling paragraph, the "Arielist" illusion:[9]

"There has been much talk of the spinning sister who prospers in the north while the creative sister dreams in the south; but this symbol is unfortunately inexact because the United States not only achieves results, but also dreams and creates. And we [Latin Americans], we have not been able to make our

9. In the history of ideas in Latin America, "Arielism" is the significant theme developed by the Uruguayan writer José Enrique Rodó. In his book *Ariel*, Rodó praises Latin America's spiritual superiority over United States materialism. I discuss his theories in greater detail on pp. 94–99.

dreams fruitful, we have not been able to impart the spirit's creative touch to our vision."[10]

For Vasconcelos, modern history is the unfolding of a struggle between two ethical systems, the Latin and the Anglo-Saxon, and there can be no doubt as to the outcome of this confrontation: witness such landmarks as the defeat of the Armada, Nelson's victory at Trafalgar, Dewey's at Manila, and Sampson's at Santiago de Cuba.[11]

Nowadays, the scene of this conflict is in the New World, in the Americas, and the Anglo-Saxon ethos has never been so convincingly vindicated as by the North Americans.

Latin America, however, is not only Latin. It is also Indian and black, even Asiatic, a melting pot of races. Because of its basically hybrid nature, it is the only area where a historic mutation can take place through which not only the continent but also mankind as a whole will attain an unprecedented level of development. We will be the pioneers of a universal civilization, of a *cosmic* civilization:

"History does not repeat itself. . . . No race ever reappears on earth; each defines its mission, fulfills it, and disappears. . . . The days of the ethnically pure whites, today's victors, are numbered. . . . By accomplishing their mission, which was to mechanize the world, they have unknowingly laid the foundations of a new era, the era of the fusion and unification of all peoples."

Having thus fulfilled their mission, and no longer able—according to Vasconcelos's premises—to contribute anything significant, the Anglo-Saxons are disqualified from assuming leadership in the coming historic cycle, since they have failed to create a community that integrates the colored races. They have exterminated the Indians and the blacks, or segregated them inexcusably through racial discrimination. Latin America, on the other hand, "assimilates the colored races; this gives us new rights and the hope of an unprecedented mission in history. . . ." "We are beginning to recognize an imperative of history: that 'overflow of love' which allowed the Spaniards to create a new race fusing with the Indians and the black,[12]

10. This and all subsequent Vasconcelos quotations are from *La raza cosmica*, 1925.
11. The latter two are the decisive naval battles of the Spanish-American War of 1898.
12. What in fact took place during the Conquest and the colonization was not an overflow of love but an incredible fury of sexual indulgence directed toward Indian and black women, as a result of which a very small number of Spanish men engendered a multitude of mestizo and mulatto descendants, and laid the ground for the tradition of paternal

generously spreading the seed[13] and extending the culture of
the white West. . . .

"The English continued to breed only with whites . . .
which shows their limitations and heralds their decadence.
For in taking this stance, the Anglo-Saxons merely followed
the usual proud process of a victorious race; they did what all
strong and homogeneous races have wanted to do throughout
history. But this does not answer the human problem. The
American continent was not held in reserve over five thousand
years for so limited an objective. This new and ancient continent has a much higher destiny. It is destined to become the
cradle of a fifth race which will unite all the peoples of the
world and replace the four races that have so far shaped history isolatedly. It is on the soil of Latin America that the scat-
tering of races will end: here, racial unity will be consum-
mated by the triumph of fruitful love and the sublimation of
all origins. . . . Our undeviating loyalty to this hidden purpose is the guarantee of our triumph. . . . We are the humanity of tomorrow while they [the North Americans] are on their
way to becoming the humanity of yesterday, the last great
single-race empire, the last empire of the white race. . . ."

We Latin Americans are not going to repeat one of the
constantly recurring cycles of history, one of the "partial attempts of nature." It will be our triumph "to be the definitive
race, the synthesis race, the *cosmic* race . . . combining the
genius and the blood of all peoples . . . and therefore able to
achieve genuine fraternity and to project a truly universal
vision of the world."

There is something moving, but also something equivocal,
and therefore typically Latin American, in this 1925 adaptation of Marxist themes—class struggle and the resolution of
history through the triumph of one of the contenders. In Vasconcelos's interpretation can be seen an exact parallel to the
Marxist notion of class struggle as the basic pattern of history,
with "Latinity" taking the place of feudalism, the Anglo-Saxons
that of the bourgeoisie, and the Latin Americans (the only
people able to transcend the limitations and egoism of other
dominant races or classes of history) that of the proletariat.
And if the Latin Americans can take on this heroic role, it is
precisely because of the degree of their former humiliation. In

---

irresponsibility that is one of the greatest plagues of Latin America.
13. Note the wording used here, as well as the "ethnic synthesis" quoted
earlier. Vasconcelos speaks as a Spanish white and gives in to racism,
as fair-skinned Latin Americans so often do.

fact, we know only too well that Latin-American society has been particularly inhuman and brutal, having been unable to rid itself of the social norms of domination and submission earlier imposed by the conquistadors. If one is to look for signs that someday man may be able to find a different and better way to live with his fellow man, it is far-fetched to seek them in Latin America. Such signs, if they exist, can only surface in evolved societies: Scandinavia, West Germany, the Netherlands, Great Britain, France, Japan, and particularly the United States. These are the countries from which we have imported practically all our ideals, all our humanist and humanitarian institutions, socialism included.

This is something that Latin Americans know perfectly well, to the extent that they are able to face the truth about themselves and their history. Vasconcelos, who was among the most intelligent, cultivated, and lucid Latin Americans of his day, certainly knew it. But he nevertheless expounded his fable of the "cosmic race"—one of those lies that, in Octavio Paz's terms, "reflect both what we lack and what we desire, both what we are not and what we would like to be," lies that we go on inventing "because we are desperate."[14] This despair clearly surfaces through Vasconcelos's apparent messianic optimism: "Anglo-Saxons were able to fulfill their mission faster than we because theirs was concerned with the immediate and had some precedents in history. To fulfill their destiny the Anglo-Saxons had only to follow in the footsteps of other victorious peoples. The white man's values reached their zenith when they were transferred from Europe to the New World. As a result, the history of North America is as the uninterrupted and heartening *allegro* of a triumphal march."

Ariel and Caliban

Theories such as those of Ricardo Rojas or José Vasconcelos were important because, unlikely as it may appear, they were taken seriously in their day and stirred enthusiasm throughout most of Latin America. Even today their power of seduction is not quite spent, for they bring into play mythical allusions of permanent significance.

Another book, whose success was far more surprising—or perhaps revealing, since it is so dull, shallow, and bloated a production—was José Enrique Rodó's *Ariel*. It is utterly un-

14. *The Labyrinth of Solitude*, pp. 40, 41.

readable today, but when it first appeared, in 1900, it was hailed throughout the hemisphere as the resounding and irrefutable manifesto of Latin America, of a Latin America that stood as the champion of the spirit fighting the gross materialism of the Chicago meat packers.

Rodó, a Uruguayan who lived from 1872 to 1917, succeeded in giving expression to all the anguish and resentment not of the continent (whose inhabitants in 1900 had mostly heard neither of *Ariel* nor, for that matter, of any other book), but of *the Latin-American ruling classes*. Particularly of the intellectuals, who took *Ariel* as the springboard for their own books and articles and gave Rodó's thought an immense resonance. *Ariel* had struck the right chord, it provided the intellectuals with the psychological compensation they craved. It is still agreed even today that this book had great importance for the history of ideas in Latin America, but actually it has few readers. Anyone who attempts to read it soon puts it down with a feeling of embarrassment at what it reveals—not about North Americans (which is not much), but about Latin Americans themselves.

Rodó belongs to the generation of Rubén Darío, the man with the hands of a marquess, to whom Latin America was so repugnant that he found relief in dreaming about the court of Heliogabalus, all of gold, silk, and marble. The opening pages of *Ariel* are quite reminiscent of this, but with a difference. Rodó was not a poet, but a *philosophe* who nostalgically harked back to the Golden Age of Athens:

"Prodigious city, which thought of life as of the concert of all human faculties, as of the free and harmonious development of all energies able to contribute to the glory and power of men. . . . Each free Athenian set limits to his activities, which described a perfect circle, its harmony nowhere to be broken by chaotic compulsions. Whether an athlete or a living sculpture at the gymnasium, a citizen at the Pnyx, a polemicist or a thinker under the porticoes, he exercised his will in all sorts of virile deeds and his thought in the most varied and fruitful meditation."

How does all this apply to Latin America? Rodó was writing for the small minority of Latin Americans who enjoyed a high economic, political, or social position—all university graduates, for instance—free citizens in a society that, like Athens, continued to depend on slave labor. These members of the Latin-American elite should, like the Greeks, "consider leisure as the noblest way of leading a truly rational life, associating leisure with the kind of thinking that is free from any base subjection to reality." As he read *Ariel*, a Latin-American poet, employed, for instance, as Vice Consul in Paris, Madrid, or Barcelona, could feel himself an exalted being, superior in his leisure to Edison and Ford, so busy in the vulgar north soiling their hands while inventing ill-smelling and noisy machinery. That his idleness was made possible by the labor of slaves in the Central American coffee plantations or in the tin mines of Bolivia made no difference.

Rodó went on to stress that we must preserve "the integrity of the human condition at all costs . . . No single pursuit[15] should ever make us forget this supreme truth. The hollowness of artificially constricted aspirations renders *ephemeral*[16] the glory of societies that have sacrificed the free development of their sensitivity and of their thought to mercantilism, as was done by the Phoenicians, or to warfare, as was done by Sparta."

Which translates into: The North Americans are piling up all the money in the world on Wall Street, they gave us a thrashing at Manila and at Santiago de Cuba, but we are Athens, hence *eternal*, and they are Phoenicia and Sparta, hence *ephemeral*.

What of democracy? So crude a political system, said Rodó, "stands convicted of debasing humanity and leading it to a Holy Empire of utilitarianism . . . Noble concern for the highest interests of the species goes utterly counter to the democratic spirit: democracy implies the crowning of Caliban and the defeat of Ariel. . . . It fatally leads to the primacy of mediocrity; more than any other system it lacks the safeguards that would protect what is highest in culture; democracy gradually atrophies any idea of superiority other than that demonstrated by greater smartness and ruthlessness in competitive struggles which themselves become the most ignoble incarnation of brute force. . . ."

The Latin-American ruling elite easily understood this allusive language. Ariel, the fairy spirit, was one of their own kindred, while the more able and enterprising North Americans were incarnations of Caliban, the symbol of animalism. Besides, Rodó soon made his meaning clear: "There are two closely interconnected components of the model usually called *Americanism:* utilitarianism as a conception of human des-

15. Launching a warship or ordering an artillery attack? For let us bear in mind that *Ariel* was among other things Latin America's response to the United States' victory in the Spanish-American War two years earlier.
16. My italics.

tiny, and equality through mediocrity as the purpose of social relations."

Regrettably, some Latin Americans were seduced by the material power of the United States, selling their souls to compete with and equal the North American barbarians. This had to be considered a major mistake. True, the North Americans were efficient, but only in the service of immediate practical goals. Their civilization, Americanism, "consequently conveys a singular impression of incompleteness and imperfection." Then Rodó went on to pontificate:

"The North Americans have no ear for the right note, the note of good taste. In such a setting, true art can come into being only in the form of individual revolt. . . . The idea of beauty has no appeal for North Americans, any more than the idea of truth. To them, any intellectual activity that has no immediate practical application appears vain and sterile, an object of contempt."

The educational system of the United States might be extensive, but "it has resulted in a generalized half-culture, and an actual retardation of genuine culture. As illiteracy disappears, so do superior culture and genius."

As a result, all the readers of *Ariel,* from the Rio Grande to Tierra del Fuego, came to the astonishing conclusion that, in a territory with an illiteracy rate of 90 percent, the conditions for a flowering of a new Athens were naturally present, for, unlike the North Americans, "we Latin Americans are inheritors of a racial legacy; we have a great ethnic tradition to maintain, a sacred bond which establishes our solidarity with the immortal moments of history."[17]

Finally, we need not be unduly concerned with the insolent power of the North Americans, which displayed itself so overwhelmingly during the Spanish-American War:

"The very character of the North Americans makes any hope of hegemony an impossibility. Nature refused to grant them a genius for propaganda and for an apostolic vocation. They lack the supreme gift of amiability—in the noblest sense of the word: the ability to be civil to others and to display that

17. This platitude about the exceptional destiny of Latin America, which sees us as taking up the torch of "Latinity" against the "Anglo-Saxon" culture, became a catchword for the generation that bridged the turn of this century. Another quote, from the Peruvian Francisco García Calderón (1883–1953): "Some day the Latin empire which gave Spain heroic Quixotism; which in Florence witnessed the harmonious development of man's faculties; which gave France serene reason, a subtle language, and all-conquering grace, will have a new avatar in the Indies of Christopher Columbus."

extraordinary power of empathy by which races entrusted with a providential mission . . . can make of their culture something akin to Helen's beauty . . . in which all recognize some trait of their own. . . ."

Almost all Latin-American intellectuals of the nineteenth and early twentieth centuries shared Rodó's feelings. Helen stood for Latin Europe, and particularly for France. It is interesting to note that the affinity and admiration that men like Miranda and Bolívar felt for England were not shared by later Latin-American intellectuals. Although they welcomed British investments and adopted British technology, the Latin Americans of the second half of the nineteenth century seemed to experience an instinctive resistance, an emotional need to reject what was Anglo-Saxon. Latin Americans may have identified the British with the North Americans, who were becoming troublesome neighbors.

Thus we countered defeat with a bad book. The remarkable reception that greeted its publication may be due to its success in re-establishing—at least in the Latin Americans' minds— some measure of balance between the power of the North Americans and our own weakness, and in quieting the conscience of Latin-American intellectuals. (The term "intellectual" is rather ambiguous among us: it includes all who are "lettered" in the sense of the French word "*lettré*." It embraces not only bona fide scholars, diplomats, et cetera, but also lawyers or political figures working as "secretaries" to the *caudillos,* and is even extended to cover the editor of the slightest pamphlet, a poet who has turned out only one sonnet, or the author of a single article.) The main cause of their "existential" discomfort, as we would say nowadays, was their privileged position in a society that remained extremely backward and that was committed to a structure that stands as a classic example of social inequality and servitude.

For some years now, Rodó and his book have reposed in the dustbins of history. Marxism now fulfills for Latin America the same function that Rodó's manifesto did earlier, and in a far superior way: it offers a cosmic vision, and can therefore act as a unifying force. Moreover, its pole of attraction lies not in a mythical Athens or in a hypothetical "Latinity," but in a power that is the very tangible, present-day rival of the United States: the Soviet Union.

Of course the Soviet Union has in recent years stood revealed as a far more repulsive and threatening Caliban figure than anything Rodó could have dreamed of, or even in his worst nightmares attributed to the United States. But it is a great power, and it is the world enemy of the overbearing North Americans. Further, it has been amply proven that the failures of Marxism in no way lessen its seductive power. For the followers of this new faith, as for those of older religions, neither bad shepherds nor the transformation of the Church into an organ of brutal repression detracts in any way from the hopes of redemption formulated by the prophets.

5

Latin America and Marxism

The Pillage of the Third World

It is not exactly Marxism but, rather, the Leninist theory of imperialism and dependence that in our day has come to bring a coherent, convincing, and grandiose answer to Latin America's chronic inferiority complex.[1]

Our culture developed alongside that of the North Americans in the Western Hemisphere, and our two histories are parallel in many ways. This closeness, this identification, leads us to painful and humiliating comparisons, and every Latin American, when his conscience awakens, needs to find an explanation for the contrast. In earlier chapters I discussed a number of significant and characteristic attempts in the history of ideas in Latin America to reduce this contrast or to reverse it. As we have seen, this can be done by arguing that Latin America's inferiority is only a surface phenomenon and that it hides a subtle and essential superiority; or by attempting to demonstrate that the inferiority has been, and continues to be, real, but that through some future historic change it will be transformed into predestined superiority.

The next step—one that was assured of instant success—was to formulate a hypothesis according to which the differences in power and wealth between Latin America and the United States were in no way (or at least not essentially) due to any North American virtue, or to any Latin-American short-

---

1. No doubt this remark can be extended to the complex—albeit more general and diffuse—with which the Third World as a whole is afflicted in its dealings with the industrialized Western world.

comings, but could be wholly explained through the operation of world capitalism. Since world capitalism has at the same time caused the development of advanced capitalist nations and the underdevelopment of colonies and dependent nations, the latter really deserve all the credit for capitalist prosperity and power, wherever they are found, since they have paid for these benefits with their poverty and their weakness.

Latin America could then be seen as a particular case of a general law whereby the advance of some countries and the lag of others are due essentially to the economic, cultural, and political relations between the two groups, a connection entirely advantageous to the first group, and entirely harmful to the second. So much so that, for instance, if the connection between them had never been established, England would be as backward as India, or India as advanced as England, or both would be in a comparable stage of development, lower than the current English level of development, but higher than India's.

Marx, of course, never held with such foolishness. In a letter dated April 9, 1870, there is a vaguely similar argument, but it is made in reference to Great Britain's relations with Ireland, a nation not considered part of the Third World; and it would be highly improper to cite this reference in support of the thesis that today is at the very core of the Third World ideology.

That the poverty of the Third World and the wealth of the capitalist West are two facets of one phenomenon is a contention that has proved enormously appealing. It invariably comes up in the books and articles of all the leftists of the first, second, and third worlds. It can also be found in the so-called progressive-development economics criticized by Gunnar Myrdal in his *Asian Drama* and *The Challenge of World Poverty*. It appears in the speeches of Third World political leaders and is in general infiltrating the thinking of the Third World—whose ranks it is therefore no surprise that Latin America has thought proper to join. In the countries where this thesis has taken hold, practically no one dares criticize or refute it.

On the Inequality of Nations

That Marx and Engels bore precapitalist or (more simply) backward nations no particular love is abundantly proven in their writing. I have noted and given the reasons for Marx's conviction that India actually benefited from its contact with England.[2] The basic text of Marxism, the *Communist Manifesto*, is equally clear. Its first part praises the bourgeois-liberal-capitalist revolution as a gigantic step forward, the most remarkable and promising historical stage before the advent of socialism. One of the reasons Marx gave was that the liberal revolution, among other benefits, succeeded in establishing links of *interdependence* between the (advanced) capitalist countries and the (backward) precapitalist countries.

This was in 1847. In a much later and, we might say, more mature analysis, Engels provided a materialistic, historical, and dialectical explanation of the naturally unequal progress of different societies through the various stages of culture, from the primitive state to industrial civilization. This explanation is a mainstay of his book *The Origin of the Family, Private Property, and the State* (1884), one of Engels's most characteristically Marxist writings, which only death kept Marx from writing himself; Engels merely completed a project for which Marx had left a very detailed sketch.

According to this joint effort, it is only in the state of primitive savagery that "we could regard the course of [social] evolution as being generally valid for a definite period among all peoples, irrespective of their locality." When we go beyond the state of primitivism, "with the advent of barbarism, however, we reach a stage *where the difference in natural endowment of the two great continents begins to assert itself*.[3] The characteristic feature of the period of barbarism is the domestication and breeding of animals and the cultivation of plants. Now the Eastern continent, the so-called Old World, contained almost all the cultivable cereals with one exception: while the Western Hemisphere contained only one domesticable animal, the llama, and this only in a part of the South; and only one cereal fit for cultivation, but that the best, maize."

The result of these natural conditions was that from the stage of barbarism on, the two hemispheres (and eventually certain regions within each of them) "became differentiated, as did their aims and the lines of separation between the different periods of their historic development."

In the special case of America, Engels noted that at the time of the Spanish Conquest, the least backward of the peoples of

2. See pp. 46–49.
3. My italics.

the New World—the Peruvians and the Mexicans—"were still in a state of semi-barbarism . . . Not knowing the use of iron, they were still dependent on stone weapons and tools." That is to say, the pre-Columbian Peruvians and Mexicans were still at a level of historic development that the Mediterranean peoples had passed at least two thousand years earlier.

But that is not all. Engels says that for this and other reasons, particularly better nutrition,[4] the *higher* level of the primitive state (and, correspondingly, a higher level of civilization) "was reached independently only in the Eastern Hemisphere."

At this higher level of primitivism, "more progress was made in production than in all the previous stages put together. . . . We here encounter for the first time the iron ploughshare drawn by cattle, making possible land cultivation on a wide scale—tillage—and, in the conditions then prevailing, a practically unlimited increase in the means of subsistence; in connection with this we find also the clearing of forests and their transformation into arable and pasture land—which, again, would have been impossible on a wide scale without the iron axe and the spade. But with this there also came a rapid increase of the population and dense populations in small areas. Prior to tillage only very exceptional circumstances could have brought together half a million people under one central leadership: in all probability this never happened."[5]

The causes and consequences that Engels describes did not materialize in America; indeed, they could not have materialized outside of Eurasia without the impact of European civilization. It follows that the myth of the noble savage, as well as the Leninist theory of imperialism and dependence and all its derivative theories, are seriously shaken by a careful reading of Marx's and Engels's thinking (which in this case is but the reflection of the most elementary common sense).

Marx's and Engels's Blindness

When I recently presented the afore-mentioned argument to a Venezuelan audience, the reaction was one of surprise mixed with some hostility. Someone argued that Marx and Engels had

4. See p. 26 (note).
5. In Karl Marx and Friedrich Engels, *Selected Works,* vol. 2, pp. 171–72, 173.

not lived long enough to witness the effects of imperialism, as we can observe and understand them today.

What this proves is that dogmatism is one thing, facts are another. Marx died in 1883, and Engels in 1895. By that time, the premises for later theories according to which the wealth of some nations and the poverty of others can be explained almost entirely by the advantages of imperialism and the disadvantages of "dependence," had become widely obvious. The first to formulate these theories were Hobson[6] and Hilferding;[7] subsequently Lenin took them up in his *Imperialism: The Highest Stage of Capitalism* (1917); and since then they have appeared and reappeared with ever-growing assurance, dogmatic and anti-Marxist in their claim to offer a blanket explanation for the unequal development of different parts of the world. (Pierre Jalée, Paul Baran, and André Gunder Frank are among the current spokesmen of this so-called theory of dependence. Latin America has of course its own crop, including the Brazilian Celso Furtado.)

The British presence in India dates back to the sixteenth century and had developed into absolute control even before Marx's birth in 1818. The Dutch set up their establishments in Java in the seventeenth century. The Spanish had secured their American empire by 1550, and the Philippines by 1600 (Manila was founded in 1571). France's influence had been paramount in Indochina since the sixteenth century, and the peninsula was made a French colony in 1858. France conquered Algeria in 1830, when Engels was ten years old. In 1853, the North Americans forced Japan to begin a process of integration into the world capitalist system. Chinese resistance to the same process was broken by the British in 1842 in the so-called Opium War. Ceylon (now Sri Lanka) became a British colony in 1796, West Africa in 1838. Egypt became a British protectorate in 1882, one year before Marx's death, and thirteen years before Engels's. From 1846 to 1848, the United States fought Mexico and annexed Mexican territory. And so on!

Let us take as a point of reference the date 1848, when Marx and Engels, then respectively 30 and 28 years old, were writing the *Communist Manifesto*. By that time, all the imperialist countries (which, according to the hypothesis under dis-

6. John Atkinson Hobson (British), in *Imperialism*, 1902.
7. Rudolf Hilferding (Austrian, naturalized German), in *Das Finanzkapital*, 1910.

cussion, achieved their development only by plundering the Third World) had in fact reached levels of economic, political, social, scientific, and technological development far superior to the rest of the world's.

It is therefore obvious that the impact of the imperialist, capitalist West on what today is called the Third World had made itself felt by 1848, and that the consequences, favorable and adverse, of this impact on both parties were already distinguishable. The contrast between the rich and the poor countries were perhaps sharper than they are today. Nonetheless, it never occurred to "the greatest thinker of the century," as Engels called Marx, speaking at his graveside, to argue that the advance of the capitalist countries or the lag of the colonial territories was due to the relations that existed between them. That these relations of domination by one group over another were unfair, and pregnant with trouble, everyone now agrees; but Marx saw in them, rather, the only chance of progress for the countries that now constitute the Third World.

And, as late as 1893, in his preface to *The Condition of the Working Class in England*, Engels once more stressed the significance that he believed colonial expansion might have—this time in counteracting the crisis of overproduction in advanced capitalist countries. But he did not for one moment argue, against all common sense and evidence, that the progress and accumulation of wealth in such countries as England, France, Holland, and Belgium (the classic imperialist countries) was primarily due to their colonial role; or that nations such as Austria-Hungary, Switzerland, Sweden, and Denmark, which had no colonies, derived some vague "indirect" benefits that would brand them as intrinsically "imperialist," aligned with the colonial powers, as others have claimed.[8]

If this thesis—that the inequality among nations evident today was determined by imperialism and dependency—were founded on sound arguments, rather than elaborated by *ad hoc* propaganda, one could justifiably ask how Marx and Engels failed to notice so fundamental a point in their ambitious search for the basic laws of past and future historic development. How could they have overlooked these premises, which today are said to derive from a gigantic historic process that began more than two centuries before their birth and reached its culmination before their eyes?

8. See, for example, Pierre Jalée, *The Pillage of the Third World*, trans. Mary Klopper, New York, Monthly Review Press, 1968.

Leninist Revisionism

The real reason why Marx and Engels did not attach great importance to the Afro-Asian and Latin-American worlds lies in the fact that they still believed in the imminent collapse of the capitalist system in the advanced countries. Such a prospect seemed plausible, and early theorists of Marxism thus did not feel called upon to explain why their prophets' predictions were not being fulfilled. By the end of the century, however, it was obvious that the capitalist system was not drawing to a final crisis in England, France, Germany, or anywhere else. Rather than witnessing the desperate, progressive pauperization of workers that Marx had predicted, the century was enjoying steady growth in the real purchasing power of earnings. Instead of the expected blockage through lack of investment opportunities for accumulating capital, the economy boomed as the ingenuity of financiers and the opportunities for further capital investment proved seemingly inexhaustible. And in the transatlantic distance, the United States stood ready to enter the arena as a major capitalist power.

The First World War revived the Marxists' hope for an imminent final crisis within the capitalist world. But it also demonstrated the futility of counting on the international solidarity of the working class to help destroy capitalism by overcoming national borders. Much concerned, the Marxists were now under pressure to provide a satisfactory explanation for the renewed vitality of capitalism, and to propose a revised statement of the prospects for future development, so as to breathe new life into the key Marxist tenet that the dynamics of history would inevitably lead to the world-wide triumph of the socialist revolution.[9]

This need serves to explain the revisionism of Hobson, Hilferding, and Lenin in attributing the unexpected strengthening of capitalism in the advanced countries, and the lowering of combativity among the industrial proletariat in these countries, to imperialism. They went on to conclude that the world revolutionary struggle against the capitalist system would have its main setting not in the Western, capitalist countries, as Marx and Engels had thought, but in the distant lands in

9. In much the same way, the disciples of Christ, when they became convinced that the Second Coming and the millennium were not imminent, reformulated Christianity on the basis of other expectations than the Messiah's immediate return.

which these countries had established colonies or dependencies. The proletariat of *men* in the advanced capitalist countries had shown it lacked the will to struggle; its individual members were too susceptible to improvements in their living and working conditions. New *nations* would have to be substituted for men, and a proletariat of nations would become the principal mover of world revolution.

This revisionist theory was particularly attractive to Lenin, since his own country, Russia, was marginal to the capitalist system, and he felt little sympathy with explanations that held his country to owe its revolution to the Germans or the English.

Here are the operative passages: "Capitalism has now brought to the front a handful (less than one-tenth of the inhabitants of the globe; less than one fifth, if the most 'generous' and liberal calculations were made) of the very rich and very powerful states that plunder the whole world. . . . Obviously, out of such enormous *super-profits* (since they are obtained over and above the profits that capitalists squeeze out of the workers of their 'home' country), it is quite *possible to bribe* the labor leaders and the upper stratum of the labor aristocracy. . . . This stratum of bourgeoisified workers . . . are the *real agents of the bourgeoisie* in the labor movement. . . . Not the slightest progress can be made toward the solution of the practical problems of the Communist movement and of the impending social revolution unless the economic roots of this phenomenon are understood and unless its political and sociological significance is appreciated."[10]

"The division of the world into two main groups—of colony-owning countries on the one hand and colonies on the other—is not the only typical feature of this period; there is also a variety of forms of dependent countries; countries that, officially, are politically independent, but that are, in fact, enmeshed in the net of financial and diplomatic dependence. . . ."[11]

" 'Imperialism' is a state of parasitic, decaying capitalism, and this circumstance cannot fail to influence all the social-political conditions of the countries affected [the colonies and dependent countries—in a manner favorable to revolution]

10. V. I. Lenin, Preface to the French and German editions (1929) of *Imperialism: The Highest Stage of Capitalism, Selected Works*, 2 vols. Moscow, Foreign Language Publishing House, 1947, vol. 1, pp. 635–36.
11. Lenin, *Imperialism*, p. 692.

. . . weakening the . . . empires [through] economic para-
sitism and . . . the formation of armies composed of subject
races. . . ."12

The following paragraph from Hilferding is particularly revealing: "In the newly opened-up countries themselves
[Lenin's "colonial and dependent countries"] the capitalism
imported into them intensifies contradictions and excites the
constantly growing resistance against the intruders of the
peoples who are awakening to national consciousness. . . .
This . . . threatens [imperialism so that it] can maintain
its domination only by continually increasing its means of exerting violence."13

Thus, it is clear that Hobson's and Hilferding's theories, as
propagated by Lenin, admirably fit in with the need of backward countries to explain their backwardness and weakness in
terms other than their own inferiority.14 As far as the revolutionary Soviet state itself was concerned, the new theories
were to prove of great interest and applicability, enabling Russia to break through its isolation and to make up at least par-
tially for its weakness vis-à-vis the advanced capitalist countries by waving the much-feared flag of subversion in these
countries' peripheries: in their colonies, their zones of influence, and their client states.

The Theses of the Third International

This is why the Second Congress of the Communist International (the Third International), which met in Moscow in

12. *Ibid.*, p. 705.
13. Hilferding, quoted by Lenin, *ibid.*, p. 720.
14. It should be stressed that there is nothing mythical or imaginary
about imperialism and the exploitation of the weak countries by the
stronger. Throughout history, strong countries have submitted weak ones
to all kinds of humiliations, punishments, and exactions. But it is manifestly false to conclude that the imperialist countries, from antiquity to
the present day, have derived their power from these exactions: It is,
rather, that these can take place because decisive imbalances of power
already existed *prior* to any contacts, before any inequitable transfer of
wealth from the weak to the strong. Further, it cannot be taken for
granted that a country's ability to act as an imperialist power, and to
transfer wealth from its colonies to itself, will necessarily turn to its
advantage. The example of Spain, ruined by its fantastic success in
America, suffices to prove that the greatest inflow of wealth can be catastrophic if the society receiving it *lacks the capacity for internal development.* The latter is far more important and decisive for a nation's own
prosperity and stability than the military and political talent required
to subdue other peoples.

1920, spent much of its time converting the Hobson-Hilferding-Lenin theses into practical advice for revolutionary action in the territories that today constitute the Third World—or at least into demonstrations of solidarity with the Russian Revolution. The propositions adopted by the Second Congress of the Third International are amazingly pertinent to an understanding of the politics and ideas of our time.[15]

The theses state that the allegedly equal relations between sovereign nations in fact cover up the enslavement of the great majority of the world's population by a very limited minority—the bourgeoisie and the workers' aristocracy of the advanced capitalist countries—and that it will be impossible to abolish this slavery and to eliminate inequalities between the rich and the poor countries without first destroying capitalism throughout the world.

Once this is understood, the theses then argue, the political evolution and history of the world will be seen to revolve around the struggle between the advanced, capitalist, imperialist countries and the revolutionary Soviet power (the U.S.S.R. did not yet exist in its present form.) In order to survive and to win, the Soviet Union will have to enroll the support of all the "proletarian vanguard groups" of the world (that is to say, all the parties affiliated, or ready to be affiliated, with the Communist International), as well as all the *nationalist* movements in the colonial territories and dependent countries. These nationalist movements will have to be persuaded that their interests and aspirations converge (and are in fact identical) with the defense and promotion of Soviet power, and thus with the progress and future triumph of world revolution.

The Communist parties, therefore, will have to follow a policy of "realizing the closest possible union between all national and colonial liberation movements and Soviet Russia"; the form of this alliance in each separate colony or dependent country will be determined by the stage of development that its Communist movement and its corresponding national liberation movement will have reached.

"It [will be] necessary . . . to explain constantly that only the Soviet regime is able to give the nations real equality [and likewise] to support the revolutionary movement among the

15. The preparation of the "Theses of the Second Congress of the Communist International on National and Colonial Questions" grew out of a collaboration between Lenin himself and the Hindu Communist M. N. Roy. It is worth noting that Roy was then sent to Latin America by the Third International, and that we owe to him the founding of the Mexican Communist party.

subject nations, [for example] Ireland, the American Negroes.
. . . The victory over capitalism cannot be fully achieved
and carried to its ultimate goals unless the proletariat [of the
advanced capitalist countries][16] and the toiling masses [of
colonial and dependent countries] rally . . . in a heartfelt
and close union. . . . One of the main sources from which
. . . capitalism draws its chief strength is to be found in the
colonial possessions and dependencies. Without the control of
those extensive markets and vast fields of exploitation, capitalism cannot maintain its existence even for a short time. . . .
Extra profits gained in the colonies and dependent countries
are the mainstay of modern capitalism, and so long as the
latter is not deprived of this source of extra profit it will not be
easy for . . . the working class [i.e., the Communist parties of
the advanced capitalist countries] to overthrow the capitalist
order. . . . Thus, it is the breaking up of the colonial empire
[and the emancipation of the dependent countries] together
with the [then inevitable] proletarian revolution in each home
country that will overthrow the capitalist system in advanced
capitalist countries. . . . In order to promote these objectives,
it must be taken into account that there are to be found in the
dependent countries [and in the colonies] two distinct movements. . . . One is the bourgeois democratic nationalist
order, and the other is the mass action of the poor and ignorant peasants and workers for their liberation from all forms
of exploitation. . . . The cooperation of the bourgeois nationalist revolutionary elements is useful for the overthrow of foreign imperialistic capitalism, which is the first step toward
socialist revolution in the colonies [and dependent countries].
. . . Thus the masses in the backward countries may reach
Communism, not through capitalist development, but directly
under the leadership of the class-conscious proletariat of the
advanced capitalist countries [i.e., the Third International]."[17]

These theories were later to acquire more subtle and veiled
formulations, while they imposed themselves throughout the
world; in a sense, whenever anyone uses the expression "Third
World," he is tacitly endorsing some of the basic assumptions

16. In Communist parlance the word "proletariat" came to be used more
and more frequently to designate the Communist party ("avant-garde of
the proletariat"), starting with Lenin's assertion in *Imperialism: The
Highest Stage of Capitalism* that "the union leaders and . . . the workers' aristocracy of the advanced capitalist countries had been bought off
and had been corrupted by the bourgeoisie."
17. *Report of the Proceedings*, Communist International, 2nd Congress,
Moscow, 1920, pp. 571–79.

contained in the "Theses of the Third International," presented at its Congress in 1920.

But before this strategy received its more shaded formulations, ostensibly straying from its initial purpose, it was stated tersely and brutally by Stalin, in *Problems of Leninism* (written in 1924).

"The road to victory of the [Communist] revolution in the West lies through revolutionary alliance with the liberation movement of the colonies and dependent countries against imperialism. . . . The revolutionary character of a national movement . . . does not presuppose the existence of proletarian elements in the movement, the existence of a revolutionary or a republican program of the movement, the existence of a democratic basis of the movement. The struggle the Emir of Afghanistan is waging for the independence of Afghanistan is objectively a *revolutionary* struggle, despite the monarchist views of the Emir and his associates, for it weakens, disintegrates, and undermines imperialism. . . . For the same reasons, the struggle the Egyptian merchants and bourgeois intellectuals are waging for the independence of Egypt is objectively a revolutionary struggle, despite . . . the fact that they are opposed to socialism; whereas . . . the British Labor Government . . . is . . . *reactionary*, despite the proletarian origin and the proletarian title of the members of that government (since it administers the national interests of an advanced capitalist country). . . . Lenin was right in saying that the national movement of the oppressed countries should be appraised not from the point of view of formal democracy but from the point of view of the actual results obtained, as shown by the general balance sheet of the struggle against imperialism."[18]

Nehru, Kenyatta, Ho Chi Minh, Chou En-lai, Sukarno, and other Third World leaders who were the product of Western influence in Asia and Africa were in immediate sympathy with these views. Leninism was the last and most decisive Western influence on these leaders, and on thousands like them who were less well known but similarly motivated. Some adopted Communism without any reservations;[19] others kept their dis-

18. Joseph Stalin, "Foundations of Leninism," in *Problems of Leninism,* Moscow, 1945, pp. 59–67.
19. Ho Chi Minh was the delegate to the Third International for Southeast Asia. In the last thirty years, the history of Vietnam, Laos, and Cambodia has illustrated the ever-increasing spread of violence, as cheerfully predicted by Hilferding in 1910. This is a far cry from the evolution to some kind of formal democracy hoped for by many Western

tance, hesitant to align themselves automatically with Soviet foreign policy, and unable to accept the premise that whatever was good for the U.S.S.R. was also good for their struggling countries, no matter how immoral or mad it might appear. To the latter group belongs the Peruvian Victor Raúl Haya de la Torre, the most interesting and influential Latin-American Marxist before Fidel Castro, Che Guevara, and Salvador Allende. All of these men are Leninists, in the sense that they believe that the advanced capitalist countries owe most of their power and prosperity to the pillage of colonies and dependent countries, which in turn owe their poverty and their backwardness to their exploitation by the developed countries. Nehru, for instance, said: "A considerable part of Western Europe's progress to industrialization was paid for by India, China, and the other colonies whose economies were under the control of the European powers."[20] Although Nehru spoke only of a "considerable part," others affirm that the West has owed—and still owes—all its prosperity and primacy in world affairs to its pillage of the Third World.

Latin-American "Third World" Character

These erroneous ideas stemmed from generous impulses, genuine needs, and justifiable nationalistic expectations inspired by Western nationalism; and they were exacerbated by imperialist domination and exploitation, by the humiliation inflicted on Third World elites through the racism, chauvinism, and overbearing pride of the West. The Leninist theory of imperialism and dependence not only offered aspiring Third World leaders the means and justification for revenge and personal compensation; it also taught them how to become effective leaders, how to acquire a following in their own countries (and, for some of them, such as Nehru and Sukarno, in other countries as well). This is why all aspiring Third World leaders became, to some extent, demagogic propagandists of the cosmic Leninist vision: it was adapted to their personal

liberals, and the benefits have accrued not to these unhappy countries themselves, but to the Soviet Union, and now also to China—the citadels of socialist power in the historic struggle against the advanced capitalist countries.
20. Quoted in Leopoldo Zea, *Latinoamérica y el mundo,* Caracas, Universidad Central de Venezuela, Biblioteca de Cultura Universitaria, 1960, p. 32.

interests; it suited the collective needs of their countrymen, who responded happily to a psychologically acceptable explanation of their lower standard of living and of the inferior position of their country on the world scene.

Leninism, as rendered by the Third International, offered a ready-made plan of action: it proposed workable methods for agitation and political action; it formulated both the theory and the rules; it explicitly told revolutionaries in the new countries that they need not wait for the development of "objective conditions" in the backward capitalist or precapitalist economies of their countries before taking up arms; they could become active immediately and force the pace of history. They were told to form political parties of a new kind to spearhead the struggle, composed of totally dedicated professional organizers who were determined to lead the malleable and immature masses by any conceivable means toward such aims as would appear historically beneficial *in the context of world revolution*. This new generation of national leaders was taught to devote itself to the furthering of world revolution even if it saw no immediate advantage for its own country (as in the case of Vietnam).

At the onset, these ideas and goals had been intended for the Afro-Asian world, in which were located the colonies and the dependent nations of the European imperialist powers. But by the end of the Second World War, the center of gravity of the world capitalist system had unmistakably shifted to the United States, so that Latin America, the back yard of this belated champion of imperialism, found itself in the forefront of the "proletariat of nations" destined to storm the bastions of capitalism.

None of the social or geographic realities of Latin America justified such a destiny, for the subcontinent is made up of a group of countries very different from those in the Afro-Asiatic world. To take an extreme example: Argentina could reasonably be compared to Canada or to New Zealand; it is certainly more culturally advanced than Australia. It should regard itself as one of the world's developed countries, on a par with the three other nations mentioned or even ahead of them and other countries that Pierre Jalée lists among the "imperialist nations."[21] Almost the same could be said of Chile, Uruguay, Mexico, Venezuela, and of pre-Castro Cuba. Other Latin-

21. Pierre Jalée, *The Pillage of the Third World.*

American countries[22] are less prosperous, but still cannot be compared to the Afro-Asian nations: essentially they are Western countries, heirs to Western European civilization as legitimately as is the United States.

Paradoxically, the fact that we Latin Americans are an extension of Western culture compounds our frustration, since we cannot explain satisfactorily why we have been unable to capitalize on the advantages we have over the real Third World. Argentina takes no satisfaction in being ahead of Australia, New Zealand, or even Canada, as indeed it is, but resents its failure to reach the level of the United States. This is why the demagogue Perón, on his return to power in 1973, strengthened his position by deciding that in matters of foreign policy, Argentina would henceforth consider itself part of the Third World.

Perón took this official stand somewhat late in his career. A lot of water had flowed under the bridge since 1956, and the Latin-American nations had not awaited Perón's return to Argentina to start militating in the "group of 77" and join the cause of the Afro-Asian bloc in the United Nations Conference on Trade and Development. This solidarity has very recently been extended to the international political sphere, on such issues as the Arab-Israeli conflict. Most of the Latin-American nations voted in favor of having the UN General Assembly hear Yasir Arafat and welcome him as head of state. Later, most also voted in favor of Israel's exclusion from UNESCO.

These two moves, as well as others since, have shown that the United States can no longer take the support of Latin America for granted. How far will this trend go? Is the day coming when the U.S.S.R. and China, the two poles of the socialist world revolution, will be able to count on the automatic support of Latin-American countries other than Cuba? This may seem unlikely, but in 1945 it seemed equally unlikely that, some fifteen years later, the U.S.S.R. would have at its disposal a satellite state one hundred miles off the Florida coast. Such future realignment of the Latin-American countries with the Soviet Union and China would conform to the predictions and goals of the 1920 Third International concerning the Third World, but would go well beyond anything forecast in the world of the twenties. Neither Lenin nor anyone else could then have envisioned the United States as the un-

22. Or, rather, Spanish American. It should be stressed again that the conclusions drawn in this book are not applicable to Brazil, which categorically refuses to be viewed as part of the Third World.

questioned center of world capitalism, and Latin America as a stronghold of anti–North Americanism.

Haya de la Torre and APRA

I said earlier that the most important Latin-American Marxist before Fidel Castro, Che Guevara, and Allende was the Peruvian Victor Raúl Haya de la Torre.[23] This requires some explanation. Castro, Che, and Allende are fashionable today; they have been, and continue to be, immensely popular throughout Latin America, because their basic political stand is in direct defiance of North American power. This position has earned them the well-orchestrated endorsement of the international Communist movement, and also the sympathy of the Western European nations. Since 1945, these nations have come to resent fairly openly the disproportionate power of the United States, and found comfort in the setbacks to Washington's foreign policy—sometimes with a measure of masochism.[24]

Haya de la Torre soon ran into trouble with the Third International, and he and his disciples have since been the victims of a masterly campaign of defamation waged by the same pro-Soviet groups that built up Fidel Castro, Allende, and Che Guevara—and with the same persistence and intensity. Haya and his disciples' main purpose has been to give the Latin-American countries democratic regimes as a transition toward social democracy. The North American and European press has shown so little interest in this important trend that even informed citizens and assiduous readers of newspapers and magazines may never have heard of Haya de la Torre or his American Popular Revolutionary Alliance.

Haya founded APRA in Mexico in 1924, under the double influence of the Mexican and Russian Revolutions. From 1910 onward, the Mexican Revolution constituted the most significant social upheaval in Latin America since the wars of independence. It had been launched spontaneously on the modest slogan of "Honest elections, no re-election [of the President]," issued at what proved to be the ripe time against a *caudillo* too long entrenched in power, whose autocracy had de-

23. Raúl Haya de la Torre was born in 1895 and is still alive.
24. Western Europe prefers to see Washington's setbacks occur in Latin America, rather than closer to home (as, for instance, in Portugal or Africa).

generated into a gerontocracy. The protracted, widespread, and bloody peasant insurrection unleashed by this apparently innocuous slogan confirmed that the surface amenability of Latin-American societies hid a constant, dormant resentment and a great potential for sudden violence, and that the agrarian problem—the latifundia and the status of the peons—had not been solved but, rather, had deteriorated in the hundred and fifty years since independence had been established.

As for the Russian Revolution, Latin Americans could not remain indifferent to the promises of its early days, when the world still had high hopes for a generalized change in production and ownership patterns, leading to the abolition of inequalities, injustices, and various forms of nationalism.

Revolution was therefore the order of the day. But what revolution? Mexico's had come to a halt, thereby demonstrating that there were but limited prospects for a primitive social conflict lacking both strategy and ideology. As early as 1924, the Russian Revolution embarked on an unforeseeable course of its own, guided according to a pattern that had little to do with the basic tenets of Marxism. Its deviations and tactical mistakes were beginning to arouse concern among those who were aware of what was really going on in Russia. At best, it was quite obvious that the conditions in Latin America—or in "Indo-America," as Haya de la Torre called it—differed greatly from those that prevailed in prerevolutionary Russia. Haya returned to the sources in Marx and Engels and found himself questioning Marx's prediction that the experience of the advanced capitalist countries would offer the backward countries a relevant model for their own development. Even less did he accept Lenin's thesis (the official thesis of the Third International, as we have seen) that it was the destiny of the backward countries to provide cannon fodder for a "world revolution," with its center in the Soviet Union and its Mecca in Moscow.

Haya argued that Latin America offered the example of a hybrid and unrepresentative sort of capitalism, which could not be expected to fit the classic pattern of development that Marx and Engels had traced for France or Germany. What was the class structure in Latin America? A burgeoning though weak bourgeoisie, connected to the import trade but unconnected to a national industrial sector (since no such sector existed) coexisted with a feudal oligarchy, whose members, the great landowners, wielded practically all power through alliances with the army and with the Church. Where industry was more than the sum of small manufacturers and cottage industries, it was in the hands of foreign capitalists. The same was true of the basic infrastructures—the railroads, port installations, et cetera—and the export of both agricultural and industrial goods. The proletariat was small in number and could in no case be expected to act as the only promoter, or even the principal promoter, of the urgently needed reforms. On the other hand, the peasants were numerous and had shown during the Mexican Revolution that they represented a considerable potential fighting force. The middle classes, including intellectuals and university students, were irked by the constrictive nature of the Latin-American social and political structures, and were ready to be enlisted in nationalist revolutionary action. Furthermore, Haya felt that the various Latin-American countries could not be expected to modify and improve their national situations in isolation: the failure of the Mexican Revolution loomed as an eloquent example. The struggle could only be considered at the level of Latin America as a whole. Haya therefore thought of the APRA as a movement that was neither national nor altogether international, but distinctly Latin-American in scope as well as in character; strengthening the political and economic unity of the continent was one of its main purposes.

The basic tenets of APRA were the following: (1) Action against Yankee imperialism; (2) unification of Latin America; (3) progressive nationalization of land and industry; (4) internationalization of the Panama Canal; (5) solidarity with all oppressed peoples and classes.

The fifth point was intended as a friendly gesture toward the Third International, but to no avail. The Communist International knew no worse enemies in the world than socialists not under its control, and immediately launched a campaign of defamation. Haya was accused of being an agent of British imperialism, because he had limited his call for revolutionary Latin-American action to the struggle against *Yankee* imperialism. This was sufficient proof that he sought to protect the British!

In his later statements, Haya made it clear that he was opposed to *all* forms of imperialism. This clarification naturally did not silence the Third International: the issue had been only a pretext. In fact they were attacking Haya and his APRA because he had dared take on the struggle for socialism without joining it to the Third International.

In his main work, *Anti-imperialism and APRA* (written in

1928, but not published until 1936), Haya provided the following explanation:

"My statement did not imply that APRA's anti-imperialism limited itself to fighting Yankee imperialism and no other, such as British imperialism. It happens that the five propositions of APRA were announced in Mexico in 1924, and were addressed primarily to the sector of Indo-American countries in the Caribbean, where United States imperialism is aggressively present. . . . Further, for most of our peoples, Yankee imperialism is a synonym for all modern imperialism. . . . But as our Communists were making use of this false ambiguity to state that my use of the word 'Yankee' reflected dark designs on the part of APRA which stemmed from secret ties with British imperialism, I clarified the matter on several occasions . . . and in particular in my book *Remarks on Imperialist Britain and on Soviet Russia* [published in 1932]."

In another passage, Haya candidly explained his difficulties with the Third International:

"At the start of the European autumn of 1926, I received a friendly letter from Lozowsky, the President of the International Red Labor Movement or *Profintern,* saying that he 'welcomed APRA.'

"I answered Lozowsky in a long letter in which I confirmed certain points we had already discussed in Moscow: the unique characteristics of America, socially, economically, and politically, its radical contrast with European realities; the need to study American and, in particular, Indo- or Latin-American problems apart, in all their complexity. I restated my sincere conviction that it was not possible, from the viewpoint of Europe, to formulate magical formulas for the curing of Latin-American ills. Assuring him of my admiration for the perfect knowledge the Russian leaders had of their own country's social reality, I told him I could not help noting their evident lack of scientific knowledge of things American. I pointed out to him that I had personally explained my views in conversations with Lunacharsky, Frunze, Trotsky, and other Russian leaders. After a long, patient, and careful visit to the great country of the Soviets, I had decided not to adhere to the Communist party, thinking then—as I still do now—that it was not the Third International that could resolve the grave and difficult problems of Indo-America."

It is easy to imagine the anger with which the Soviets received this declaration of independence from a man and a movement they counted on to promote Comintern policy in

Latin America. The next year, in 1927, they took advantage of the First Anti-imperialist World Congress in Brussels to excommunicate APRA. Immediately after this, agents of the International became active in Latin America, mobilizing a network of Communist parties that were duly subservient to Moscow, or creating parties where none existed; in this they resorted to a formula and to mechanisms too well known to require further elaboration here. It is worth noting, however, that the Mexican Communist party coordinated and made possible the series of attempts that culminated in Trotsky's assassination.

Imperialism: The First Stage of Capitalism

One of Haya's most interesting theories is that, in Latin America, imperialism, far from being the ultimate stage of capitalism, as Lenin and the Communist International would have us believe, was but the *first* stage. He argued that no economic system deserving to be called capitalist existed in Latin America prior to the influx of foreign investments from advanced capitalist countries; whatever other effects this inflow of capital may have had, it launched the process of modernization of national economies that previously had remained feudal and precapitalist.

Haya argued that the effects of capitalism fueled from abroad were varied and complex, and had both positive and negative aspects. He noted three of the latter: (1) a basic disequilibrium was triggered by investments that had been selected, not to help develop the internal economies of Latin-American countries, but to meet the capitalist countries' needs in mineral or agricultural raw materials; (2) the traditional power structures soon formed alliances with the foreign investors (and with the embassies of the foreign countries) and so further strengthened their positions;[25] and (3) the new arrangements placed even more obstacles in the way of Latin-American political unity.

Revolution in Latin America could begin only after a certain number of necessary conditions were present—the will to develop the national economy; capital to prime the developmental process; and, most important, the emergence of a modern proletariat, able to organize itself into unions and willing

25. See "The Consular *Caudillos*," pp. 224–27.

to be mobilized tactically and strategically. Massive foreign investments led to all three of these necessary steps.

What has been forgotten—and the Communists have done all they could to make us forget it—is that on this point Haya de la Torre was in agreement with Marx and Engels. It is quite clear that insofar as diagnosing the *means* by which the backward countries can reach socialism, Haya de la Torre stands as an orthodox Marxist, whereas Lenin and the Leninists are revisionists. The term will worry only those who think, argue, or fight their battles around quotes and references to Marxist and Leninist holy writ. But if we leave aside matters of ideological orthodoxy, simple common sense appears, in this case, to be on the side of Marx, Engels, and Haya de la Torre, whereas it is Lenin, the Leninists, and the Stalinists who have tailored the historic facts to fit their purposes. They did this when they had to face up to the fact that the revolution had started in backward Russia and not in England or Germany. They did it when they argued that the revolution could live and develop even though it was bottled up in one country (the same backward Russia), with all the Stalinist corollaries that entailed. They have done it since 1945, rejoicing over such odd (from the point of view of Marxist orthodoxy) "socialist" triumphs as the political developments in China, North Korea, Albania, and Cuba. And they do it when, in forecasting the future of socialism, they go on brandishing the theses of the Second Congress of the Communist International: they argue that the role of Third World countries in bringing about the future consists in sacrificing themselves on the altar of World Revolution, and therefore goad these countries on to policies designed to provoke the advanced capitalist countries into self-destructive punitive actions, such as the Cuban blockade, or the French and subsequent North American military action in Vietnam.

The Communists' anger and acrimony toward APRA grew in direct proportion to Haya de la Torre's success and influence. By 1929, "Aprist" parties (or parties influenced by APRA) had developed in Peru (Haya's homeland), and also in Mexico, Guatemala, Costa Rica, Puerto Rico, Bolivia, Chile, and Argentina. In general, what could loosely be called Aprism has been the Latin-American socialist alternative to Marxism-Leninism. And the Aprist, proto-Aprist, or Aprist-inspired parties have shown themselves far better able in practice to influence the political evolution of Latin America than have the Communist parties. Throughout their history, all Latin-American Communist parties except Chile's have been paralyzed by their need to adhere to the dictates laid down in Moscow. The Aprist or APRA-inspired parties, on the other hand, have remained creative and democratic during the same period. Aprism has supported attempts at armed, revolutionary insurrections, including one in 1933 that, with North American help, succeeded in overthrowing the Cuban dictator Machado. It must be noted, however, that Aprism has not aimed for "dictatorship of the proletariat" but, rather, for the abolition of oppressive, traditional power structures; it has aimed for the establishment of reformist democracies that would respect the rights of man and thus contribute to freeing the peasantry from the servile conditions under which it still lives. Aprism has militated to have foreign investments made subject to regulations (for the first time!), with the ultimate purpose of nationalizing all the basic sectors of the economy. It would at the same time stimulate national capitalism, a step without which no socialist revolution is conceivable, or even desirable, according to Aprism (and according to Marx and Engels). In a later part of this book, I will tell the story of the Aprist party with which I am most familiar, the "Democratic Action" party in Venezuela. I would like to make it clear that Aprism deserves far more attention and study than it has met with, either within Latin America or outside, from those who knowingly or not accept the Communist version of contemporary Latin-American history. Any Latin-American political development that succeeds in uniting social and economic progress with freedom and the rights of man will owe a great deal to Aprism.

The Communist Parties

Until the time of Fidel Castro, the Latin-American Communist parties, with the exception of the Chilean Communist party as noted above, were small groups kept from effective action by their subservience to Comintern and Cominform directives.[26] The fact is that, until 1935, the Latin-American Communist parties were practically paralyzed. They were the object of fierce repression by the authorities, and the excommunication

26. The Communist parties were of course important and influential in stimulating political activity, and many leaders of what may globally be called Aprism started careers as Communist militants or sympathizers.

of Aprism decreed by Comintern in 1927 kept them from any contact, even tactical, with the only group with which they could have felt any affinities.

This isolation was not broken to any significant degree until the Seventh Congress of the Communist International, in 1935, when Moscow, preoccupied with the growth of fascism, decreed that in the future the worst offense for a good Communist would be "the sin of left-wing sectarianism." This meant that henceforward Comintern would authorize any alliance, under any conditions, with any group "opposed to fascism and imperialism." At the same time it abandoned the impossible requirement, which it had previously enforced, that any non-Communist allies of a national Communist party, whatever their origin, first had to agree to subscribe without reservation to the tactics and strategy of Comintern, as represented by the party.

This "supple line" was dominant until Stalin felt certain that the U.S.S.R. had successfully resisted the Nazi assault. It ended with the French Communist leader Jacques Duclos's denunciation of "Browderism," so called after Earl Browder, head of the United States Communist party, who was selected as a scapegoat to help launch the new course. A number of leading Latin-American Communists who had spent almost ten years supporting the antifascist front and the war effort against the Berlin-Tokyo-Rome axis were suddenly disavowed, and in some cases expelled from the party.

Cominform was created in 1947 in order to lead the international Communist movement back to "leftist sectarianism," an attitude that reached a peak during the cold war years, coinciding with Stalin's terminal paranoia. For the Latin-American Communist parties, these years represented a new period of isolation, even of implacable persecution, and, once again, of underground activities.

The party line was to change again after Stalin's death and the U.S.S.R.'s development of the atom bomb. Cominform, which had been created in 1947, was dissolved in 1955, and the Twentieth Congress of the Communist Party of the U.S.S.R. (the same Congress that heard Khrushchev's secret report on Stalin) once again authorized the Communist parties of the West and of the Third World to revert to popular-front tactics. Thus it implicitly condemned the insurrectional approach that might have led to confrontation with the United States and conceivably to an atomic war. This terrifying possibility had become the Soviet Union's only fear, and peacekeeping its main object. The Communists of Western Europe were now in the doldrums: they had to accept a long period of waiting and preparing, working for a peaceful transition to socialism at some indefinite future date.

The Leninist theses on national and colonial questions continued to prevail in the Afro-Asian countries (the only Third World countries at that time) and found their confirmation in developments in China and Vietnam (as well as in Nehru's India, Sukarno's Indonesia, and Ceylon and Burma).

As for Latin America, it was, at the time and for all the foreseeable future, within the North American sphere of influence. Neither the U.S.S.R. nor a Communist party as disciplined as Cuba's would have dreamed of encouraging the petit-bourgeois, individualistic terrorist named Fidel Castro, considered by orthodox revolutionaries a quixotic adventurer.

Nixon Goes to Caracas

During the periods when the "hard line" prevailed, the Latin-American Communist parties were under orders from Moscow to stir up as much public unrest as possible. When, on the other hand, the international situation became delicate for the U.S.S.R., the "soft line" obtained, and the Communist parties were instructed to act as agents of moderation and conciliation. The latter was policy at the height of the fascist period and during the war, and again while the Soviet Union was consolidating its conquests, following the Korean truce and Stalin's death. The United States had become the keystone of world capitalism; its deep and complex relations with Latin America made it natural for the Communists to turn their attention to our subcontinent, and to use it as a testing ground for the Leninist theses. Thus they started to build up tensions between the two Americas. But the Soviets were aware that the United States was too powerful to be directly provoked in its zone of immediate influence, just as Washington had resisted the temptation of intervening in any way in the Budapest insurrection in 1956. Whatever the rhetoric, both superpowers knew there was no alternative to peaceful coexistence.

The resolve to steer clear of any headlong confrontation in no way altered the Marxist-Leninist purpose of "burying capitalism," which Khrushchev invoked in the famous declaration he made while visiting the United States. But back in the Soviet Union, he made it clear that the purpose was to bury capitalism "under mountains of meat and butter," by exceeding the United States' production of consumer goods.

The Latin-American Communist parties, obliged to react like faithful weathercocks to the least change in the "wind from Moscow," consequently had to adopt a passive stance, refraining from any direct, militant action. An example: In January 1958, one year before Fidel Castro's triumph in Cuba, Venezuela moved from a brutal dictatorship of the right, which had lasted ten years, into a state of semianarchy. A whole year went by before the provisional government could call for elections and establish a new legitimacy. During that interval, the Venezuelan Communist party could have attempted a *Putsch* with good hopes of success. Circumstances seemed favorable, and the party was at the zenith of its prestige and influence because of its heroic role in the clandestine struggle against the dictatorship. *Nixon's visit to Caracas took place at this point, triggering the public demonstrations that endangered his life.* Proof was established that the Communist party was able to dominate the streets, that the Caracas masses were ready to be mobilized, and that the other parties and other important organized groups that might have blocked Communist action—the armed forces, the Church, the media, the labor unions—were all either impotent or unaware of what was happening, or else in *active sympathy* with the Communist, anti–United States slogans. The President pro tempore, an Admiral of the Fleet, went so far as to say: "If I had been a student, I, too, would have joined the anti-Nixon demonstration. . . ." But the Venezuelan Communist party did not for one moment consider the possibility of seizing power: such direct action would have been contrary to the current soft party line. Instead, after the Nixon carnival—for this is what the demonstrations against Nixon were—it went back to the effort of building up a "democratic front" and concentrated all its efforts on "defending democracy" and collaborating with the Aprist and Christian Democratic parties in preparing elections. In conforming to the "soft line," it conceived no greater ambition than collaborating in a leftist electoral front, with the hope, if that front was successful, of having some say in the future government, all within the severely limited goals defined at that time by Moscow for Latin America.

Fidel Castro in the Sierra Maestra

In Cuba, the Communists had entered upon a tactical alliance with Batista and had even agreed to hold posts in his Cabinet. When he was discredited, they withdrew their support. But at the same time they continued to keep their distance from the "*Putschist* petit-bourgeois adventurer Fidel Castro"—all except a few who were either heterodox Communists or, possibly, men on an assignment to join the Fidelist ranks, ready to take the risk of being later excommunicated as deviationists.

Thus the Cuban Communist Party had opposed Castro's assault on the Moncada barracks on July 26, 1953. During the second half of 1958, the Cuban Communists militated for the formation of a wide political front that would include not only the "anti-imperialist" sector (that is to say, themselves and their sympathizers) but also any Cubans with democratic aspirations and sentiments who wanted to see Batista's dictatorship replaced by a government that was ready to implement Aprist theories. Thus the Communist party found itself defending the very kind of government it had so virulently attacked as "proimperialist" or "traitor to the fatherland" when the hard line prevailed.

In fact, Fidel Castro's 26th of July Movement corresponded to Aprism, and certainly not to Marxism-Leninism, in its theoretical principles. But in 1958 the Communists criticized Castro's group for its tendency toward terrorism (in the tradition of the struggles carried on by the Cuban students) and for the romantic adventurism of the guerrilla fighter. The *guerrillero* represented nothing new in Latin America; he belonged to the age-old tradition in rural, backward, and unorganized societies of taking up arms against established power—the very antithesis of the Marxist concept of revolutionary action.

At the end of 1958, the Batista dictatorship met its end much in the same way as Pérez Jiménez's in Venezuela some eleven months earlier. It was exhausted; dissension was rife among high government officials; further, the dictatorship had alienated the high military cadre at a time of general discontent, when all the population, including the middle and upper classes, had gained sufficient courage to demonstrate openly their opposition to administrative corruption and repression. Fidel Castro's guerrilla tactics had served as a catalyst in this evolution, but it is certain that even without him, Batista could not have maintained himself in power: for *the United States had come to look upon him only as a dead weight and a scoundrel.*

There were two reasons for the unexpected turn of events that followed in Cuba. The first, no doubt the less significant, was that the corruption of Batista's regime had penetrated the armed forces, already discredited by their poor showing in the struggle against the *guerrilleros*. The army's inglorious confrontation with them put it, as an institution, *irrevocably* against the bearded heroes come down from the mountains.

The second factor was Fidel Castro himself. With the initial exception of the Communists, Cubans and Latin Americans alike were unanimous in their acclaim for the triumphant revolutionary, and important sectors of opinion in the United States looked with favor on his rise to power. Within a few months, the process he had launched led to results the Communists had long viewed as their ideal objective, but had considered too risky ever to pursue. Fidel had decided upon direct confrontation with the United States, even at the cost of a complete economic and political rift. This was followed by a governmental take-over of the Cuban society and economy, starting with North American firms—an accelerated take-over that was soon to convert Cuba into a country more strictly Communist than Poland, Hungary, or even the U.S.S.R.

By 1968 ("the Year of the Heroic *Guerrillero*"), no trace remained of any private economic activity or services; all had been taken over by the state, labeled as intolerable and dangerous buds of "individualist tendencies" and "anti-Communist activities." Fidel effected this radical transformation through the Cuban Communist party. Initially the main instrument of his policy, it later became the dominant faction of the United Revolutionary party, which Fidel created in order to accommodate the diverse revolutionary tendencies among the population. Somewhat later he dissolved this, and the Communist party has remained the only party, dominating the government in the best Leninist tradition. The party was made responsible for the control of all activities, including radio, television, and the universities, the publication of all books, magazines, and news releases, and of Cuba's one remaining newspaper (this daily is the only successor to the vast array of newspapers of all political sides that had continued to flourish even during the darkest moments of the Batista dictatorship).

But the main point was that Fidel Castro radically changed Cuba's alignment in the international geopolitical configuration. Formerly dependent on the United States, Cuba now became a client state of the Soviet Union. So unquestioned is the Soviet Union's control over the use of Cuban territory for the purposes of its own overall strategy that neither in 1962, when it decided to make the island a nuclear base against the United States, nor later, when it abandoned this project, did it bother to take the views or the will of Cuba into consideration.

Why and how did Castro choose this course? Was he a disguised Communist before 1969, or a Marxist of a different shade from Aprist Marxists, an even purer Marxist, in the true sense, than the Leninists? I shall try to answer these questions later.[27] But whatever his motives may have been, the fact remains that Fidel Castro won one of the most significant and spectacular victories for the Leninist theses on the role of colonial and dependent countries in the destruction of the world capitalist order. And this a mere one hundred miles off the North American coast, in one of the countries most closely connected to the United States.

This would suffice to explain, and in fact to justify, the immense repercussions that the Cuban Revolution had throughout the world. The events in Cuba between 1959 and approximately 1962 (by which time it had become obvious that the island was a Soviet satellite) made it clear to people everywhere that they were not in the presence of the kind of governmental change endemic to Latin-American countries. Something altogether new had occurred. What had happened might well be compared to the flight of Apollo 11, when man first set foot on the moon. With the Cuban Revolution, the Marxist-Leninist world view succeeded for the first time in being anchored in a specific national government in the Western Hemisphere. This would have been as unthinkable a few years earlier as interplanetary travel, and its consequences may prove to be even greater.

It is a development that shook the West and continues to undermine it. Could one conceive of the Portuguese crisis of 1975 without the Cuban Revolution of 1960? The effect was equally great on socialism, in the widest meaning of the term. Nothing remained quite the same after the Cuban Revolution, everything had been shaken: men, ideas, tactics, and Marxist-Leninist, as well as social-democratic parties. And this transformation occurred because of a revolutionary process triggered in one small Latin-American country: an ongoing process was started that soon was to affect the rest of the subcontinent. With the Cuban Revolution, Latin America

27. Chapter 9, pp. 283–88.

ceased being merely a part of the American continent, and was inserted, as it were, into the world scene. For the many Latin Americans whose feeling of inferiority toward North America had grown into a complex, the fact that their national destiny had finally become relevant to world history as a whole came as something like revenge.

The "Good Revolutionary"

Castro's Marxist-Leninist confession of faith in December 1961, and his successful resistance to North American pressure and to the machinations of the CIA—the high point of which was the disastrous landing at the Bay of Pigs—understandably made him the object of world-wide attention and adulation. Cuba had become a "socialist democracy," and Fidel one of the stars of world Communism. Journalists and simple busybodies (such as the French novelist Françoise Sagan) flew in from all over the world to witness firsthand this novel way of turning to socialism.

For the U.S.S.R., this turn of events, coming at a time when the Soviet position was very weak, was literally providential. Khrushchev's denunciation of Stalin's crimes and "personal deviations" before the Congress of the Soviet Union's Communist party in 1956 produced an echo in world opinion that the Soviet leadership, little aware of the power of the modern media, had hardly foreseen. Shortly upon this followed the Budapest insurrection and its brutal repression by Soviet tanks, and the uprising of the fifteen thousand Polish workers at the Poznan railroad-car factory who openly attacked Communism and the Russians, clamoring for "bread and freedom." Sino-Soviet relations, which were cold in 1960, further deteriorated and led to the kind of confrontation that may yet result in war; the world witnessed a *power rivalry* between the two main revolutionary countries, a scandalous and depressing exhibition. In August 1961, the Berlin Wall was the only response that the Communists could find to the East Germans' "voting with their feet," and showing how many were eager to trade their part in "building the future" of their country under Communist rule for personal freedom and a decent life in the present.

In this dark picture, the emergence of revolutionary Cuba had a double meaning: it demonstrated the resilience of Leninism, and, more important, it briefly renewed the old socialist hope of a regime that could combine Communism and human decency. Old dreams were rekindled. Centuries earlier, prior to the discovery of the New World, European thinkers had imagined that somewhere there existed an island uncontaminated by civilization and original sin, peopled with noble savages free from ambition, cruelty, and envy. For the revolutionary mystique as it had developed since 1917, this myth now assumed a new form. The noble savage became a virtuous revolutionary, uncontaminated by Stalinism, able to build a just world without resorting to Stalin's cruelty and ruthlessness. And what more suitable cradle could this virtuous revolutionary have than a tropical island?

The Cuban Revolution briefly fitted this illusion, just as the Chinese Revolution had done somewhat earlier. The incarnation of this illusion was not so much Fidel Castro, whose image as a virtuous revolutionary—bearded, dressed in rumpled battle clothes—soon gave way to the reality of a ruthless political animal and strongman. The myth settled on Che Guevara and on his theory of the purifying function of guerrilla warfare and of the "new man."

For "El Che," the *guerrillero* and the new approach to guerrilla warfare were to bring not just revolution, but—finally—a pure revolution, a *humane* one. The *guerrillero* was the saint of the revolution, superior to other men not only because of his personal worth and his revolutionary conscience, but also because of his charity and his willingness to take upon himself the sufferings of the oppressed. A disciple of El Che, the Colombian guerrilla-priest Camilo Torres, went so far as to say that if Christ had lived in Latin America in our time he would have been a guerrilla fighter. (See p. 167.)

These pure, ascetic revolutionaries, hardened by danger and privations, were expected after conquering power to exercise it with the same goodness, the same fervor that they had displayed in gaining it; they were expected to communicate their fervor and altruism to the masses, and thus bring about "the advent of the new man" through an unprecedented sociological mutation.

El Che expected the virtues of the *guerrillero* to spread as by contagion throughout socialist society and to transform it into an "armed democracy," a society of *guerrilleros*, very largely, if not entirely, made up of social reformers. Material inducements would be unnecessary; work would be done on a voluntary basis; money would disappear along with man's mercenary instincts; in an economy organized "for service and not for profit," abundance would be general; each individual would draw from the communal holdings the goods and the food that fitted his needs.

Che was not the first to formulate the idea that socialism would lead to material plenty and that it would simultaneously eliminate human selfishness, salaried work, and the commercial basis of society: Marx and Engels had done this before him. But the emphasis with which he speaks of the virtues of the *guerrillero* is striking. The advent of this "new man" precedes and heralds the postrevolutionary conditions that will lead to the elimination of individualism and social conflict, which, according to Marxism, inevitably result from private property and the class warfare attendant upon it.

All theorists of socialism, without exception—even the pre-Marxists—took for granted that one of the primary tasks of the revolution was to create conditions favorable to the emergence of a new type of man. This superman would be an avatar of that old noble savage whom civilization had driven back into our subconscious, and who would now rise again, enriched by all the marvels invented by that same loathsome civilization. Thus equipped, the new man would be truly a superman in a world become a superworld. According to Fourier, harmful animals would disappear in socialist society, and all surviving species would endeavor to serve man and save him the trouble of doing any work: "A super-beaver will see to the fishing, a super-whale will move sailing ships; a super-hippopotamus will tow the river boats. Instead of the lion, there will be a super-lion, of wonderful swiftness, upon whose back the rider will sit as comfortably as on a well-sprung carriage." William Godwin predicted that man might well achieve immortality once private property had been abolished. Karl Kautsky said that with socialist society, "a new type of man will arise . . . a superman . . . an exalted man." Trotsky embellished this concept: "Man will become incomparably stronger, wiser, finer. His body will be harmonious, his movements more rhythmical, his voice more musical. The average human being will reach the stature of an Aristotle, a Goethe, a Marx. Above these heights, new peaks will arise."[28]

It is, therefore, perfectly clear that the marvelous originality

28. See Charles Fourier, *Oeuvres complètes,* Paris, 2nd ed., 1841, vol. 4, p. 254; William Godwin, *On Property;* Karl Kautsky, *Die soziale Revolution,* Berlin, 3rd ed., 1911, vol. 2, p. 48; Leo Trotsky, *Literature and Revolution.* These authors are quoted, with references, in Ludwig von Mises's *Socialism,* New Haven, 1951, pp. 163–64.

and profundity with which current fashion credits Che Guevara are without substance, and are founded on ignorance or, perhaps, on the propagandists' calculation that certain key and constant ideas of socialism seem far more attractive if attributed to Che than if traced to their origins in Fourier, Godwin, Kautsky, Trotsky, or even Marx and Engels. The martyred *guerrillero* is more appealing in the guise of prophet of the "New Man" than his waistcoated Victorian predecessors.

"Revolution Within the Revolution"

El Che died in Bolivia in 1967. He fell victim to his attachment to the Leninist vision of a world revolution brought about by the insurrection of the "proletarian countries." Specifically, he died because of the failure of his own theory of the "insurrectional focal point,"[29] which he thought would catalyze the revolutionary potential of the masses in the Third World.

This notion was of prime importance to Che's view of revolutionary strategy. He had seen how Castro had been radicalized by his experience of guerrilla warfare, and had witnessed Castro's transformation into one of the most successful of anti-imperialist leaders. Fidel's success in forcing a Caribbean country to change its alignment from the capitalist to the socialist camp had gone counter to the calculations of all the Communist ideologists, and El Che thought that this success could be explained only through some factor implicitly connected to guerrilla action itself. For Fidel had been able to achieve what neither the labor movement nor the traditional strategy of the Communist parties had been able to bring about in Latin America: to forge a *real revolutionary avant-garde,* and to organize the early materialization of the conditions requisite to the revolutionary process.

The theory of the "insurrectional focal point" was popularized by Régis Debray in his pamphlet *Revolution Within the Revolution?* (1967). It assumes Latin America to be ripe for a revolutionary explosion and views the survival of the existing

29. *"El foco insurreccional."* For this key concept of Che Guevara's thought I have adopted the English equivalent, "insurrectional focal point," as used by Theodore Draper in *Castroism: Theory and Practice,* New York, Praeger, 1965, p. 65. J. P. Morray, one of the translators of Che's *La guerra de guerrillas,* renders the term simply as "the insurrection," but, as Draper points out, there is a perfect Spanish equivalent (*insurrección*) for this term, which Che Guevara did not choose to use. —TRANS.

power structures as owing only to the alliance of the oligarchies and the armies that are betraying the fatherland with
North American imperialism. Revolutionary strategy therefore
must set itself the double aim of breaking up this alliance by
disorganizing the armies and demoralizing the bourgeoisie,
and of eliciting the participation of the masses in the conquest
of power and the building of a socialist society. Both these
purposes can be served by the tactics whose efficacy was
demonstrated in Cuba—the insurrectional focal point—a
localized focus of guerrilla warfare. At first glance this formula
may seem to describe only a tactical necessity or an expedient.
It goes far beyond that, however, allowing the revolutionary
movement to strive for three decisive political objectives
simultaneously: (1) to create a sizable revolutionary avant-
garde; (2) to draw the antirevolutionary armies of "the traitors
to the fatherland" into battle before they are ready for conflict—and so destroy them; (3) to politicize the masses. The
insurrectional focal point achieves this triple end by its very
existence. It may be seen as the trigger that sets the revolutionary movement going. Thus the insurrectional focal point
clears the ground for the final act of the revolutionary drama:
the general strike or urban insurrection that will result in the
take-over of the government.

Naturally, these ideas proved instantly attractive. They provided an alternative to the deservedly discredited traditional
Communist parties and to the policy of automatic compliance
with the Soviet line; they had the freshness of a new way of
making the revolution, starting with what is simplest and
easiest to implement—the insurrectional focal point—and
building up from there to the most complex—the generalized
revolutionary movement. Furthermore, by proceeding thus, the
virtuous revolutionary would avoid contamination by the "old
politics," which "rot away" the purity of intentions and compli-
cate action.

This seductive concept has appealed as much to the dilettantes of the revolution as to its more serious practitioners. In
the years that followed its formulation, chic magazines and
leftist salons in Europe and North America buzzed with
gingerly discussions of Che's theories as interpreted by Régis
Debray. Meanwhile, men and women of flesh and blood—
mostly very youthful university students—were sacrificing
their illusions, and sometimes their lives, testing the new revolutionary theories.

In their insistence that the forces of revolution should not attempt a take-over before conditions were ripe, the earlier Marxist theorists showed good sense. Latin-American Communists spent so much time observing Moscow, and so little studying their own countries, that they failed to notice when the objective conditions necessary for action had in fact arisen, as, for example, in Venezuela in 1958.

But with the onset of the Cuban Revolution and the theory of the insurrectional focal point, several Latin-American Communist parties jumped into action and set out to emulate Fidel Castro; there was a *guerrillero* behind every tree. Even the Aprist parties lost their left wing and their following among the young to Castroism and Guevarism.

But the tactics discovered empirically by Fidel Castro turned out to be inapplicable to the rest of Latin America without some adaptation to particular national situations. And even if conditions had been ripe for a comparable *coup de force* in other countries (I am again reminded of Venezuela in 1958), an attempted take-over would probably have miscarried, for lack of a Fidel Castro able to force the hand of destiny. Further, there is little doubt that the Cuban Revolution robbed subsequent insurrections of the advantage of surprise. Everyone—the army, the several political groups (liberal, conservative, Aprist, Christian Democrat), middle-class management, the labor unions, the Church, the media, and, in general, all elements of society, including the non-Communist workers and the overwhelming majority of peasants—had been forewarned and was on the alert. The North Americans, for their part, were ready to send help, and if necessary to intervene "in time," as they actually did in the Dominican Republic in 1965, "to prevent a new Cuba."

Rural Guerrilla Warfare and Urban Terrorism

In the decade that followed the Cuban Revolution, insurrectional focal points comparable to Castro's in the Sierra Maestra developed or were planted in ten or twelve other Latin-American countries. For a revolutionary the decision to take to the hills was unnatural. The new type of *maquis* demanded by Guevarist theory was reminiscent of the 1920's—of Zapata or Pancho Villa during the Mexican Revolution, or of Sandino in Nicaragua—ghosts from the past, appropriate no doubt to a rural, precapitalist society in which the revolutionary was of the peasantry and shared its habits and know-how. But the Latin-

The Latin Americans

American *guerrillero* of the 1960's was a bourgeois intellectual and, typically, a student who knew nothing of the outdoors, who had never carried a knapsack, seen a snake, or lit a fire without matches. A boy scout would have been better prepared for life in the open.

This is reflected in a conversation Fidel Castro had with a Venezuelan Communist in 1963:

F.: You might make a good *guerrillero,* although you are a little fat. The mountain will trim you down. . . .

v. c.: In Venezuela, Fidel, the cities have played a significant role in the political struggle. In any case, our "urban plan" puts the government on the defensive. It would be silly to withdraw to the countryside, and give up our positions.

F.: Listen, Mendoza, the only thing guaranteeing the survival of the armed strength of the revolution and the development of a real rebel army is guerrilla warfare. Urban terrorism is easy. Many prefer to die in the cities, rather than fight in the mountains.[30]

The fact is that taking to the hills was neither easy nor any less dangerous than confronting established power in the cities. One has only to recall Che Guevara's failure and death in Bolivia in 1967, and the easy capture of Régis Debray. These examples give the clearest and most eloquent proof of the limits of the "revolution within the revolution," which turned out to be a one-shot weapon. Some *guerrilleros* are still obstinately holding out in several Latin-American countries, but they are increasingly isolated and are taken less and less seriously. Paradoxically, they now manage to stir public opinion only when they strike in the cities, robbing a bank to secure funds or taking hostages for ransom.

Meanwhile, sociological reality has quite disproven the rural-warfare theory. For several years now, the young Latin Americans who, inspired by the cult of Fidel Castro and Che Guevara, persist in "open warfare" have been operating almost exclusively in the cities. The movements that have best managed to make the headlines have been the Tupamaros in Uruguay, and the Montoneros and the People's Revolutionary Army in Argentina. In Uruguay, urban terrorism has caused a formerly liberal regime to turn brutally repressive. Kidnappings, holdups, and other acts of violence are daily occurrences in Argentina. This has given the government, with or without Perón, a perfect excuse for the liquidation of left-

30. Quoted in Rafael Elino Martínez, *¡Aquí todo el mundo está alzao!* (Here, we are all heroes!), Caracas, El Ojo del Camello, 1973, pp. 277–78.

☙ 134 ☙

wingers, and has reminded the Argentine Marxists, albeit a little belatedly, of Perón's true personality and origins.

In some cases, left-wing subversive action (the "armed struggle") has been denounced as being manipulated by the CIA—the supreme insult. This charge was leveled in 1974 against some *guerrillero* groups operating in Mexico, for instance, when one such group of leftist extremists held captive the father-in-law of the Mexican President.

Chile: A Case of Terminal Childhood Disorder

There is no doubt that the emotional and ideological tremors caused in Latin America by the Cuban Revolution were among the main causes of the failure, or at least of the brutal outcome, of Chile's experiment with a popular front. Salvador Allende would probably still be alive today if he had not felt obliged to prove himself the equal of Fidel Castro and El Che, and if he had not been subject to Castroist and Guevarist pressures from the left. He would probably have remained the President of Chile until 1976, when, by due process, the presidency would have gone to a constitutionally elected successor —most likely the Christian Democrat Eduardo Frei. The Chilean economy would have been largely nationalized, less radically than it actually was between 1970 and 1973, but sufficiently to prove irreversible. Thus the Chilean Communist party would have been rewarded for its patience, for its organizational ability, and for its resolve to combine tactical dexterity with unwavering attachment to the U.S.S.R.

Of Latin America's Communist parties, Chile's is the only one that has been more than a political coterie, the only one that has been able to set a course of its own, rather than trail in the footsteps of APRA and other populist parties; it is the only Communist party that was able to implement the "united front" called for by the Seventh Congress of the International, participating in a leftist coalition—albeit in a secondary role—from 1938 to 1941, and then again from 1946 to 1947. In 1956, together with the Socialist party led by the Aprist Salvador Allende, it organized an electoral coalition known as the Front for Popular Action, using the acronym FRAP.[31]

31. As I am sure I shall be accused of vilifying Allende when I call him an Aprist, let me specify that in his basic position, Allende was closer to Haya de la Torre than to the Communists. Besides, once the term Aprist

In the 1964 elections, which the Christian Democratic candidate Eduardo Frei won with 55.6 percent of the votes, the FRAP polled 28.6 percent, thanks to the support of some smaller parties, including the extreme left wing of the Christian Democrats, radicalized by the Cuban Revolution.

Six years later, the Chilean Conservatives, disconcerted by what they interpreted as a dangerous leaning toward the left on the part of Frei's government, put up their own candidate, which they had refrained from doing in 1964, in fear of the FRAP. The result was a narrow victory for Allende, with a plurality of 36.2 percent of the votes against 34.9 percent for the Conservative candidate and 27.8 percent for the Christian Democrat.

The Chilean Constitution held that in a case such as this, where no candidate secured an absolute majority, the final decision lay with Congress, which had the right to choose between the two candidates who had ranked highest in the popular election. This method was essentially similar to the one that prevails in France, where, however, a second popular referendum decides between the two leading candidates. In the case under consideration, the Christian Democrats were given a chance to cast their votes in Congress for the Conservative candidate. But they preferred to give them to Allende, in return for a series of concessions and his assurance that he would not try to subvert the Constitution.[32]

Whereto? And by What Means?

The Chilean nightmare has forced the more serious among Latin-American Marxists to submit revolutionary tactics and strategy to a basic re-examination. The cycle that started in 1959 with the Cuban Revolution ended with the rout of the "Chilean Popular Unity" (the name the FRAP gave itself when it came to power in 1973). Another dream has come to an end. In Cuba, the Castro regime has become a replay, adapted to tropical conditions, of the worst and most depressing aspects of the kind of Communism with which we have been growing

---

is freed of the pejorative connotations forced on it by the Communists, it describes better than any other the many different efforts made at different times to bring about a democratic, Latin-American form of socialism, and not just an instrument of Soviet foreign policy.

32. The ensuing tragedy of Salvador Allende, and of Chile, will be discussed in Chapter 9, pp. 258–63.

all too familiar in Europe since 1917. In Chile, on the other hand, the attempt to lead a Latin-American society to socialism without first eliminating the army and without suppressing public liberties has led to an implacable dictatorship. What course are Latin-American Marxist-Leninists to follow now? And by what means?

Some, citing what has been called the "Peruvian revolution," have concluded that nothing can be achieved without first winning over the armed forces to the revolutionary cause. Other Communists (or perhaps the same ones) have decided to break away openly from the U.S.S.R. They continue to find satisfaction in the existence of a Communist state in Russia, but consider that the Soviet Union's political backwardness, its low economic productivity, and its imperialistic domination over Eastern Europe and Cuba daily discredit the revolutionary cause.

On might argue that the survivors of the "insurrectional focal point" tactics have been made wiser by failure, in particular by the manner in which Castroists and Guevarists led Allende to disaster. I think they have begun to take stock of themselves, and to see that the policies recommended by Haya de la Torre were perhaps not quite so mistaken after all.

One of the shrewder movements of Marxist renovation in Latin America is the MAS, the Venezuelan Movement Toward Socialism, whose platform is similar to the views expressed by Roger Garaudy.[33] The MAS firmly refuses to set its policy in accordance with the tactical requirements of the Soviet Union, which, as we have seen, submits the Latin-American Communist parties to a pendulum swing between the two poles of a united front and leftist sectarianism. Furthermore, the MAS does not limit its appeal to true believers of the Marxist faith, but seeks to enroll all groups that have some grounds for disaffection. It appreciates that Venezuelan Aprism has been successful in achieving this wider appeal, and limits its criticism of the Aprist Democratic Action party now in power to deploring the contradictions between its words and its deeds—the party's stated platform and the policy that four Democratic Action Presidents have implemented in their nearly seventeen years in power since 1945.

At the same time, the "neo-Communist" MAS tacitly concedes that the shortcomings of the Democratic Action party

33. *The Crisis of Communism: The Turning Point of Socialism,* trans. Peter and Betty Ross, New York, Grove Press, 1970.

may have resulted from its historic circumstances; this "anti-imperialist" (i.e., Marxist) movement originated, survived, developed, and came to power before the Cuban Revolution, Nixon's trip to China, and the Communist victory in Vietnam. Given the changed world situation, has not the time come for a fresh team of men to renew the Aprist goal? Should they not launch a new anti-imperialist alliance among workers, peasants, the middle classes, and "nationalist entrepreneurs"? Or even better, are not conditions ripe for the absorption of Aprism by Leninism, along the lines of Lozowsky's unsuccessful attempt in 1926? Surely, that attempt failed partly because of its historic situation and partly because of the brutality of the Soviet Union's strategy of dominating the development of world revolution, on the assumption that what was best for the U.S.S.R. was necessarily best for the final triumph of Communism.

In any case, the MAS and other neo-Communist Latin-American movements that have been defining their strategy in conformity with "objective conditions" hold some trump cards in their effort to link Latin America to the Third World. It is clear, for example, that the Aprist parties have learned from Fidel Castro that one could go faster and further in the direction of anti-imperialism than they have done. Anti-imperialism means something very specific in Latin America: it means confrontation and an eventual break, not with the advanced capitalist world as a whole, but with the United States.

Latin Americans now largely accept the idea that our position of inferiority vis-à-vis the United States is due for the most part to that country's exploitation of our subcontinent through the mechanisms of imperialism and dependency. Thus we have fallen prey to the most debilitating and pernicious of the several myths through which we have tried to explain our destiny.

One, Two, Three . . . Many Vietnams

This myth is debilitating because it attributes all that is wrong in Latin America to external factors; it follows that Latin America can do nothing to improve itself, short of adopting the Cuban pattern and breaking its dependence on North America. Even the best-directed and most heroic efforts at "reformism" must be counterproductive, since they can only postpone the development of the indispensable revolutionary mutation.

Latin America and Marxism

There is another reason why this myth is pernicious. Latin-American countries may be led to assume that they share no common interests with the United States, and so be led to self-destructive patterns of behavior; this may be true even of countries on the verge of decisive progress and a historic breakthrough, such as Venezuela.

I must point out that neither the détente among the super-powers, which resulted from Kissinger's efforts, nor the replacement of the United States–Soviet bipolarity with the United States–China–Russia "tripolarity" has in any way reduced the deadly rivalry between the three main powers. These factors have not lessened the Soviet Union's or China's use of Marxism as an instrument of foreign policy, or made any less urgent the dilemma facing each Latin-American country having to choose between liberal and Marxist models of social organization—with all the diverse, contradictory, and incompatible demands this choice must address in their domestic policies and international relations.

Actually, the détente among the three superpowers is more apparent than real, and it blurs the realities of rivalry in much the same way that the earlier spotlight on cold war and bipolarity probably had been too sharp, lending them exaggerated clarity.

In this new situation, China and the Soviet Union—the Communist superpowers—are in an excellent position to fan the fires of anti–North American sentiment in Latin America. In doing so, they are not concerned with the true interests of Latin-American countries, but more likely are making use of these countries for their own shared or national purposes.

Nobody seems to have even tried to get at the bottom of Che Guevara's statement that every Latin-American revolutionary must strive to make his country a new Vietnam. For could anyone maintain that the Vietnam War served Vietnam's true interests? It seems evident to me that the war was a ghastly calamity for the Vietnamese people. Their legitimate nationalistic aspirations were shunted off course to fit in with the Leninist theses on the national and colonial problem. Vietnam became a pawn in a world-wide confrontation between two large geopolitical groups—a confrontation that lately has been taking the form of a series of mutual adjustments through which each group contends for secondary advantages while steering clear of a world conflagration. In this struggle, which does not even aim for a permanent equilibrium, Vietnam was reduced to the role of strategic stronghold, to be fought over, taken, and lost in the changing tides of war. It is Vietnam's misfortune that ideology no longer plays the basic role in the process of readjustment between world powers, and the same misfortune will be the lot of any Latin-American nation that follows Cuba's example and takes the Leninist bait. Ideology may play a significant role, but not a decisive one. While ideological confrontation may highlight public debates, mutual arrangements between the great powers determine settlements. As a result of such arrangements, Vietnam, after having lived through thirty years of hell for the sake of world revolution, must now accept that its sacrifice has only resulted in a new era of cooperation between the United States and the Soviet Union, and in China's full-fledged membership in the club of superpowers.

After that lesson, who in Latin America would dare to proclaim the need for two, three, or more Latin-American Vietnams, to fulfill the dreams of the "virtuous revolutionary" Che Guevara?

6

Latin America and the Church

By the Church and for the Church

No other institution has contributed as much as the Catholic Church to determining what Latin America has and has not become. The Spanish Conquest was made in the name of the Faith and in the service of the Faith. Conquest and colonization were one with Catholicism. Up to the nineteenth century—throughout the three hundred and fifty years during which the political and social structures of Latin America were being decisively shaped—Catholicism was both the brain and the backbone of Latin-American society.

The evangelization of the New World constitutes the most successful instance of Christian proselytizing since antiquity. It coincided with the Reformation, when half of Europe was shaking off the rule of the Papacy. This would have been reason enough for Rome to look upon Latin America as its fairest daughter, and to take special interest in its development. There are three hundred million Catholics in Latin America; given the rate of population growth, there may be five hundred million in a quarter of a century. The Church's future will be threatened if its political and social influence over our continent continues to decrease, but if, on the other hand, the Church succeeds in recovering some of its past influence, or at least in holding its present ground, it will preserve one of the main branches of world Catholicism.

It is only fair, therefore, to assume that Latin America looms large in the Vatican's appraisal of the state of world Catholicism. Certain of Rome's broad policies and important decisions, such as the détente in its relations with the Communist world, may well have been made in order to further the present and future development of the Latin-American Church, allowing it to take on a new role in the social dynamics of countries in which it once controlled practically all aspects of the lives of individuals and set the basic pattern of society as a whole.

From Omnipotence to Bankruptcy

Emancipation was the first major social initiative in Latin America in which the Church played no role; but at the same time, this was not a step *against* the Church. The Constitution of the first Venezuelan republic (1811) codified the religious intolerance that existed under the old Spanish empire: "The Catholic, Apostolic, and Roman religion is the religion of the state, and the only religion of the people of Venezuela, to the exclusion of any other. One of the first duties of our National Representation will be the protection, the maintenance, the purity, and the inviolability of the Faith. We will never allow any cult, private or public, or any doctrine contrary to the teachings of Jesus Christ on the territory of the Confederation."

Similarly, in Mexico, the 1814 Constitution of Apatzingán, though inspired by the radicalism of José María Morelos, specified that "the Catholic religion will be the only one, and none other will be tolerated." An autonomous tribunal was set up outside the secular authority to defend Catholic dogma. Morelos himself, in his *Sentimientos de la Nación* (1814), had said, "We must uproot any plant not planted by God." Iturbide's Plan of Iguala (1821) demanded as the first of its bases "the Catholic, Apostolic, Roman religion, without tolerance of any other"; the republican Constitution of 1824 declared that "the religion of the Mexican nation is, and will always remain, Catholic, Apostolic, and Roman. The nation protects it by wise and just laws and prohibits the practice of any other faith."

Similar provisions are to be found in practically all the first constitutions of the Spanish American republics. In the first decades of independence, one of the extravagant privileges that the Church maintained, unchanged, in the several republics was the monopoly over education. Conflicts between Church and State appeared only after about 1850, when the liberals began to try to reduce the power of the Church, in keeping with the spirit of the new times. The Church, in taking, as an institution, a stand against Latin-American emancipation, had correctly foreseen the crumbling of the old regime and the abolition of its own customary rights and privileges.[1]

The Church steadfastly fought the waning of its power and influence, acting in close alliance with the so-called conservative parties. But ecclesiastical policy did not rule out cooperation and the exchange of services with some of the "liberals," who were more interested in capturing and holding power than in engaging in ideological confrontation. Certain "liberal" leaders and dictators at the end of the last century and the first half of the twentieth did in fact govern with staunch ecclesiastical support, in return for which they made agreements and concordats favorable to the Vatican and to the local clergy.

Further, until recently, the Latin-American Church clearly appeared to have allied itself with United States hegemony. I have already had occasion to note that until the Cuban Revolution, it was impossible to exert power in Latin America without being actively pro–North American, or at least without refraining from active anti–North Americanism. The Catholic Church has always been, and still wishes to remain, a key element in the power structure—the temporal power structure if possible, but certainly the spiritual power structure. And who in good faith can distinguish where the first of these two demands begins and the other ends?

To understand the problems raised in Latin America by this traditional duality of the temporal and the spiritual, we would have to assess the basic ambiguities within Catholicism, the contradictions and accommodations that have sprung from its double character as spiritual messenger and temporal power. Others, more competent and better informed, have focused on this question. I shall simply say that in the Spanish American empire, and later in the Latin-American republics, these ambiguities and contradictions inherent in Catholicism were intensified by ecclesiastical actions and hardened into extremes of

1. The encyclical *Et si longissimo* issued by Pope Pius VII in 1816 called the Hispano-American emancipation "seditious" and exhorted Latin Americans to remain faithful to the King. South American bishops went much further in interpreting this encyclical. In a pastoral letter, the bishop of Arequipa referred to independence as "irrational, prejudicious, injurious, and criminal before God." The bishops of Popayán (in Colombia) and Mérida (in Venezuela) and the ecclesiastical governor of Caracas called the insurrection an "extremely grievous sin."

idealism and Machiavellianism. Both resulted from the situation: the Church had to apply its methods and gear its purposes to a very complicated social context, while taking upon itself the role of prime creator and leader of a basically unsound society. In due course, the Latin-American Church was itself affected by the many and various weaknesses inherent in the society to whose development it had so greatly contributed; these came, by feedback, as it were, to afflict the priest as well as his parishioners, the shepherd as well as his flock.

Having previously been all-powerful in Latin America, the Church has lost more strength in that part of the world than in any other where it once held sway. It has now but a shadow of its former power: Catholicism finds itself pushed into a marginal existence, and faith, once a living force, has largely given way to meaningless, formalistic assent.

Thus, in the modern era, which has seen the extension of European culture to the American continent, Latin America's history bears witness to the failure of Catholicism in contradistinction to Protestantism, or, at least, to the defeat of the Catholic ethic by the Protestant ethic, which shaped the development of the United States.

The Other America Again

The Chilean Francisco Bilbao (1823–1865) was one of the first Latin Americans to diagnose the painful contrast between the two Americas. He attributed that difference to the presence in the Northern Hemisphere of "free thought, self-government, moral freedom, and the policy of open immigration." All of these factors he found directly traceable to Protestant America's freedom from the material, moral, political, and spiritual subjection that Catholic absolutism imposed on the southern half of the continent.

One century later, just before the Second Vatican Council, the same concern appeared in the words of another Latin American, speaking in modern terms. According to Juan José Arévalo, Protestantism is in "sympathy with democracy. Sociologists . . . have established a connection between Protestantism and the origins of modern capitalism. The Pilgrims aboard the *Mayflower* were Protestants, and they were responsible for the civil and religious consolidation of democracy in America, in opposition to the monarchical principles of the

Roman Church and the authoritarian principles of the Anglican Church."[2]

Worse still, the difference between the two Americas lies not only at the level of economics and politics, but also at that of public and private morality. This is a point of special importance to those, believers and unbelievers alike, who see in Christianity more than a hypocritical cover for games of power and interest, for cynical and immoral behavior. To them, the North American, Protestant society appears more Christian, or perhaps less anti-Christian, than Latin-American, Catholic society. It demands of its followers a pattern of social behavior that dictates reasonably good faith in daily affairs and in interpersonal relations and requires socially constructive action even of those in opposition. An example: North American culture presents no parallel to the cruel rejection of unmarried mothers characteristic of Latin-American society, where *two children out of five are conceived out of wedlock*. In North American society, the generation of child-bearing age normally assumes the care of the children it begets. In Latin-American society, it is almost the norm for the father to refuse responsibility for his offspring; the mother does not have this option, but infanticide and child abandoning are common practices. One is reminded of the "overflow of love" referred to by Vasconcelos[3]—the conquistadors' fulfillment of the male dream of having *all* women available to them. This perversion of love and sexuality seems to have flawed Latin-American society from the Conquest to the present day, without Catholic morality's having been able or much inclined to do anything about it.

Catholic and Protestant Morality

Naturally, the history of both North and South America has included the development of behavior patterns that, unchecked, would have threatened the collectivity or nation with frustration, impotence, or even civil war or disintegration. The Protestant North, one can venture to say, has been better able than the Catholic South to inhibit such trends at their incep-

2. Juan José Arévalo, *AntiKomunismo en América Latina*, Buenos Aires, Palestra, 1959. There is an English translation, *Anti-Kommunism in Latin America: An X-ray of the Process Leading to a New Colonialism*, trans. Carleton Beals, New York, Lyle Stuart, 1963.
3. See p. 92.

tion, through appropriate sanctions and other social mechanisms.

Of this power of self-correction North American society has lately given a dramatic demonstration. It recently checked two of its Presidents—keeping one from seeking a second term and forcing the other to resign—in a process that originated in public protest against an iniquitous and aberrant foreign war and reached its apex with the Watergate affair. In the spring of 1975, a United States Congressional committee studying the behavior of North American multinational corporations made public the fact that some of these, including United Brands in Honduras and Gulf Oil in Bolivia, had bought off Latin-American leaders. The threat of exposure will obviously act as a deterrent to venality in the future. Are we going to reach the paradoxical situation in which Latin-American Presidents and Cabinet members will avoid corruption in fear of having their transgressions brought to light under the North American parliamentary and judicial systems?

The fact is that the judgment of national public opinion has been a more powerful deterrent in the United States than the legal decisions of its courts or Congressional committees. Public opinion in the United States is far from being cynical and powerless, as it is in so many other countries; if it were, the proper judicial mechanisms could not play their role, whatever the extent of their formal power. It is true that the decision requiring Nixon to make public the incriminating tapes (and thereby concluding the Watergate affair) came from the Supreme Court, the highest level of the country's judiciary; but the problem was launched at grass-roots level, with the revelations reaching the reading public via investigative reporters backed by their newspapers. In a wider sense, this process was started even earlier, when Lyndon Johnson's handling of the Vietnam War prompted public discussion on excessive executive power.

I was a college student in the United States when Senator Joseph McCarthy was at the height of his power. To the young Latin American that I then was, it seemed evident that McCarthy's unscrupulous demagogy, unfettered at a time when the cold war was at its peak, would lead him to the White House. "Don't worry," my North American roommate assured me, "he doesn't have a chance." My friend went on to explain that his parents, conservative Republicans, had until recently been the Senator's fervent admirers, warmly endorsing his attacks on the "crypto-Communists." But they had just watched him on TV, at a Congressional hearing held to shed light on his allegations. The Senator had been brilliant, incisive, convincing. But when the time came for one of his victims to speak, and the witness began to meet the Senator's extravagant allegations with a factual refutation, McCarthy picked up an ashtray and started hammering his desk with it to keep his opponent from being heard. *The start of his political decline can be traced to that moment.* My friend's parents, and the majority of those who thus far had seen McCarthy as a sincere defender of North American society against Communist subversion, suddenly understood the Senator's basic dishonesty, and turned against him.

It is easy to brush such a story aside as naïve and childish, particularly for someone who belongs to what we Latin Americans consider a "normal" society, who knows from long experience that government is not his business and who has become a cynic about public affairs. I, for one, want to state what seems evident to me: every kind of immorality, corruption, fraudulence, and even crime among men of power may be fairly common practice in the United States, may often go unpunished; but impunity is less common in the United States than anywhere else, with the possible exception of Great Britain and the Scandinavian countries. In these countries— all Protestant—such matters are quite often eventually brought to light. I also think that North American society is better able than Latin-American society to show up charlatans in its own midst—persons who pretend to be what they are not, and seek to play a role in society for which they are not qualified.

This is an important point. Catholic, Latin-American society is readily satisfied with appearances: with a show of being a good parent, of behaving well, of possessing talent, honesty, erudition, patriotism; with the outward trappings of revolutionary radicalism, or proper sexual conduct; *with a show of religion.* At the same time, our societies have set very strict limits on openly permissible behavior. Only North American influence has in recent years led us to become somewhat more tolerant of nonconformist behavior patterns.

Protestant North American society, by way of comparison, demands men and women far more strictly to give proof of what they really are, as against what they claim to be. This pragmatic, common-sense requirement has given the country its dynamism, for it insures a constant number of tried citizens with dominant roles in the key sectors of national policy and development.

The Uses and Abuses of Intelligence

We Latin Americans do not like to consider such examples. We prefer to forget them altogether, or else we seek to compensate for what we so obviously lack by appealing to values higher than those behind the practical and prosaic conduct of daily affairs. Such virtues appear to us suitable for shopkeepers. What are thrift and frugality compared to a good existential anxiety or a nice case of *in articulo mortis* repentance?

In *The Labyrinth of Solitude* (pp. 21-23), Octavio Paz acknowledged the existence, in the United States, of a "criticism [that] is valuable and forthright, of a sort not often heard in the countries to the south . . . But it is a criticism that respects the existing systems and never touches the roots. I thought of Ortega y Gasset's distinction between uses and abuses, in his definition of the 'revolutionary spirit.' The revolutionary is always a radical, that is, he is trying to correct the uses themselves rather than the mere abuse of them. Almost all the criticisms I heard from the lips of North Americans were of the reformist variety: they left the social or cultural structures intact and were only intended to limit this or that procedure. . . .

"When I arrived in the United States I was surprised above all by the self-assurance and confidence of the people, by their apparent happiness and apparent adjustment to the world around them. . . . On the other hand, I had heard a good deal of talk about American realism and also of their ingenuousness, qualities that would seem to be mutually exclusive. To us a realist is always a pessimist. And an ingenuous person would not remain so for very long if he truly contemplated life realistically. Would it not be more accurate to say that the North American wants to use reality, rather than know it? In some matters—death, for example—he not only has no desire to understand it, he obviously avoids the very idea. . . . American realism, then, is of a very special kind, and American ingenuousness does not exclude dissimulation and even hypocrisy. When hypocrisy is a character trait it also affects one's thinking, because it consists in the negation of all aspects of reality that one finds disagreeable, irrational, or repugnant."

Latin America and the Church

Another Mexican writer, Leopoldo Zea, sees "Western Man" —a category chiefly defined by the Protestant ethic—as having "thrown overboard, without much regret, a past that weighed him down . . . This was not true of the Iberian who remained set on extending his past into the modern future. The Westerner . . . even created a sort of Christianity designed to serve his future: Protestantism."

Zea admits that Spanish Catholicism was destined to become fossilized and a dead weight, both in Spain itself and in the Latin-American colonies; but he attributes to the faith of Rome a *moral* superiority over Protestantism. In settling America, the Catholic Church supposedly recognized "the humanity of all men, independent of their race, their character, their culture, etc."[4]

The same argument had been presented earlier, at greater length and in greater depth and subtlety, by Octavio Paz, whose *Labyrinth of Solitude* first appeared in Spanish in 1950. Paz has the same leitmotiv as other Latin Americans seeking to understand their nations' destiny: he compares his own world to the United States, and comes to conclusions favorable to his nurturing ground:

"It is very easy to laugh at the religious pretensions of colonial society. It is still easier to denounce them as empty forms intended to cover up the abuses of the conquistadors or justify them to themselves or to their victims. To a certain extent this accusation is true, but it is no less true that these other-worldly aspirations were more than [a mere trick]: they are part of a living faith. . . . Catholicism was the center of colonial society because it was the true fountain of life, nourishing the activities, the passions, the virtues and even the sins of both lords and servants, functionaries and priests, merchants and soldiers. Thanks to religion the colonial order was not a mere superimposition of new historical forms but a living organism. The Church used the key of baptism to open the doors of society, converting it into a universal order open to everyone. . . .

"The fate of the Indians would have been very different if it had not been for the Church. . . . I am not thinking only of its struggle to improve their living conditions and to organize them in a more just and Christian manner, but also of the opportunity that baptism offered them to form a part of one social order and one religion. . . . This possibility of belonging to a living order, even if it was at the bottom of the social

4. *Latinoamérica y el mundo.*

pyramid, was cruelly denied to the Indians by the Protestants of New England. The flight of their gods and the death of their leaders had left the natives in a solitude so complete that it is difficult for modern man to imagine it. Catholicism re-established their ties with the world and the other world.

"New Spain [Mexico] committed many horrors, but at least it did not commit the worst horror of all: that of denying a place, even at the foot of the social scale, to the people who composed it. There were classes, castes, and slaves, but there were no pariahs, no persons lacking a fixed social condition and a legal, moral, and religious status." (Pp. 102, 103.)

Paz's interpretation views Latin-American culture as revolutionary, realist, radical, humanist, open, replete with human brotherhood and Catholicism; as such it has nothing to envy in the North American culture, which is reformist, hypocritical, conformist, racist, individualistic, Protestant, atomistic, and preoccupied with correcting abuses, rather than aspiring to perfection.

Much as I admire Paz, this view of Catholic, Spanish American colonial culture seems to me idealistic, a far cry from reality. Where in Latin-American culture today can we find a trace of all these fine qualities? We cannot assess the influence of Catholicism on Latin America by referring only to the colonial period. Even today, most of the Latin-American leaders in all sectors of life have spent years of study in Catholic schools and universities; they have of course received baptism and communion, but neither education nor the sacraments seem to have made a dent in the selfishness, the ineptness, the instinct for dissimulation characterizing the ruling classes. And this includes not only the rich and the politicians, but also those "progressive" intellectual elements that earlier conceived such admiration for *Ariel* and that, in more recent years, have begun to discover the virtues of strictly hierarchical societies, which, unlike the much-hated liberal societies, offer every man a place in society, albeit on the lowest rung.

Religious Orders and the Conquest

The religious conquest of the New World was no less astounding than the military. At the end of the fifteenth century, Spanish Catholicism was a militant and militarized faith, totally committed to a war of reconquest against the Muslim infidels, which culminated in the conquest of Granada in 1492, the very year of Columbus's discovery of the New World. It has often been pointed out, but bears repetition here, that Columbus's discovery, coinciding with the end of the politico-religious wars, provided new opportunities and opened a new field of action to human energies that would otherwise have lacked an outlet. But for the discovery of America, Spain would no doubt have committed itself fully in North Africa. When Columbus returned with the glad tidings that he had discovered a new route to the Indies, he presented the Spanish with a far more attractive focus than North Africa for their surplus energies. And in this enterprise, the concern with Christian evangelization was mixed in with political and economic purposes; proselytism, if anything, was primary. The first colonial organization contained as many churchmen as administrators, and they played a more significant role. In the strings of settlements set up in the newly claimed land by representatives of the metropolis, churches and their dependencies were invariably the first masonry buildings to be erected.

The great, tortured debate that soon arose about the nature and rights of American aborigines bears witness to the seriousness and sincerity of the Christian faith in sixteenth-century Spain. If the "Indians" were human beings, endowed with a soul, sons of God on a par with the Christians who had subjugated them, their enslavement would be a sin, and slaveholders and conquerors would forfeit their salvation, as would the King whose flag they were raising in the New World.

It was altogether to the intellectual credit of Spain and Catholicism that for the first time in history, a debate was settled, in theory if not in practice, *against* the right of the stronger to enslave the weaker. Though some theologians were willing to defend the Aristotelian thesis of natural servitude, they were opposed by clerics come over from America specifically to plead and win this case.

The most remarkable of these clerics was Fray Bartolomé de Las Casas. In 1550, during a debate personally launched by Charles V in his imperial court of Valladolid, Las Casas defended the thesis that American Indians were human beings, equal in every respect to Europeans, and able to do whatever Europeans could do, except shoe a horse. He admitted that the American Indians performed human sacrifices, but then, following a line of reasoning later to be retraced in his own way by the contemporary French anthropologist Jacques Soustelle, he went on to argue that the most deeply religious men are those who offer up the greatest sacrifices to God; thus any culture that made human sacrifices on the altar must have a very high conception of divinity. This comment is characteristic of Las Casas's way of thinking, at once fiery and inclined to paradox. By temperament he belonged among those who, once having made up their minds and reached certain conclusions, are moved to violent indignation, willing to resort to exaggeration and even misstatement to defend their thesis; and ready to impose it by force if possible. The present-day Latin-American "revolutionary priests" are thus quite right to see in Las Casas a hero and a precursor; they consider him a witness to the presence of the Holy Ghost in the historic drama that was about to take a tragic turn for the Indians.

In 1597, a papal bull settled the question theoretically. Indians were recognized as men, endowed with a soul, exactly as were the Europeans. But as they were pagans and savages, they might be considered inferior, children who had not yet reached the age of reason. The role of the Spanish colonizers was therefore to *protect* them and to *bring them to the faith of Christ.* They could be used for labor, but with moderation: as workers, and never as slaves.

The Church as an Instrument of Social Control

It goes without saying that these fine principles were nowhere applied. In Cubagua, Indian pearl-divers were forced to dive to such depths that they burst their lungs; in Peru, Indian miners were not allowed to return to the surface, but lived and died underground. Each settler who was granted an encomienda received at the same time a number of native "souls" whom he was supposed to protect and evangelize, but the organization of labor had the earmarks of the most ruthless slavery.

The sternest critics of Spanish colonization contend that such practices led to the near-extermination of a very large sector of the native population. Actually it is doubtful that the pre-Columbian population of Spanish America was ever very numerous. According to the most plausible estimates, the population of the Aztec empire did not exceed one million. The capital, Tenochtitlán, covered less than four square kilometers, reflecting a limited population. Cuzco was the only city of any consequence in the Inca empire, and a new system of calculation, based on the optimal use of land according to the farming methods that were prevalent before the Conquest and Spanish colonization, has recently led to the conclusion that the area that is now modern Peru could not at that time have fed more than a million and a half inhabitants.

In sixteenth-century Mexico and Peru, one of the colonizers' most serious problems was the shortage of Indian labor for the encomiendas; as these regions were the most heavily populated in the hemisphere, we may infer that the same was true in other parts of the continent.[5]

This contradicts the extravagant but long-accepted claims behind the legend of the Spanish colonizers' wholesale extermination of the natives. In fact, notwithstanding the cruel treatment meted out to the Indians and the introduction of smallpox and other eruptive diseases that decimated them, the native population seems never to have undergone too sharp a drop; toward the end of the sixteenth century it probably exceeded that of the pre-Columbian period, and it has not stopped rising since. The natives were not exterminated; they continued to make up the majority of the population, along with the mestizos, whose numeric growth reflected the Spanish sexual frenzy. The Church soon found itself playing a role very different from that which Fray Bartolomé de Las Casas had hoped to witness. It became the key element in a system of authority and control that enabled a relatively small number of white settlers and their legitimate descendants, the Creoles, to remain the masters of docile masses of Indians, mestizos, blacks, mulattoes, zambos, et cetera. In the Catholic colonial order, all these serfs were to have their place, as Octavio Paz pointed out, on the lowest rung of the social ladder.

The Triumph of the Inquisition

There is no doubt that this structure reflected deliberate social planning. When the new viceroy, Francisco de Toledo, arrived in Peru in 1569, he carried instructions designed to check the efforts of clerics such as Las Casas, who had embraced the cause of the Indians. Henceforward, any difficulties arising from the treatment of Indians were to be referred directly to the bishops; this would keep agitators from creating scandals that might threaten the Crown and the Church. One of Toledo's first steps as the new governor of the colony (the most important in the Spanish empire in the Americas) was to meet

5. Bailey W. Diffie, "Estimates of Indian Population in 1492," in Lewis Hanke, ed., *History of Latin American Civilisation*, London, Methuen, 1969, vol. 1, pp. 193–94.

the high ecclesiastical authorities of Lima and Cuzco. The Inquisition had just been introduced in Peru, and the purpose of the meeting was to agree on more efficient use of the Holy Office in insuring the submission or silence of churchmen who preached opinions that threatened official policy. Indeed, it was the specific, stated purpose of the Inquisition in Latin America to stamp out reformist elements within the clergy. Its formidable machinery was not intended to identify and punish heretics among the Indians: the unconverted Indians were not heretics but innocent pagans; hence they could be the object of proselytizing efforts, but the purity of their faith was not in question. Toledo, however, inaugurated his viceroyalty by executing the Inca Prince Túpac Amaru for refusing to submit to the Spanish Crown and the Catholic faith: this left no doubt as to his policy and resolve.

The same pattern soon became evident in New Spain (Mexico), where the Inquisition was established the following year (1570). This sinister organization was rapidly to acquire powers all the more pervasive for being ill-defined. Its anathemas, proscriptions, and warrants for arrest brooked no appeal. The "secular arm" of civil authority in principle owed it unrestricted obedience and support, and the viceroys themselves came to stand in fear of it. It would have been unnatural for authority so extensive and unchecked to limit itself to its stated purpose of maintaining the correct political line and checking heresy; the Inquisition ended up as a self-serving organization concerned with the privileges and wealth of its members, and with the political power of the Church as a whole.

The close of the sixteenth century saw the end of the heroic days of conquest and colonization. In the seventeenth and eighteenth centuries, the Church rid itself almost entirely of its idealists and agitators, and was solidly entrenched as an equal partner with the secular authorities, sharing their power and spoils and living with them in a relationship of symbiosis and simony. The priests had become sedentary lovers of the good life, prominent in the first rank of the Creole oligarchies, and the spiritual arm was less interested in saving the souls of its flock than in reinforcing its moral dominion over society and increasing its patrimony. Tithes, legacies, and donations from the Crown or from individuals flowed into its coffers, till the Spanish colonial Church became the foremost owner of land and slaves. In Mexico it owned one-fifth of the national territory.

Clerics like Las Casas never entirely disappeared: they could not have, as long as the Scripture was not placed on the Index. There were, at all times, humble parish priests whose concern for social justice drove them to sympathize with the emancipation movement, and who, sometimes, were its direct instigators. In Mexico, two such men were Hidalgo and Morelos, both poor priests serving poor parishes. Actually, Morelos was a mestizo at a time (1810) when the Mexican Creoles were scrupulously faithful to the Spanish Crown. But the Church as an institution became an integral part of the "Establishment," sharing in its wealth and its privileges, very early in the history of the colonies. The French Revolution, and the previous, "scandalous" example of the threat of enlightened anticlerical liberalism, further confirmed the Church in its convictions, and led it to an even more uncompromising defense of the political and social structure of the *ancien régime.*

The "Reducciones" of Paraguay

Only the Jesuits were in favor of the independence of Latin America, for special reasons inherent in the history of their order. By 1767, when they were expelled from all lands under the control of the Spanish Crown, they had succeeded in creating in America a theocratic Christian state that, though it might hold little attraction for a modern liberal, presents one of the few examples of a socialist regime that actually governed in accordance with its principles.

The Jesuits arrived in Paraguay in 1588. By 1700, they had established in this hinterland some thirty missions, called *reducciones,*[6] grouping at least a hundred thousand laborers in all. Each *reducción* radiated outward from a central plaza, with one side occupied by the Church and its sacristy, and the three others by dormitories designed to house one hundred or more families, each in separate quarters. In the morning, the men of working age would be led off to work by a Jesuit brother, all marching to music behind the statue of a saint borne by two men. On the way to the fields, the procession would stop and pray at several stations that served as oratories. As the procession made its way, small working crews would be dropped off at the field where they were to be em-

---

6. From the Spanish verb *reducir:* "to persuade or attract someone by reason and argument; to lead to obedience" (*Dictionary of the Spanish Royal Academy*).

ployed for the day. When all had been safely deposited, the priest and the musicians would turn around and head back for the barracks. Further devotions and a rest period followed at noon, before lunch. Then, more work till sunset, at which time the same padre and musicians would return to escort their wards back to the fold for the night.

Other inmates of the *reducciones* herded cattle or practiced handicrafts. The economy was simple; all property was held in common. Thus they put into practice a concept that today has been adopted by the Social Christian parties, even though no one quite knows how to apply it in a modern society, where paternalism and the "socialization" of property lead to dire results that by now have become clearly predictable. In exchange for their labor, the members of these Communist societies were entitled to a share of what the community produced, as well as a fraction of what it "imported" in exchange for its produce: knives, scissors, spectacles, et cetera.

The Jesuits' attitude toward the Indians was that of adults entrusted with the care of children who would never reach the age of reason. The "neophytes," as they were called, were taught not to take initiatives, but only to obey. In retrospect, the *reducciones* appear as the best possible materialization of a *City of God* on earth, of a Platonic Republic. One wonders whether Christian political thought did not find its permanent and imperishable ideal in this society that the Jesuits fashioned in the seventeenth and eighteenth centuries.

The Jesuits Outside and in Opposition to the System

It would have been interesting to trace the growth of this extraordinary social experiment, had it been allowed to proceed. But its apparent success was the cause of its ruin. The Jesuits' wealth and power in Paraguay (and in all the Spanish empire) was used as a decisive argument against them by all their enemies, from those within the Church itself to members of the Masonic Order, which reached the height of its power and activity in the eighteenth century.

Further, the Jesuit missions in Paraguay stood as an implicit criticism of the system of colonization and *reducción* of the natives being applied throughout the rest of Spanish America. Their wealth was a source of temptation to the Spanish settlers in the south and to the Portuguese in the north. The latter, in fact, undertook slave hunts in Jesuit mission territory —under the indifferent or approving eye of the Spanish, who themselves hoped to lay claim to the Jesuits' lands and Indians.

In 1767, King Charles III succumbed to the pressure of "enlightened" ideas and ecclesiastical intrigue and expelled the Jesuits from the Spanish empire. He confiscated their property for the benefit of the Crown and dispatched non-Jesuit clergy and civilian administrators to Paraguay to take over the *reducciones*. Within a few years, the Indians had all been dispersed: some had reverted to traditional life, others had been enslaved. The missions were left to fall into ruin; the cattle were killed or allowed to run wild; jungle reclaimed the cultivated land.

The Jesuits dispersed throughout Europe and became eloquent enemies of the Spanish American empire, while the rest of the clergy remained loyal. Francisco de Miranda, who dreamed of destroying the empire and setting up independent republics in its place, was well aware of the advantages that his cause could derive from this large group of educated exiles. So were the English, who had reasons of their own for endorsing the Spanish American independence movement. Documents still extant quote conversations between Pitt and Miranda on how to exploit the presence of so many eminent, disaffected Spanish Jesuits in Europe. In 1806, a Creole member of the order, Juan José Godoy, joined Miranda the Precursor in the expedition, planned in the United States, that led to a landing near Caracas and to revolt against Spain.[7]

Of the Jesuits expelled in 1767, the best known is the Peruvian Juan Pablo Vizcardo y Guzmán, the author of a *Letter to the Spanish Americans*, one of the most eloquent and impassioned of the many documents that cleared the way for the emancipation of the Spanish colonies in America. Miranda had this *Letter* printed in French in Philadelphia in 1799, and in Spanish in 1801, and had it widely distributed from Mexico to Buenos Aires.

But it is perfectly clear that the exiled Jesuits constituted an unrepresentative minority group within the body of the Church. In a judgment delivered in 1810, the Holy Office declared Vizcardo's *Letter* to be "one of the most deadly, libertine, and disruptive productions ever seen, far more threatening and dangerous to America than is the propaganda of the present-day tyrant and usurper, Bonaparte."

7. Miranda is called "the Precursor," just as Bolívar is "the Liberator."

Latin-American Anticlericalism

The nineteenth century was a dark night for the Catholic Church throughout the world, but especially in countries in which it sought to cling to its ancient privileges through alliances with reactionary powers dedicated to the preservation or restoration of the *ancien régime*. In the countries where it pursued this policy, the Church paid dearly for the usually brief and precarious tenure of the privileges it pretended to, contrary to its evangelical mission: it met with growing popular disaffection and even active hostility.

We have seen that in Latin America the first revolutionary tremor had left the Church almost unscathed. But from the middle of the nineteenth century onward, and with few exceptions (notably Colombia), the Spanish American republics evolved into *liberal, secular* states. This may not always have worked to the advantage of the common people, but for the Church it constituted an unmistakable setback. For the "liberals," at best democratic oligarchs (in Argentina and Chile), were more often autocratic leaders who compensated for a lack of any real liberalism with radical anticlericalism. They stripped the Church of its privileges and possessions, curbed or suppressed religious congregations, replaced parish with civil registration, made civil marriage a precondition for church weddings, forbade worship outside the church precincts, encouraged secular education, and legalized divorce. Certain republics, such as Mexico, Cuba, and Uruguay, even broke off diplomatic relations with the Vatican.

A document recently issued by the Venezuelan Episcopate declares: "The position of the Church is still affected today by the discriminatory measures of which it was the victim at the end of the last century; for several decades these measures rendered impossible the normal functioning of a number of ecclesiastical institutions such as seminaries."[8]

What this document does not mention is the Church's discovery of how tenuous its evangelical work of three and a half centuries proved to be when it lost its alliance with secular authority. Once the Church stopped being an instrument of domination, faith lost its attractiveness for the men of the Latin-American ruling class, and churchgoing became

8. Press Bulletin of the Permanent Secretary of the Episcopal Conference of Venezuela, Caracas, January 10, 1975.

"woman's business."[9] Actually, the ladies, too, viewed their religion, their Mass, and their confession as pastimes, perhaps the only source of distraction in their lives of boredom and mediocrity. Faith retained its vitality only among the masses, and even there it had an ambiguous character, since the mestizo people of Latin America practice a form of Catholicism that is contaminated with all sorts of pagan superstitions. Among the pure Indians of Mexico, Guatemala, Colombia, Ecuador, Peru, and Bolivia, Catholicism has been merely superimposed on a substratum of pre-Columbian beliefs. The following comments of a pureblood Mexican Indian describe his feelings toward the statues in his village church, and show what such symbols mean to him and his people:

"This is Señor San Manuel here in this coffin; he is also called Señor Salvador or Señor San Mateo; he watches over people and over the animals. We pray to him to watch over us at home, on the road, in the fields. This other figure on the cross is also Señor San Mateo; he is showing us how he died on the cross, to teach us respect. . . . Before San Manuel was born, the sun was as cold as the moon, and the *pukujes,* who ate people, lived on the earth. The sun began to grow warm after the birth of the Child-God, Señor San Salvador, who is the son of the Virgin."[10]

Christ dying on the cross to teach us to respect our betters! . . . What can one possibly add to this? We see what the Church intended from the viewpoint of social control; and we see why it enjoys so little respect among us today.

The "Judeo-Protestant-Masonic-Liberal-Marxist Anti-Christian Conspiracy"

The Church's role in the world and in Latin America up to the Second World War was not precisely conducive to restoring its prestige. Yet a certain renewal of evangelism, in both transcendent and human terms, did begin to take place following the *Rerum Novarum* encyclical (1891), in which Pope Leo

9. An anecdote from the present: At a certain beach club near Caracas, a large number of families (all from the ruling class) are in the habit of attending 10 AM Mass. But one Sunday, TV retransmitted a motorcycle world championship held in Italy, in which a Venezuelan champion was the favorite. That day the ladies went to Mass by themselves.
10. Ricardo Pozas, *Juan Pérez Jelote: Autobiography of a Tzotzil,* quoted in Octavio Paz, *The Labyrinth of Solitude,* p. 107.

XIII recognized the existence of the *social question,* as well as the Church's need to counter the challenge of Marxist socialism. The Social Christian and Christian Democratic political movements drew their inspiration and guidelines from this encyclical, and from others stressing the social question. In two countries (Chile from 1964 to 1970, and Venezuela from 1969 to 1973), these parties succeeded in being elected and holding power for one constitutionally approved term. But until the death of Pope Pius XII in 1958, the Church seemed obsessed by its defeats at the hands of liberalism and unable to distinguish between liberalism and Marxism.

Confusion on this point has been so great that some Christian Democratic leaders, highly respected today and, in some cases, true liberals, were drawn in their earlier years to the Spanish *Falange* and taken in by Franco's image of himself as defender of the faith against the red hordes.

What the Church meant until recently to Latin-American liberals and democrats was vividly expressed in a book mentioned earlier, *AntiKomunismo en América Latina,* by Juan José Arévalo, the Aprist President of Guatemala from 1945 to 1950. Writing in 1959, Arévalo showed how the Church deservedly lost most of its influence over the continent, even in the crucial sphere of education. "The Church in Latin America never abandoned its struggle against secular influences. . . . In Guatemala, secular influences and popular government waned at the same time. . . . In Colombia the Church never lost its political power. The Archbishop of Bogotá has been the Lord Elector of the Republic. . . . Argentina has suffered from the clerical reaction since 1943, when the Pink House [the presidential palace in Buenos Aires] was taken over by pro-Hitler officers. The first presidential speech of this 'revolution'[11] was written by a priest. We who represented the liberal, secular 'Old Guard' in the University[12] had occasion to witness from the inside the anti-Kommunist[13] revenge unleashed against anyone who had sympathized with the Allied cause during the Second World War. . . . Peronism enacted the revenge of the Church. . . ."

11. Actually a preamble to fascist Peronism.
12. When in exile in Argentina, Arévalo was a professor at the University of Buenos Aires.
13. Arévalo wrote "anti-Kommunism" with a *K* so as to ridicule the identification made by John Foster Dulles—and by the *entire Latin-American Church*—of any kind of liberal reform with "international Communism."

Latin America and the Church

Many youngsters have never known, and many adults have forgotten, the explanation that used to be given by Catholic authorities of the evolution of Western society from the eighteenth century to the present. Arévalo quoted a certain Msgr. José María Caro (a Latin American whose 1918 book was brought up to date and reprinted in 1954), who explained this evolution simply as the product of a universal conspiracy "against the altar and the throne," aiming at man's regression to the "state of nature." Caro expected that once this evolution had been completed, the Freemasons, the liberals, and the Communists (all lumped together) would propose a new religion: the cult of Satan. Caro was convinced that Freemasonry had long worn the mask of liberalism, and that in a later stage of its truly diabolical plan, it would take the form of Marxist socialism. All this, of course, would be done for the ultimate benefit of the Jews: "Contemporary authors have shown the close relationship between Judaism, Freemasonry, and the revolutionary parties, from socialism to bolshevism. . . . Their ultimate purpose is the ruin of Christianity, which will bring about world domination by the Jews."[14]

According to this Catholic author, the high points of the Judeo-Masonic conspiracy were the English revolution of 1649, the expulsion of the Jesuits from Portugal in 1759 and from the Spanish empire in 1767, the American Revolution of 1776, the French Revolution of 1789, the Spanish American emancipation (1810–24), the Italian *Risorgimento* (1859–1870), the Russian Revolution of 1917, and the Proclamation of the Spanish Republic in 1931.

This perspective considers as part of the Judeo-Masonic conspiracy all human institutions that in some way helped weaken the influence of the Catholic Church, or that failed to serve the cause of the Church when they were in a position to do so. As can be imagined, the list is long; it includes, for example, the League for the Defense of the Rights of Man, the Boy Scouts, all secular education, and the YMCA.

One factor that is difficult to analyze or to explain from this perspective is the role of the United States on the world scene. As the world's foremost liberal and Protestant power, the United States could only be viewed as a useful support for the Judeo-Masonic conspiracy. In 1953, Gustavo Rojas Pinilla, the military dictator of Colombia, declared: "The activities of Prot-

14. Msgr. José María Caro, *El misterio de la masonería*, 1954, quoted in *Antikomunismo en América Latina*, p. 122.

estant missionaries in Colombia constitute the gravest danger to national unity and to American solidarity." He added that these activities were driving back the Faith, and thus further-ing the cause of Communism. In Colombia, forty-seven Protes-tants were assassinated between 1949 and 1957. In 1957, Pope Pius XII listed Communism and Protestantism among the dangers threatening the Catholic Church in Latin America. To cite Msgr. Caro again, as quoted by Arévalo, "In the United States, Freemasonry has progressed from its temples to the skyscrapers, and from the skyscrapers to the Pentagon." Puerto Rico is but "Masonic spoils won by the heretics on the Potomac."

But in 1954, when Caro's updated version appeared, the United States was also the foremost anti-Communist power; its Latin-American policy supported a social order to which the Church was also deeply attached, and for the same anti-Com-munist reasons. When, in 1957, Colonel Castillo Armas, the CIA puppet used in the overthrow of President Jacobo Arbenz of Guatemala, was murdered, the Bishop of Guatemala, then in Washington, promptly flew home—in an American Air Force plane, accompanied by President Eisenhower's son, who had been sent to represent his father at the funeral. Astounding as it may seem, Arévalo affirmed that in his funeral oration for the dead tyrant, the Archbishop said Castillo Armas had been "as good as Christ."

The Church on a New Tack

The chapter on the Church in *Antikomunismo en América Latina* seems singularly dated today. It is difficult to believe that only seventeen years have gone by since the publication of this book, which even then told us nothing we did not know about the staunchly reactionary attitude of the Church throughout the world, and particularly in Latin America.

On the other hand, it is not hard to imagine that even years before the death of Pius XII, some men of influence in the Roman hierarchy and members of the Roman Curia saw the utter anachronism of the Church's attitude in facing the prob-lems of the modern world. The future Popes John XXIII and Paul VI were among them; they had witnessed the Communist empire occupy the center of Europe in 1945 and draw China to itself in 1949. Given this steady progress, how could the

Church continue to interpret history as crudely as Msgr. Caro, or as inflexibly as that unbending spokesman of anti-Communism, Cardinal Mindszenty, who, in 1956, had found refuge in the American consulate in Budapest?

Another highly interesting evolution now took place. In the Catholic countries where Communism had become the state religion, such as Poland or Hungary, not only was the Church of Rome not destroyed, but it also found itself benefiting from two unhoped-for and complementary advantages. First, the Church became the only remaining nongovernmental institution, the only representative body to which the government could address itself or with which it could carry on some sort of dialogue. Second, it became a center of attraction for individuals and social groups that so far had remained indifferent or hostile to its teachings, including some that formerly had been entirely secular or even anticlerical. The nonpracticing Jew or Catholic caught in the bleak universe of Communist totalitarianism has to find a meaning in human life to make his existence bearable. Unless he is a Stoic philosopher, and able to live in peace with whatever world surrounds him, he will seek some relief for the oppressive, numbing indoctrination with which Communism weighs down all aspects of social life, and will recognize the Church or Synagogue as the only setting in which to find it.

Finding itself a focus of attraction under Communism, the Church can choose to renounce its militant anti-Communist stance, discuss with the government the conditions of its own survival under the Communist regime, reach an agreement guaranteeing its survival, and then hope that, with time, the normal course of events will play in its favor.

This strategy seems to me to provide the only explanation for Church policy since 1958—in particular, for a number of political initiatives that would otherwise seem to go well beyond the policy of *"aggiornamento"* (the general modernizing trend defined by the Vatican II Council) and beyond such encyclicals as *Mater et Magistra* (1961) or *Pacem in Terris* (1963) of Pope John XXIII, and *Populorum Progressio* (1967) of Pope Paul VI. Such a trade-off between the Church and the party would explain a number of positions the Church has taken in recent years that appear to legitimize the established Communist regimes and to give a measure of tactical Catholic support to Marxist-Leninist-inspired revolutionary movements in the Third World.

A Gift from Heaven

Such mutual tactical support between Catholics and Leninists, wherever it may occur, but especially in Latin America, has been made easier by a radical reorientation in socialist propaganda. Marxist-Leninist socialists at first promised the common man an abundance of consumer goods, once the economy had been freed of the shackles of private property and the profit motive. But the promise failed to materialize; what the man in the street witnessed instead was a growing contrast between the Eastern and Western parts of Europe. Unable to keep their word, Communists have ceased to predict unlimited abundance for all, and have instead become ardent defenders of universally shared austerity. In the new formulation, they describe austerity as a praiseworthy alternative to the vulgar indulgence of capitalist, consumer society, in which individuals, egged on by advertising, are driven to consume more and more, and to strive for personal satisfaction rather than the collective good.

By contrast, though the new man in Cuba, China, and Vietnam may not have much wealth at his disposal, he is supposedly master of himself. There are no refrigerators, vacuum cleaners, or cars to alienate him from his deeper self; nor is he troubled by radio or TV programs that advertise these gadgets and a thousand others, at the same time that they convey information and opinions contradictory to what he is supposed to think and believe. The new man's only joy in life should be the certainty that his sacrifices as an individual will help bring about the reign of justice. Good will triumph over evil, and *all shall be saved.*

Thus Communism has unexpectedly reached a position that fits in remarkably well with very ancient and deeply rooted ascetic and antimercantile beliefs—the very beliefs it had earlier rejected as obscurantist and deceitful, conceived by capitalists and priests to fool men by promising them "pie in the sky" to make up for their steady lack of bread in this world.

In effect, after several centuries of concern, if not panic, in the face of rising liberalism, free thinking, and secular capitalism, the Church has now received a gift from heaven. In the past it saw socialist Marxism as far more of a threat to its existence than liberalism—a judgment in which Marxism itself concurred. Now it has come to see that accommodation is possible, and perceives in socialist Marxism a tactical ally, the common enemy of capitalism, ready to help propagate the message that the merchants are the great enemies of man's salvation, and that the most urgent task is to chase them from the temple.

It is not at all certain that the Communists will end up having the upper hand in this curious alliance, as they firmly expect. One may remain unconvinced about the exact accordance of Catholic dogma with the transcendent design of the universe, and in doubt about the existence of a Supreme Being concerned with leading the Church of Rome to ultimate victory over all infidels; yet it is clear that there is in Catholicism a deep and relevant answer to the fundamental anxieties inherent in the human condition. The Catholic faith does offer comfort in many existential quandaries, as well as a method for confronting the diverse problems and challenges of life. Next to this, Marxist "humanism" is shallow and vapid; and as a consequence, the societies that are actually being run under the guidance of such a philosophy have proven indeed very propitious seedbeds for the rebirth of the religious spirit.

Communism, in turn, can tolerate religion, though it rightly feels threatened by liberalism, the free discussion of ideas, criticism, systematic questioning of all authority, and, of course, by the ever-increasing access enjoyed by groups and individuals in open, liberal societies to constantly improving and less expensive means of communication.[15] Communism takes good care to stamp out such intellectual endeavor whenever it becomes discernible. Similarly, Communism now plays down man's aspiration to material comfort, a motive it stigmatizes for leading to an alienated consumer society founded on the exploitation of the proletariat by the bourgeoisie.

In liberal societies, including the Latin-American countries that are less weighed down by Spanish Catholic feudalism, we find that churches today are deserted, that public opinion is concerned with issues that have nothing to do with religion, and that the young would not for the most part dream of studying for the priesthood, though they flock to secular universities. In contrast, the Catholic faith is nowhere more alive than in Poland or Hungary. This being so, how can we be sure that some similar return to the Faith might not take place in Cuba? And eventually in other Latin-American countries, if they, too, are taken over by Communism?

15. In Communist countries, private citizens may not own a copying machine, and in certain places, they must even register their typewriters with the police.

If, as I have argued, the Church has indeed made a radical reappraisal of its strategy vis-à-vis Communism, such a decision can only have been made at the highest level, and probably after the death of Pius XII. That is, it may have originated earlier, but Pope Pius XII could not possibly have presided over such a change.

There are a number of reasons why the Church's previous policy of setting itself up as the spearhead of world anti-Communism appears with hindsight to be a monumental error. These reasons are worth summarizing:

(1) A Protestant, liberal, secular, and materialistic society (the United States) is at the heart of the opposition to the expansion of the Communist empire.

(2) Ever since the Second World War and the Communist take-over in China, the Communist empire has been a political reality of such magnitude that an eternal and universal institution such as the Church could not systematically continue to refuse any accommodation to it.

(3) Catholicism has not been crushed in the Catholic countries taken over by Communism, such as Poland and Hungary. Rather, as a faith, it has resisted and prospered.

(4) In these countries, the Church has derived new importance through being the only other institution within the totalitarian state with which the government can entertain any kind of dialogue. It is the only *lung* of these asphyxiated societies.

(5) In the countries they do not control, the Communists are now preaching a kind of asceticism and an antiliberalism much in line with the Church's own obsessive fixation on the twin menaces of materialism and liberalism.

(6) In Latin America, anti-Communism is rightly identified with the United States, and even with *complicity* with the United States. It follows that insofar as they successfully resist Communism, Latin-American countries can only draw closer to the cultural and political values of the liberal, capitalist North American civilization, thus further weakening the Catholic influence.

(7) The Church in the Third World, and particularly in Latin America, has nothing to gain from identifying with forces to which Communist jargon has affixed the label "imperialism and its local minions." Particularly when the leading class among these "minions" evidently is more interested in watching a motorcycle race on TV than in attending Mass.

You Scratch My Back . . .

In 1968, Paul VI took advantage of the meeting of the 39th International Eucharistic Congress in Bogotá to make the first papal visit ever to Latin America. The Roman Pontiff was careful to keep his distance from those who, like Camilo Torres, affirmed that if Christ returned to Latin America today, he would preach rifle in hand.[16] Nor did the Pope endorse positions such as the one proclaimed by the Nicaraguan priest Ernesto Cardenal, who said: "A man can be a revolutionary without being a Communist, but he cannot at the same time be a revolutionary and an anti-Communist. I am myself in no way an anti-Communist, for though I am a Catholic and a priest, I consider myself a Marxist and a Communist. I have even come to think that in Latin America today, to be a revolutionary, one has to be a Marxist and a Communist. And even more, a genuine Christian in Latin America has to be a Communist . . . ."[17] There is no reason to think that Paul VI deliberately sought to further the trend that led the Latin-American Confederation of Christian Unions (CLASC) to declare some years later: "The legal road is blocked in Latin America. We can count only on armed struggle, on violent revolution." In fact, Paul VI had only this to say: "In Latin America, I saw a great need for social justice, so that large numbers of poor people might lead happier, easier, more human lives. . . ."[18]

But since 1968, through a coincidence that can hardly be fortuitous, the Latin-Amercan Episcopal Council (CELAM) has led the Catholic Church to take increasingly leftist positions. The same year the Pope visited Latin America, the

16. Camilo Torres was a Colombian priest, the son of one of the "twenty-four families" in what was the most traditionally Catholic society of Latin America. Born in 1929, trained for the priesthood in Colombia, he later studied sociology at Louvain. On his return, during the high point of Castroism and Guevarism, he adopted an increasingly radical stance, which might have been understood and accepted by authorities less conservative than those of his country, but which in Colombia forced him to give up the priesthood. In October 1965, he joined a guerrilla group, and in February of the next year he was killed in an encounter with the army. Even though Camilo cannot compete with Che Guevara for the title of first "saint" of the Latin-American revolution, it is in the Church's interest not to neglect this martyr, buried near the spot where he was killed under a humble aluminum cross bearing this inscription: "Any Catholic owes it to himself to respect this grave."
17. Cardenal is the author of *En Cuba*, an enthusiastic defense of the Castro regime.
18. Paul VI, speaking in Rome, September 28, 1968, shortly after his return from Colombia.

bishops of the continent met at Medellín, Colombia to discuss the application to Latin America of the guidelines for renewal set by the second Vatican Council. They decided that the new basic goal of the Latin-American Church should be "liberation from any kind of servitude," a directive that in concrete terms has been interpreted as follows: Christians are called upon to denounce and oppose structures of oppression, situations of excessive dependence, "massification," and exploitation, and to restructure society so as to establish true justice, equality, and participation.

The language of the Latin-American Episcopate became "Third Worldly" and Leninist at a more recent meeting of CELAM, held in Mar del Plata, Argentina, in May 1975. CELAM's Secretary General himself, Msgr. Alfonso López Trujillo of Colombia, declared, "We cannot talk about God as long as men are dying of hunger," and, "The United States and Canada are rich because the nations of Latin America are poor. They have built up their wealth at our expense."

In this way the Church can ride the crest of the formidable Leninist wave, while clearing itself of any responsibility for the shortcomings of Latin America: these are *all* due to imperialism!

Do the peoples of Latin America have that short a memory? In any case, the Church may be assured of finding interested supporters for its effort to spread confusion. In 1969, the year following the Pope's visit to Latin America and the Second CELAM meeting, Fidel Castro himself exonerated the Catholic Church of conservatism and submission to the United States. On July 14 of the same year, he admitted *for the first time* that the "insurrectional focal point" was not necessarily the only way to Communist revolution in Latin America. The revolution need not break out with irresistible force, overcoming national borders and distance, as he and El Che had maintained earlier. Rather, he now recognized that the path of revolution might take a different course in each country, according to prevailing conditions, and that in each a distinct process of gradual change might take place, *in the direction of the revolution.* Fidel recognized that, in such a process, the new, post-Council Church would certainly have an important, and possibly a decisive, role to play.

High-Level Diplomacy and Politics

In August 1973, Pedro Arrupe, General of the Order of Jesuits (the same Jesuits who had been expelled from Latin America by the old regime) visited socialist Chile and Cuba, and had *political* talks at the highest level in both those countries. In September, shortly before Allende's overthrow,[19] Arrupe made some sibylline statements to the press, saying that he was persuaded that "world Catholicism, which has been following the Cuban developments with much interest, will soon be able to discern the different aspects of this unique historic phenomenon."

The following year, a high dignitary of the Roman Curia, Secretary of the Vatican's Council for Public Affairs, Msgr. Casaroli, visited Cuba and met Fidel Castro. There is nothing ambiguous about the declarations Msgr. Casaroli made immediately upon his return: "Cuban Catholics are happy under the Socialist system. They have not the slightest problem with the Cuban Socialist government, no more than other Cubans. . . . The Catholics on the island are as free to worship as any other citizens. . . ."

It is true that the last sentence allows for more than one interpretation, especially as Msgr. Casaroli at the same time deplored the fact that there were only two hundred priests to serve all of the island, and he admitted having personally negotiated with Fidel Castro to loosen the restrictions placed on public worship. But the ambiguity lies less in Msgr. Casaroli's words than in the facts. Whatever Ernesto Cardenal and the other "new wave" priests may have to say about it, the Church cannot view Marxism other than as an abominable heresy; but evidently it is aware of the Leninist strategy of encouraging confrontation between Third World countries and the advanced capitalist countries, and of the formidable threat with which this approach arms world Communism. Given these facts, the Church must have concluded that it cannot confront the Communist heresy head on, that it had better seek to live in peace with it and to define a *modus vivendi*. This course is further suggested by the many indications that the new heresy is a reaction to the liberal revolution, rather than its fulfillment, as the Church had feared earlier.

19. For a time, President Allende had excellent and close relations with the Cardinal Prelate of Chile, Silva Henriquez, Archbishop of Santiago.

The Power and the Glory

The Vatican's new policy is not easy to implement, and it presents dangers not only to the Church itself, but also to individual believers, among whom perplexities, deviations, and abjurations have appeared. Most of the unsophisticated believers, but also many advanced laymen and ranking churchmen, simply cannot understand or accept Arrupe's or Casaroli's mission in Cuba, or Cardinal Mindszenty's deposition as Hungarian Archbishop; or the trip that Cardinal Willebrands, President of the Secretariat of the Union of Christians, made to Moscow in 1971.

At the same time, there is no doubt that many lay Christians and even many priests have taken refuge in indifference, or are being won over by the Marxist heresy. In 1972, speaking over Radio Vatican, the French Cardinal Daniélou remarked that certain priests "view evangelical counsel no longer as springing from a consecration to God, but rather from a sociological and psychological angle. Priests nowadays are concerned with not appearing as bourgeois, though on the individual level few of them practice poverty. They are involved with group dynamics, rather than with religious obedience. They tend to abandon all discipline on the pretext of reacting against formalism. . . . Men and women in the religious orders are giving up wearing their distinctive habit and are seeking admission into secular institutions, abandoning the worship of God for the benefit of social and political activities."

In Chile in 1971—the first year of the Allende government—a group of twenty-four Chilean priests formed a movement called "Catholics for Socialism" that argued that the injustices of the capitalist system, particularly the deplorable condition of the *dependent* countries, could only be remedied by Communist revolutions on the Cuban model. The movement spread like wildfire to other countries in Latin America and Europe. One year later, in April 1972, four hundred priests from all over Latin America met in Santiago, clamoring that Christianity and Marxism ought to work hand in hand.

Nor did matters rest there. In January 1973, nearly two hundred Spanish and Latin-American believers, both secular and ordained, met secretly in Avila, Spain, and resolved that the duty of a good Christian was to struggle for socialism, not merely as a sympathizer or "fellow traveler" of the Marxist parties, but as a *disciplined party member*. A similar resolution was passed at a meeting of two thousand Catholics for Socialism in Bologna in September 1973.

Several episcopal conferences have worried about these excesses. A synod that met in Rome during the first half of 1975 drew attention to the fact that "to the temptation of binding the Church to a political power or ideology, we now must add the equally dangerous temptation of seeking to please public opinion. The peaceful struggle for liberation which is the duty of Christians everywhere should concern itself not only with colonialist socioeconomic structures in the Third World, but also with the spiritual, ideological, religious, and moral oppression prevalent in the Second World, in the Communist world. *But fear of public opinion keeps us silent about this.*"[20]

The last is a telling phrase. It would seem to indicate that the upper hierarchy of the Church considers the general public in the Third World, and in particular in Latin America, to be ready to swallow the Leninist ideology, and at the same time unwilling to criticize oppression within the Communist empire.

It will be a long wait before we know who will have the upper hand in this ambiguous and dangerous game. But we know that the Church is patient and can count in centuries. For Christians, the temptation to fall into temporal messianism and to become overly politicized is not new—it goes back to the early Church. No doubt the risk has never been greater, but neither has the challenge, nor the opportunity. At no time has it been more pertinent to say that a *new cycle* of centuries is beginning, though perhaps not a Golden Age. And for the future, the Church will obviously not be inclined any longer to follow the beaten path traced by Msgrs. Caro, Ottaviani, and Mindszenty.

In any case, of the several regions of the globe where the Catholics and the Marxists have to choose between forming a tactical alliance and confronting each other, the most important for the Church is Latin America, which already includes half, and will soon include much more than half, of the world's Catholics. Here Marxism may be able to win some of its most significant victories in the years to come, possibly with the decisive aid of Catholics.

20. My italics.

7

Some Home Truths

The "Truly National"

The Catholic Church, the influence of the United States, and more recently the influence of Marxism, must not be viewed as elements acting on Latin America from the outside; they are integral components of the essence of Latin America, contributing to make Latin America what it is. These influences should be viewed along with other cultural, political, and economic contributions of the West to Latin-American culture, which were incorporated at first through the somewhat deforming prism of Spain, and later, starting in the eighteenth century—the century of the Enlightenment and of the North American and French Revolutions—through the channel of countries more centrally "Western": France, England, and the United States.

Another basic element of Spanish America was the contribution made, against the will of the conquistadors, by the "Indians" who occupied the land before the Conquest. Still others came from the black slaves brought in from Africa, and from the European immigrants (Spanish, Italian, Portuguese, German, Russian and Polish Jews, Yugoslavs, et cetera) who began coming over in the second half of the nineteenth century and have kept on coming to this day. To the distinct effects of these various ethnic and cultural strains must be added the complex interaction resulting from their forced fusion, begun in the sixteenth century and at work ever since.

But when we Latin Americans attempt to understand who we are, we find ourselves unable to synthesize these different elements in an even approximately objective or scientific manner. Indeed, we do not try to be objective or scientific. We all have our own preferences and phobias when it comes to choosing and emphasizing some components of our personality, either as individuals or as a community, while arbitrarily eliminating others from the picture, or even rejecting them as irrevocably alien.

In Mexico, Hernán Cortés and the other Spanish conquistadors and colonizers—whether administrators or men of the sword or the cross—are looked upon as execrable *invaders,* as soldiers of a foreign occupying power that the pre-Columbian Mexican nation expelled some three hundred years later, thereby renewing the pattern of its own history, which had been only temporarily interrupted. And this is but the extreme manifestation of a general Latin-American historic distortion: we had occasion to see earlier that the romantic leitmotiv of the war of independence against Spain was, everywhere in Latin America, the *restoration of liberties lost in 1492.*

Marx and Freud both, in their own ways, have taught us that the phobias or fixations of nations or communities, as of individuals, reflect some deep psychological need. The most deeply anchored convictions, as well as the most subtle reasoning invented in their support, reflect a search for psychic equilibrium or for self-justification.

It can therefore happen (and it *has* happened in the case of the so-called Third World, with its easy, enthusiastic acceptance of demagogic explanations for its lag) that successful demagogues identify and analyze collective neuroses, and play upon them in order to further their own ends. Thus we can say that the Latin-American generation of 1810 took up the myth of the noble savage candidly, with no idea that they were playing with dynamite. The same can be said of the anti–North American phobia of the generation of Rodó and the Spanish-American War. But in the second half of the twentieth century, the Leninist world view has left behind all such candor and innocence; it has made a shrewd inventory of Latin-American phobias and myths and exploited them as an arsenal in its struggle to defeat Western liberalism. Such arguments are effective precisely because they are carefully attuned to the emotional needs—the neuroses—of Latin America. Thus, it becomes clear that this kind of propagandistic thinking in no way strives to examine the constituent elements of Latin-American social reality vis-à-vis their contribution to that society. Its purpose is only to praise what can help overall revolutionary strategy, and to condemn what cannot. The present strategy is to widen the rift between Latin America and the West, particularly the United States, as a first step in separating it from the Western political-economic system. And this purpose in turn serves the long-range strategy of harassing and eventually abolishing the political-economic systems founded on the values and achievements of the liberal revolution.

The overriding nature of their ultimate goal enables Leninist activists to resort to cultural and technological techniques and to ideas and hardware that are "non-native," i.e., Western, in their campaign to *de-Westernize* Latin America (manifestly the most Westernized part of what is called the Third World). Leninism is not concerned with logical coherence or intellectual rigor, but with *efficiency*. Thus it appropriates the methods and the language of the social sciences as they were developed in the West. It approves of using computers, cameras, magnetophones, video equipment, et cetera, but only for the purpose of "serving the revolution," not for the sake of disinterested research. In fact, whenever these same disciplines and methods fail to serve the "good cause," they are promptly denounced as instruments of imperialist cultural penetration.

A candid confession of this is found in an article on "revolutionary anthropology" by R. Buijtenhuijs: "Suppose that a committed [i.e., Leninist] anthropologist, during a period of residence in one of the liberated territories of the Portuguese colonies, finds political, social, and economic reality far below the claims of the revolutionary leaders, should he publish his findings or not mention them? If he publicizes them, he runs the risk of serving counterrevolutionary propaganda, which will make immediate use of his writing."[1]

This explains why Oscar Lewis saw his work, the product of a year's residence in Cuba under the Communist regime, confiscated by the Cuban police, and heard himself labeled a CIA agent. Equally enlightening is the following exceptionally unguarded testimonial by a Marxist Latin-American sociologist; he states that in the struggle against cultural dependence, "we must view as truly *national* whatever is opposed to imperialist domination."[2]

It is in this context that we should view the recent trend

1. "L'Anthropologie révolutionnaire, comment faire?," *Les Temps modernes,* no. 299–300, June–July 1971, p. 2389.
2. Alfredo Chacón, "¿Qué es la cultura nacional?" (What is national culture?), *El Nacional,* Caracas, February 15, 1975.

toward an overblown, *"engagé"* enthusiasm for all that is "Indian" in Latin-American culture. At first sight this emphasis would seem to reflect the justified concern all Latin-American reformers have had for the original Americans, oppressed from the time of the Conquest to the present day, even though the wars of emancipation against Spain and the Mexican Revolution were fought in their name. But the Leninists' concern is different. The myth of the noble savage serves them well because of its *nationalist, anti-imperialist, "virtuous revolutionary"* impact on societies that in fact owe relatively little to the pre-Columbian past, societies from which either Indians are totally absent or in which they play a passive and marginal role.

There are from fifteen to twenty million pureblood Indians in Spanish America today (less than ten percent of the population), concentrated in particular in Mexico, Guatemala, Colombia, Ecuador, Peru, Bolivia, and Paraguay.[3] They live under the most unacceptable conditions, and the governments of their countries should make it a primary concern to restore the Indians' dignity and give them a decent standard of living. Policies that aimed toward solving the Indians' problems by *integrating* them into the dominant Western and Hispanic culture seem at best naïve today. It is far more effective and acceptable to try to give the Indians the means to rebuild their own cultural heritage, insofar as this is still possible today.

But it is absurd and sterile for Latin-American society as a whole to claim that its primary roots lie in pre-Columbian cultures, and that Western culture, from its introduction during the Conquest and colonization, has led to a downward trend in Latin America's destiny. This interpretation, which we discussed earlier, sees our history since the Conquest as a story of steady deterioration due to the intrusion of imperialism (viewed in this case as one continuous, organic process, lasting from 1492 to the present). It claims that our situation, once supposedly authentic, autochthonous, happy, and free, has since become false, alienated, unhappy, and dependent. This is the myth of the Fall (of the noble savage), which can be reversed and avenged only by the virtuous revolutionary.

---

3. Indians are still living in a wild or semiwild state in the Brazilian, Peruvian, and Venezuelan part of Amazonia. Although the Latin-American writers who attribute all of Latin America's problems to its invasion by "foreigners" in 1492 are not uninterested in these representatives of the Stone Age, they do not consider them as mythical ancestors, on a par with the Incas or the Aztecs.

The Demographic Lie

The truth is altogether different. Western thinking has recognized for the first time that all men and all cultures are equally deserving of respect; naturally this applies no less to the Indians of Latin America than to any other ethnic group. But at the same time we should admit that the culture of the Incas or the Aztecs, not to mention that of other American Indian groups, was far from having the significance and splendor that legend has bestowed on it, and that today is being further exaggerated in an effort to convince us Latin Americans that we are its descendants and that, *like our alleged ancestors,* we are the victims of massive Western intrusion. We must recognize that our indebtedness as a people and as a culture is primarily to the so-called invaders, and after that to the North Americans and Europeans who over the years have contributed to the Westernization and modernization of our continent.

The first lie presented to us on the subject of the pre-Columbian Americans concerns their number. In his desire to prove that the Spaniards exterminated the native population, Father Las Casas, in his *Very Brief Relation of the Destruction of the Indies,* assures us that in 1492 Cuba had a population of no fewer than 200,000 aborigines. An even more extravagant claim is that there were 1,000,000 Indians on the island in 1511, of whom barely 14,000 were alive *six years later.* The eighteenth-century Spanish writer Antonio de Ulloa set America's population at the time of the discovery at 120,000,-000 inhabitants.[4]

These figures would imply that, at the close of the fifteenth century, the population of the American continent was more than a quarter of the world's total population, and was equal to the number it attained in the mid-twentieth century. The greater part of this enormous population would obviously have lived under the Inca and Aztec empires.

The sixteenth-century writers who thus inflated pre-Columbian population figures were prejudiced; they had witnessed, and they were seeking to expose, the Spanish Conquest and colonization. But even if these statements had been made in an objective state of mind by contemporary eyewitnesses, we would still have to receive them with skepticism.

Alexander von Humboldt, one of the first scientific-minded observers to view the Spanish American world as one entity,

4. Bailey W. Diffie, "Estimates of Indian Population in 1492," in Lewis Hanke (ed.), *History of Latin American Civilisation,* vol 1, pp. 193–94.

commented on the unreliability of population estimates by citing those made for Otaheite (Tahiti). When Captain Cook arrived at this island in 1769, he estimated its population at
100,000 souls; missionaries who followed· him set it at half
that figure; a later navigator set it at 16,000, and another eye-
witness at 5,000. Humboldt logically concluded that, since it
was so obviously impossible in the eighteenth century to reach
any sort of agreement concerning the population of a small
island, it was preposterous to give much credence to similar
assessments made two hundred years earlier for a vast and
mostly unexplored continent.

But any scientific concern with the accuracy of population
estimates is cheerfully brushed aside by those who for some
reason of their own wish to exaggerate the numerical significance of the pre-Columbian cultures. It is human nature to
want to adopt a hypothesis that magnifies the importance of a
topic in which one has invested much effort, and we have no
reason to expect Jacques Soustelle to escape this temptation
when he writes: "I know and regret that this estimate can only
be arbitrary, but for lack of a better one, we can admit that
Tenochtitlán-Tlatelolco had from 80,000 to 100,000 house-
holds of seven people, say a total population of between
560,000 to 700,000 souls."[5]

For lack of a better one! Modern historiographers (or anyone using common sense) can simply apply logic to this sort of
problem. Diffie makes the following elementary observation.
Since Tenochtitlán covered only about three and a half square
miles, including canals and lagoons, its population in 1520
was obviously limited. Besides, he asks a question that is as
simple as it is decisive: if we suppose the Aztec capital to have
had a population of more than a few tens of thousands, how
can we imagine the logistics of supply or garbage disposal in a
city that had no navigable river nearby, beasts of burden, or
draft animals, and did not know the use of the wheel?[6]

I have already quoted the same author's view that the present territory of Peru could not have supported a population of
over a million and a half, given the methods, tools, and plant
and animal resources in use before the Spanish colonization,
even *supposing an optimal use of the soil.*[7]

Animal species unknown in America before the arrival of

5. Jacques Soustelle, *La Vie quotidienne des Aztèques à la veille de la
Conquête Espagnole*, Paris, 1955, p. 34.
6. Diffie, "Estimates," in Hanke, vol. 1, p. 195.
7. See pp. 152–53.

the Spanish included the horse, the donkey, the pig, the goat, the rabbit, the bovines, and domestic fowl. Plants unknown in America included not only the eucalyptus so dear to Jorge Luis Borges, and the rose, but also wheat, rye, grapes, olives, mangoes, sugar cane, the citrus fruits, bananas, coffee, and many others. In short, of 247 plants used for food or in industry and cultivated systematically in America today, at least 199 originated in Eurasia or Africa, and one in Australia, while only 45 are known with certainty to have originated on the American continent. In 1652, the Jesuit Father Bernabé Cobo understandably voiced the opinion that the New World gained more profit from the transfer of these plants and animals from the Old World than Spain ever gained from the gold and silver harvested from the American colonies.[8]

Friedrich Engels's lucidity protected him against Third World prejudices. In 1884, as I have already discussed, he reasoned that the American pre-Columbian societies could not have grouped even half a million men under one leadership—and certainly not in a single urban agglomeration.[9]

Inca Socialism

Engels's reasoning notwithstanding, the Incas appear to have succeeded in establishing and administering an empire of approximately one million subjects, and this without ever having developed writing. They must be credited with exceptional political genius. But the praise of Inca socialism, which is often expressed, seems as arbitrary as the unwarranted inflation of pre-Columbian population estimates. The argument is put forward for propagandistic and not for scientific reasons: Inca socialism is held to be relevant to the contemporary anti-imperialist struggle, and thus to be the "national" heritage of all Latin America, not just of Peru, Bolivia, and Ecuador, the territories where the Incas held sway. In any case, it is absurd to base a defense of socialism on what is known to us of Inca practices. We may praise the Inca system as a model *totalitarian* state, or as a successful structure for the apportioning of basic foods in a situation of chronic shortage (for there must have been a critical dearth of food in pre-Columbian Peru, as

8. James A. Robertson: "Some Notes on the Transfer by Spain of Plants and Animals to Its Overseas Colonies," in Lewis Hanke, ed., *History of Latin American Civilization*, Boston, Little, Brown, 2nd ed., 1973, vol. 1, pp. 34–41.
9. See pp. 101–02.

in an increasing number of Third World countries today). Certainly we cannot propose Inca socialism as the model of a system affording liberty in the midst of plenty.

Through a paradox that is only apparent, the first to attribute extraordinary virtues to the Incas were the Europeans, and first among them, the Spanish discoverers of the new continent. The last survivor of the group of adventurers who conquered Peru under Pizarro repented on his deathbed for the part he had played in the destruction of a supposedly perfect society and in the corruption of the American noble savage. It is in fact more than likely that Mancio Sierra de Leguízamo's last will, in which these thoughts are recorded, was written in his name by some churchman, but this in no way detracts from their value as the expression of the prevalent opinion, or, rather, prejudice, that was earlier formulated by Christopher Columbus in his letters to the Catholic Kings.

According to Sierra de Leguízamo's will, the Inca empire, before the arrival of the Spanish, presented the model of so perfect and virtuous a society that it included not a single thief, not a single corrupt or slothful man, not a single adulterous woman. A man could leave a hundred thousand pesos in gold or silver lying unguarded in his house, and go out without having to fear theft. He merely left a broom or a piece of wood on the threshold to show that the master was away.

Sierra de Leguízamo's will was the primary source of later statements on the supposedly perfect virtue of ancient Peru. The romantic North American historian William Prescott (1796–1859) stated: "If no man could become rich in [pre-Columbian] Peru, no man could become poor. No spendthrift could waste his substance in riotous luxury. No adventurous schemer could impoverish his family by the spirit of speculation. . . . No mendicant was tolerated. . . . Ambition, avarice, the love of change, the morbid spirit of discontent, those passions which most agitate the minds of men, found no place in the bosom of the Peruvian."[10] As a utopian and romantic socialist, Prescott never considered that these conditions—if they ever had existed in Peru—could hardly have stemmed from a spontaneous appearance of "natural" virtue in the noble savage prior to his "fall"—a fall inevitably brought about by a civilization of merchants, by the ambitious, Faustian, Western civilization. Louis Baudin argues that the functioning of Inca society was made possible by the absolute control the state had

10. *History of the Conquest of Peru,* Philadelphia, David McKay, n.d., 2 vols., vol. 1, p. 83.

over the individual.[11] It was a system in which each individual lived in strict submission to a plan formulated at the top; the living conditions of all ordinary men were pegged down to the lowest level; privileges increased progressively for the higher rungs of the strictly hierarchical and sacred ladder that structured society. All power and responsibility lay with the leaders, who conceived and formulated the norms for production, distribution, and consumption that regulated the activities of the entire population.

In this system, a peasant practically never left the valley in which he had been born, and the only leader he had contact with was his centurion. These "simple" peasants, who comprised 99 percent of the population, received only the summary instruction pertaining to their specific skills. Each individual owed blind obedience to his superiors, under threat of the most cruel punishments. Centurions were allowed to leave their valleys and were entitled to some education. The class that held the highest positions in this machinery for social control had exclusivity of knowledge and prestige. None but the highest personages of the realm could travel for any private reasons, let alone for pleasure; except for the Incas, only messengers or officials were allowed to travel within the empire. Any subject found away from his place of work and residence without proper excuse was severely punished. In his preface to Baudin's book, Ludwig von Mises stressed that under the collectivist Inca regime, the individual was deprived of any freedom of action or decision. The subjects of the Inca Kings were human beings only in the zoological sense. In fact, they were treated as domestic animals; their personal efforts had little influence on their own material welfare.

The problems besetting some regions of the globe today may suggest political schemes reminiscent of those put in practice by the Incas, although a system perfectly parallel to the Incas' would hardly be applicable in our era. Most of the conditions that characterized the Inca empire have vanished forever: the total isolation, the ignorance of alternate forms of society, the backward science and technology. Leaders who preach comparable programs may call them "socialist" if they wish, but it is absurd to seek to base a model of social organization for Latin America on the myth of the noble savage—all the more so in such countries as Argentina, Chile, and Venezuela, whose

11. Louis Baudin, *A Socialist Empire: The Incas of Peru,* Princeton, Van Nostrand, 1961.

aboriginal societies never resembled the Inca empire or had any significant contact with it. Yet we hear our pre-Columbian past praised as a model of what is *authentically national,* and used as an argument in anti-imperialist propaganda.

The pre-Columbian American Indians were few in number and little advanced in their political development, science, and technology. They were physically weak because of defective nutrition, and lacked a higher religion that might have allowed them to resist Christian proselytism. Neither on the military nor on the cultural level were they able to withstand the shock imparted by an absurdly small number of Europeans. And the societies that were least able to resist were the most *advanced,* the Inca and the Aztec, for the total absence of popular participation in the Peruvian and Mexican systems made it impossible for the masses to get over the capture and death of their leaders; the Spanish were able to assume control simply by taking over the positions earlier held by the ruling class.

Cortés conquered Mexico at the head of 600 men, and Pizarro took the empire of the Incas with only 180. Such prowess may be reminiscent of the novels of chivalry then in fashion, but the authenticity of these figures has been established beyond doubt. While recognizing the uncanny daring of the conquistadors, we should realize they did not have to confront millions or even hundreds of thousands of warriors, but only the small ruling groups, more priestly than military, that reigned over communities limited in numbers and lacking the ability to strike back.

The population of America began to grow around the time of the Conquest and has risen progressively to the present level of "demographic explosion." I stress two reasons for this: the conquistadors' and colonizers' astounding capacity to engender mestizo (and, a little later, mulatto) offspring; and, what was more significant, economic factors such as the introduction of new varieties of animals and plants, and of techniques of Eurasian origin that allowed the land to support a far greater density of population. This process has gone on uninterruptedly since, and has gained further momentum from the industrial revolution and from involvement with the United States, today the world's principal center of scientific research and technical innovation.

Thus we see that the factor most frequently cited by those who wish to stress the present and future importance of Latin America, namely its immense and steadily growing population, stems directly from those relationships of dependence and imperialism in which some claim to find the source of all our ills. But for these relations, Latin America simply would not exist.

A Culture of Transients

I must again bring up the basic fact that, unlike Asia or Africa, America was practically an empty territory when it first experienced the impact of European civilization. In this New World, it was the historic good luck of the North Atlantic seaboard to be colonized by England, the European nation then endowed with the greatest energy and creativity in all fields, and particularly in science, technology, economics, and political theory. Thus the English New World colonies were caught up in the ascending historic fortunes of seventeenth-century England. The English settlements in America benefited from the very start from this momentum, while at the same time they succeeded in discarding the obstacles to growth inherent in a number of Old World institutions. Nor did the settlers have to accommodate pre-existing institutions and cultural patterns, as the British colonists who went to heavily populated Asia and Africa had to do.

By contrast, it was Latin America's destiny to be colonized by a country that, though admirable in many ways, was at the time beginning to reject the emerging spirit of modernism, and to build walls against the rise of rationalism, empiricism, and free thought—that is to say, against the very bases of the modern industrial and liberal revolution, and of capitalist economic development.

At the same time—and for reasons that may not necessarily be connected with its rejection of modernization—Spanish society in the sixteenth century was starting to move into a phase of decadence. It was growing tired, and displayed a tendency toward disintegration that affected even its medieval, precapitalist value system. The "new countries" that Spain founded in America not only took over these disintegrating tendencies, but further exacerbated them. The Spanish American New World was the Spanish Old World, with a few serious additional problems.

Ortega y Gasset wrote that "everything which has happened

in Spain [since 1580] is disintegration and decay,"[12] whereas a society in the ascent is characterized by *amalgamation,* in the sense that every individual and every group *feels* itself, and knows itself to be, part of the whole; that whatever affects the part affects the whole, and vice versa.[13] In the same way, decay occurs when the different constituent elements of the community no longer feel involved in a common destiny, either as groups or as individuals; in discovering their particularism, they lose their sense of belonging to an organic whole, and each ceases to share the feelings and interests of the others.

From the outset this was even more true of Spanish America than of Spain itself. The Spaniard's selfishness, his aversion to identifying with the interests of society as a whole, only increased when he was transplanted to America, the land of conquest, plunder, and slavery.

If the man from Estremadura, Castile, or Andalusia who landed in "the Indies" did not feel Spanish, he was to feel even less American. The opposite was true of the British settlers who came to the New World; they not only became Americans, but also pre-empted the name. From the start and still today, the emigrants to "America" have never felt that they were mere visitors to the new land. They came to integrate themselves, in Ortega and Mommsen's sense: they threw in their individual lot with the common destiny of the new country, which they viewed as a far better place to live in than the old, clearly destined to perform better as a society.

Among the characters in any Spanish village even today can be found *"el Indiano,"* the local boy who made good in the Indies and has now come back, pockets filled, to live out his declining years at home—and home means not Spain, but his province, the very village of his birth.

Many Spaniards who had come only to seek their fortune did, of course, stay on. But they, and the children of mixed blood whom they fathered, did not remain willingly. They stayed not as owners of the land, committed to the land, but as transients, strangers to the soil. They were not members of a society "built to last," but unwilling participants in an ephemeral adventure, the by-product of the disintegration of Spanish

12. José Ortega y Gasset, *Invertebrate Spain,* trans. Mildred Adams, New York, Norton, 1937, p. 34.
13. He was inspired by the opening sentence of Mommsen's *Roman History:* "The history of every nation . . . is a vast system of amalgamations." (Quoted in *Invertebrate Spain,* p. 20.)

society that became evident from the sixteenth century onward.

The difference between the English settlers in North America, who built a dynamic new society, and the Spanish, who viewed the colonies as a centrifugal extension of the homeland, was reflected in the character of the towns they founded. In the English settlements in the New World, urban agglomerations sprang up and developed to fill the needs of the settlers and farmers; in the Spanish American colonies, towns were ends in themselves, and the rural population was reduced to slavery to serve their needs. The English settler came to the New World to live on the land as a farmer. In fact, he aimed to be a *free* farmer, assured of independence by drawing all his sustenance from the labor of his own hands. The Spaniard bound for America (the would-be *Indiano*) came to found cities as a base from which to exploit the land. The agricultural or, preferably, mining work was done for him by slaves who were organized into encomiendas and later into haciendas —institutions that displayed all of the defects and none of the good qualities of the socioeconomic structures of medieval Europe.

Agrarian Reform

There has been a great deal of argument lately that all of Latin America's ills are the result of inequitable land distribution. Those who hold this opinion fail to appreciate that the inequity is a symptom, rather than a primary cause, of the social ills associated with the latifundium—as it exists today and as it has long existed in Latin America's changing land-tenure patterns. The basic problem goes deeper.

I do not wish to argue in defense of the haciendas, marked by low productivity as well as other failings, but I see no intrinsic reason why large land holdings should be unproductive or socially harmful. The King Ranch, in Texas, said to be the largest expanse of land owned by a single family, is also one of the most efficient and productive operations of its kind; it carries on cattle breeding on an industrial scale; the workers receive excellent salaries and live in dignity and freedom. Their way of life is privileged even in contrast with that of workers in the North American cities: they enjoy all the advantages of urban life without having to cope with its disadvantages, its tensions, its overcrowding and pollution. Similar patterns of land ownership exist in Canada, Australia, and New Zealand, and cannot be viewed as intrinsically harmful. Given certain conditions, the concentration of much land in the hands of a single owner permits mechanization and a rational distribution of labor; it makes possible greater productivity and therefore a higher standard of living for the farm laborer.

But large private ownership can be a crippling liability when its historical roots lie in a slave society such as that of the Spanish empire. Slavery necessitates certain behavior patterns among masters and slaves, and among the descendants of both groups, which are hardly compatible with freedom and progress, and which tend to be passed on long after slavery ends. The freed peasant who inherits the land that his forefathers tilled as slaves tends to inherit his forefathers' dependence on the dominance of others. His new status as owner of his land will not change him overnight; he will continue to look for some paternalistic control. It is in this relation that he will now stand, as peon and as *voter*, to a political party or to a government locally represented by a cacique.[14] The feudal spirit and attitude toward work continue to prevail, and with them the same primitive forms of production and the same low productivity. And as there is no longer a master to blame, the failure of agrarian reform (an expression that is constantly heard once the euphoria over land distribution has subsided) will be blamed on bad government, on the Minister of Agriculture, on the dearth of government loans, on the poor quality of seeds, on marketing difficulties, et cetera. That is to say, failure will be attributed to every conceivable cause except to the essential one, which is that the social structure set up in the sixteenth century continues to weigh down Latin-American society in the twentieth. The peasant still has the attitude of a slave; he still expects others to make his decisions for him, and prays only that these new masters will be less demanding and better-intentioned toward him than the former landowners.

By and large, the Latin-American farmer can hardly conceive the dream of owning a plot of land that he can farm himself, without fear of another man's interference or oppression; he does not yearn to be a free man accountable to no one but himself, indebted to no one's paternalism. The Anglo-Saxon idea of the free farmer, which in itself contained the

14. Caciques were originally chiefs of native American tribes. Both in Spain and Spanish America, the term has come to designate the person who exerts pre-eminent influence in the political or administrative affairs of the village or district. "Caciquism" describes the dominance of these rural political leaders.

seed of all the political evolution of the English colonies in North America before and after independence, knows no counterpart in the Spanish American rural world.

Quite the contrary. When a Latin-American farmer does aspire to change and improvement, he generally hopes to move to the urban areas, which have been the home of the idle classes since the sixteenth century and are a great status symbol. It follows that the existence of the landless peasant is paradoxically matched by that of the peasantless land. In Venezuela, where the new oil wealth has led to the overdevelopment of cities and to the building of a communications network that makes travel within the country considerably easier, much praise is usually bestowed on agrarian reform programs; but large areas of land near (and not so near) the border would be lying fallow today but for the clandestine emigration of squatters from a poor and less fortunate neighbor, Colombia.

The difficulties or downright failures of all the attempts at agrarian reform in Latin America to this day have their most serious effect on the non-Hispanized Indians, who traditionally live outside the money economy and whose standard of living is extremely low. Can they be blamed for their continued attachment to their old mode of life, an attraction that represents a form of passive resistance to assimilation by Spanish American society? The material advantages held out to them by well-intentioned reformers hold no attraction for them. The gifts of land and the other benefits that they have received through the better-conceived and better-executed agrarian reform programs have led to little improvement in their lot. Whatever changes may have occurred in their circumstances, they tend to produce no more than they require for their own use and that of their families. If by chance they happen to come into some cash, they are likely to spend it in a pitiful splurge. They see no reason to look ahead, to save, or to produce a surplus to feed a distant (and *foreign*) urban world. To appeal to them, an agrarian reform program would have to be aimed toward bringing back some of the substance of their ancient civilization, thereby allowing them to build a living connection to that lost heritage. In this sense, their aspirations, if they could formulate them, would be reactionary and incompatible with the modernization being sought by the apostles of agrarian reform.

As a result, in most countries in which agrarian reform has been attempted, the division and distribution of large land holdings among the peasantry has had very little social impact, and its net economic effect has usually been a loss. The former landowners, when dispossessed, invest their money in real estate or mortgages, or transfer it abroad. In the village, once the fiesta celebrating the transfer of deeds is over, the peasants, now landowners, do not find themselves better off than before. As long as they remain on the land and work at farming, they are weighed down by the legacy of the old colonial structure.

The Hacienda

"Hacienda" is the one Latin-American word that is understood throughout the world. There are good reasons for this. In Spanish, the term originally meant the sum of a man's goods and wealth, or, simply, his wealth. The Ministry of Finance of a Spanish-speaking country is the Ministerio de Hacienda, comparable to the United States Treasury Department. When the Spanish colonizers in search of a fortune finally understood that gold and silver were not to be panned by the bucketful in Latin-American streams, and that, moreover, mining was the privilege solely of the King, to be undertaken by his subjects only under royal patent, many of the more ambitious among them turned their attention from mining to agricultural pursuits. It is in this sense that the freehold ownership of large stretches of land, which after independence carried no royal taxation, came to constitute rich Latin Americans' hacienda, in the true sense of the word.

The hacienda as an institution reached its maturity at the close of the seventeenth century. But at that very moment it began to stagnate, in line with the stagnation of Hispanic culture. The patterns of land ownership, social organization, and production inherent in the hacienda system present notable points of resemblance, but also of contrast, to those of feudal Europe. Land in Latin America theoretically remained the property of the King of Spain; as was the case under the European feudal system, its use and occupation gradually came to confer inalienable rights, and those rights were in certain cases transferable by sale. Another parallel to the social order of medieval Europe lay in the labor pattern, analogous to serfdom, through which the Indians and the blacks were attached to the land by established customs, social necessity, or institutionalized slavery.

But a very significant difference lies in the fact that, operating in a world economy far more complex than that of the Middle Ages, the Latin-American haciendas soon ceased to be self-sufficient economic units, entered the world market, and started producing for export—at first to Spain, later to Europe as a whole, and finally to the United States. Most of the arguments that today attribute the subcontinent's marginal role in history and its developmental lag wholly to a division of labor allegedly imposed by the world capitalist system—which assigns the role of producers of wealth to certain countries, and of consumers to others—can be traced to this early connection of Latin-American production to foreign economies.

Another point of difference was that neofeudal Spanish American society was spared the constant warfare that characterized the European Middle Ages. Peace was maintained practically without standing armies. The social order was based on unfortified cities, which were the hub of civil and ecclesiastical power, surrounded by a network of haciendas. This system proved to be remarkably stable. Revolts did occur, some of them serious, such as the uprising of the second Túpac Amaru in Peru (end of the eighteenth century), the uprisings in Mexico at the end of the seventeenth, and some black slave revolts. There were also sporadic attacks of English corsairs on certain Caribbean ports. But these disturbances were rare, the exception rather than the rule, and Spanish America enjoyed a basically peaceful era. At the end of the eighteenth century, on the eve of the great convulsion of the wars of emancipation, Alexander von Humboldt traveled through Peru, Ecuador, Venezuela, and New Spain (as Mexico was then called), on a sort of scientific safari, making notes that are still valuable today on geography, fauna and flora, and also on Spanish American society. Humboldt was escorted not by an armed guard, but only by bearers to carry his scientific instruments. He crossed forests and mountain ranges and traveled as far into the wilderness as the Rio Negro, at the border of present-day Venezuela and Brazil. Yet his travel diaries contain no reference to any kind of attack or threat—and this in a region where, shortly after, no unprotected traveler could have ventured without risking his life.

Within the *Pax Hispanica,* the hacienda was not only a political and an economic institution, but also the basic cell of the social structure. Its head was the *hacendado,* or, in his absence, his bailiff. The colonial *hacendado* was an agent of social control as well as a producer. His rule was harsh and punishments were heavy; flogging to death was not a rare practice. The system was further characterized by paternalism, and of course by the sexual rights that the master and his legitimate sons could exercise over all the serfs' and slaves' wives.

The institution of the hacienda was almost justifiable at the time of its establishment, since it represented a distinct improvement over the brutality of the encomienda, in which the Indian was a machine to be worked to the breaking point. But Spanish America was to pay a heavy price for the new institution: the social mold it imposed became set, and almost all the land suited for tilling fell into the hands of a very small group of owners. Moreover, when population increased in the eighteenth century, part of the population could not be productively employed and became superfluous. These "useless" men settled on the lands left fallow by the haciendas, built themselves huts, and started cultivating their own patches of ground. They, too, became vassals of the *hacendado*. Even the cities could not expand without the approval of the *hacendados*, which further increased the power of this landowning class.

Such was the *norm* of the society. The system, which came to be generally looked upon as equitable, vested all power and wealth in a few hands, while withholding the most elementary rights, including the right to own property, from the overwhelming majority. The *hacendado* became a man to be deferred to, and sometimes revered. But the insurrection that occurred in neighboring Haiti at the end of the eighteenth century, with the attendant massacre of the French *colons*, was to show how habitual submissiveness can be converted into bloodthirsty hatred overnight.

The Sickness of Slavery

Because the Spanish American colonizers were not prepared to do manual work themselves, either in the mines or in the fields, whereas the English settlers were intent on becoming free farmers, on working with their own hands, these two groups had widely different attitudes toward the Indians. To the English and to their descendants, the Indians were only a source of trouble, to be got rid of by extermination: they were wild animals, not domestic ones, as to the Spanish. The Spaniards set up a symbiotic society in which the slaves—Indian, black, half-breed, and mestizo—were soon to be an indispensable part.

This difference is fundamental to an understanding of the success of North American society and the relative failure of its Spanish American counterpart. The same comparison can, up to a point, be made between the South and the North in the United States. In the South, the Anglo-Saxon settlers developed a slave society, as the Spaniards did in Latin America; the Europeans, rather than being free farmers, became gentlemen dependent for their farming on a slave labor force. As a result, Southern society grew to resemble Latin-American society; the South ended up losing a Civil War and being "annexed" by the North. It continued to be different from, and poorer in all respects than, those regions of North America that had remained untainted by the institution of slavery.

In a slave-owning society, a parasitic relationship with a dialectic of its own develops between slave and master, undermining both and the whole social body as well. In such a context, it is practically impossible for any human being, whether master or slave, to achieve his full potential, or even to have a thoroughly honorable character; society is afflicted as if by a cancer.

The American sociologist and historian Eugene D. Genovese has commented on the rhythm of life that slavery imposes on the society that lives by it.[15] The slave's labor knows neither regularity nor reason. In theory, he works from sunrise to sunset, but in fact he frequently pauses, speeds up his work (when the overseer appears), or slows down (when he walks away). No direct relation exists between the slave's effort and its reward or remuneration: there is no rate of exchange between the two. As a result, slave society exists outside the notion of progress, without seeking to improve its living conditions, without trying to accumulate capital (the masters do accumulate it "accidentally," but their sole motivation is the primitive desire or instinct to own more and more land). In such a society, power and respectability are in no way equated with punctuality and productivity. The slave is justified in making as little effort as possible, and his master considers work an activity suitable only for slaves. *And this is a belief that is shared by all free men, the richest as well as the poorest.*

In a slave society, the ownership of a plantation, a haci-

15. *Roll, Jordan, Roll: The World the Slaves Made,* New York, Pantheon, 1974.

enda, and slaves becomes the highest social ambition and the earmark of a self-styled aristocracy. Any other activity or vocation seems unworthy of respect; a man may have to take on other employment out of necessity, but only as an expedient. The doctor, the lawyer, the financier, the industrialist, the businessman—all dream of becoming planters one day, of ending their lives as gentry or country gentlemen, the owners of land and slaves.

Further, a slave society does not require or promote technical progress. It actually rejects such progress, instinctively and even consciously, as a potential source of trouble and social upheaval, and this rejection will affect the behavior (and the capabilities) of society well after slavery has been abolished as an institution. In Argentina, the country that was to reach the highest level of technical development in Latin America, for instance, foreigners had a monopoly in technical trades until well into the nineteenth century, a situation unchanged since colonial times. (In 1607 the authorities prohibited the emigration of the Flemish bakers then working in Buenos Aires: no one able to work the mill in their stead could be found.) The improvements made in meat and leather processing in Argentina, starting in the second half of the nineteenth century, were initiated by Englishmen and Frenchmen. In other Latin-American countries, until very recently, even the mechanical *trapiches* (sugar-cane mills) and the coffee huskers were generally assembled and periodically inspected and serviced by Europeans or North Americans. A division of labor along ethnic lines could be witnessed by anyone who observed a plantation's working day: the blacks or the Indians working the fields and bringing in the harvest; the mestizo foreman standing by and giving orders; the white owner looking on or, more frequently, altogether absent.

The Contempt for Work

We have seen that the institution of slavery had deep and pernicious effects wherever it developed, and that in Latin America these effects have been reinforced by factors specific to the continent. A Venezuelan observer has provided this explanation: "Just as the world was entering the technical age and was beginning to accept economic values, Spain expelled the Jews and Arabs [who played such a key role in the technical and economic functions of society]. As a reaction, in the

fifteenth century, 'pure' Christians fearing to be identified with
the infidels repudiated any kind of work—whether intellectual
or technical." Even earlier, "especially in Castile, which from
the tenth century on had to bear the brunt of the war against
Islam, the high adventure of the Reconquest consecrated the
pre-eminence of the religious life as of knighthood."[16] That is
to say, the Castilian considered fighting, or saying or hearing
Mass, as masculine activities par excellence; rejecting labor as
we conceive it, men lived on bounty extracted from Moorish
territory—or, later, from the Americas. Such an approach
could only confirm the view that it is better to live freely and
adventurously by one's wits and personal daring, then to eke
out a mediocre living in a stable and organized society.

The Spanish themselves, like the Latin Americans in their
moments of truth, admit to finding regular work singularly
unattractive. According to their mood, they view it as either a
vice or a virtue: "All occupations in which we engage out of
necessity are painful to us. They weigh down our life, hurt it,
tear it to pieces. . . . And what troubles us most in work is
that, in filling up the hours of our day, it seems to be taking
these hours from us. The time spent working seems not to be
truly ours; it ceases to be a part of our lives, it shortens our
days. . . . The man who works does so in the hope, more or
less remote, that work will lead to his liberation, that some day
he will stop working and start really living."[17]

The conquistadors illustrate this attitude better than anyone.
They were prepared to embark on the hardest labors, but they
did so in the hope of never having to labor again. They are
portrayed in contemporary writing as hewing boats out of un-
seasoned wood, with only their swords for tools, burned by the
sun and surrounded by the perils of the Florida coast or the
Amazonian forest. This is attested by the boats that the survivors of the Hernando de Soto expedition built to escape from
Florida; by the launch built by Francisco de Orellana, the first
white man to navigate the Amazon; and by the comment of the
Inca Garcilaso de la Vega: "Gonzalo Pizarro, that great soldier,
was ever the first to split wood for the fire, the first to forge
iron, to make charcoal, or to undertake any other task, however
menial; he set an example to all, that none might find an
excuse not to follow his lead." But all this was done with the

16. Angel Rosenblat, "El Hispanoamericano y el trabajo" in *La primera
visión de América y otros estudios*, Caracas, Ministerio de Educación,
1965, pp. 60, 61.
17. José Ortega y Gasset, quoted by Rosenblat, *ibid.*, p. 57.

hope—not a vague, distant hope, but an ardent expectation—that someday they would be freed from the harsh obligation of having to work for a living, that they might finally "begin to live."

The setting in which the newly landed Spaniard found himself in the New World—a slave society served by Indians and blacks—exacerbated these negative character traits to a monstrous degree. The mere fact of having made the trip, of having "crossed the pond," made any Spaniard, however base-born, a hidalgo, a gentleman. Rosenblat says that from the very beginnings of Spanish American society in the sixteenth century, the proportion of hidalgos, churchmen, clerics, academics, and other "cultured" men—that is to say, men who did not work with their hands—was higher than that in contemporary European society. Nor does this take into account the adventurer, the soldier, the conquistador, who, the moment he set foot in the New World, or even before, when he left Cadiz or Seville, considered himself a hidalgo or even a nobleman. "Saint Teresa describes how one of her brothers who had just returned from the Indies could not resign himself to farming his land again. He had been a Lord in the tropics: how could he be expected to go back to being a plowman in Spain?"[18]

Even today in Latin America, we speak of "working like a Negro" or "like an Indian" to refer to strenuous effort. Only the influence of other Western countries, particularly of the United States, has been able to make a dent in the Latin American's contempt for work.

The Pioneers of "Third Worldism"

A slave society is inefficient in terms of productivity, and it stands in conflict with the industrial, liberal, and capitalist revolution. Further, because it is so deeply inhumane, it manifestly runs counter to the ideals of humanism, freedom, and equality fostered by that revolution. It is not surprising to find that a number of factors inhibit the development of societies formerly based on slavery: the passive resistance to work that is the earmark of the slave; the absurd prestige of idleness that afflicts his master; and, finally, a rhythm of life so little concerned with punctuality that a civil servant who has made an appointment for three o'clock in the afternoon may not show

18. Rosenblat, *La primera visión de América*, pp. 70, 71.

up till five-thirty, or may even not appear at the office till the following day.

The conditions and the development of the Spanish American world invite, as already mentioned, certain parallels with the American South. These two slave societies have interpreted their history in a similar way; or, rather, they have required the same self-justification. In 1816, the fledgling North American republic imposed tariffs to protect the development of its budding industry against the massive influx of English manufactured imports. The most ardent among the protectionists were the Virginians and the North and South Carolinians, who felt that, with their inexpensive cotton and cheaper manpower, the Southern states would become textile producers able to rival Manchester.

Eventually, the United States did develop a textile industry, under the protection of the new tariffs, but in New England, far from the cotton fields; and the South found that it had to pay higher prices for industrial goods manufactured in the Northern states, without being able to raise the price of its cotton. Though it started from a position that was theoretically inferior, the North within a few years succeeded in industrializing itself, while the South could only step up its cotton production, using more and more slaves, exhausting the soil, and causing a collapse in the prices of its one major crop. Wealthy Southerners, who were richer than their counterparts in the North, often considered setting up shipping companies and banks of their own, in order to free themselves from their dependence on the transportation system and capital of the North, but these projects aborted, and they invariably ended up investing in the purchase of more land and more slaves.

Barely fifteen years after Southern Congressmen such as Calhoun and Lowndes of South Carolina had established themselves as effective spokesmen for tariffs on goods brought in from Great Britain, the South began to justify its subsequent failure by charging that protectionism had been invented by the North as a means of enriching itself at the expense of the South. Southern leaders stirred up their audiences by claiming that of every hundred bales of cotton sold in Boston or New York, forty had been "stolen" from the South. They were preparing the dialectics of the Civil War. The argument became more heated, and the North found itself charged with having accumulated capital, in the late eighteenth century and early nineteenth, by defrauding the South through financial trickery. One contemporary writer says: "When they [the Southerners] see the flourishing villages of New England, they cry, 'We pay for all this.' "[19] A myth was manufactured that attributed Northern prosperity to the South's paralysis, and vice versa. Southerners went to war in 1860 quite convinced that if they succeeded in *breaking their dependence* on the North, not only would they prosper miraculously; the abhorred Yankees, deprived of raw materials and the Southern market for their manufactured goods, would be condemned to an economic crisis as well.

Thus, well before the birth of Hobson, Hilferding, and Lenin, the "Third World" arguments had been invented by Southern slaveholders.

19. Harriet Martineau, quoted by Morison, *The Oxford History of the American People*, p. 436.

8

More Home Truths

The "Utopian Republics"

The welter of ideas and passions, whether false or accurate, complementary or contradictory, that today are associated with the word "imperialism," make us forget that after three hundred years, the Spanish imperial presence in America so permeated the society that Spain no longer made much distinction between motherland and colonies. It had effectively transferred, or perhaps adapted, its civilization in an organic manner to the Spanish American societies. The notion of "decolonization," as it was to be acted out, for example, in Algeria—where the French continued to regard themselves as Christian European *colons* (settlers) while the Arabs remained indigenously Moslem—finds no parallel in Spanish America. The government in Madrid sent over viceroys or captains general in order to enforce a policy of centralization; but it did so in the same spirit in which even today it nominates provincial governors in the Iberian Peninsula and in the Canary Islands.

The policy of political repression that Spain extended to its American possessions was not distinct from that which it applied at home, a blend of obscurantism and antiliberalism born of the Counter Reformation. In sharp contrast, the British settlers in North America, even before independence, were probably the freest social group that the world has ever seen. No less important, those areas in the northeast of the country destined to shape the aims and principles of the American republic, and to confirm that definition during the Civil War, were at no time afflicted by the institution of slavery.

More Home Truths

One might say that as early as the eighteenth century, the colonial American from New England, New York, Pennsylvania, or New Jersey had had more practice in the exercise of civic freedom than even his English forebears. The English who emigrated to the United States left behind all the institutions and practices that were relics of the Middle Ages and that would have constituted an impediment in their new life: the tutelage of the nobility and the Church; the inequality of men before the law; the shackles that mercantile practices had imposed on economic activities. Another medieval condition, the shortage of arable land, was also removed in the New World. The settlers left behind the prefect, the churchman, the tax collector, the extortionate squire, as well as the press gang on which the army, the navy, and all shipping depended. By 1735, the "Americans" had secured the rights of free speech and free press, of free assembly and of *self-government*. They fought the War of Independence not so much to win these liberties, for they already enjoyed them, but to confirm them and give them a proper legal base.

The North Americans' decision to declare themselves politically independent, however much self-questioning it may have involved, did not entail moral soul-searching, or a radical change in their way of life. The United States freed itself from its political link with Great Britain without breaking with the positive aspects of English political and cultural tradition. It remained part of this tradition, which it went on to improve. In the new nation, all "the mystic chords of memory which make a people one"[1] continued to vibrate in response to legacies from its British past: the Magna Carta, the Virgin Queen, the Revolution of 1688, the Bill of Rights, Drake, Marlborough, the Reformation, Freedom of Conscience, *et al.*

The Spanish Americans' accession to independence, however, occasioned a profound moral, intellectual, and spiritual crisis, a denial of their own national character as it had been forged by Spain. To define their new identity they had to appeal, on the one hand, to the mythical pre-Columbian past of the "noble savage" and, on the other, to political ideas and practices that were quite foreign to them and that they did not know how to use. In this difficulty is rooted the "constitutional lie" of Latin America on which Octavio Paz has commented at length. After the failure of the first Venezuelan republic in 1812, Bolívar analyzed the causes of its defeat in the following terms: "The legal code on which our lawgivers based

1. Abraham Lincoln, quoted by Morison, *Oxford History*, vol. 2, p. 171.

themselves was not of a nature that would have taught them the practical science of government; it was a code that had been formulated by certain wayward visionaries who set out to imagine utopian republics, predicated on the perfectibility of the human species. So that we ended up having philosophers for leaders, philanthropy for legislation, dialectics for tactics, and sophists for soldiers. . . . But what most weakened the Venezuelan government was the federal form it took in its desire to implement inapplicable maxims on the rights of man, which, by allowing men to act as they wish, break the social contracts and give the country over to anarchy. . . . Each province was granted an independent government; following suit, each town claimed the same right . . . basing its claim . . . on the theory that all men and all peoples enjoy the prerogative of establishing the government they feel is best for them. . . . Popular elections held by illiterate peasants and by scheming city dwellers set another obstacle in the way of the smooth functioning of the federation . . . for the former are so ignorant that they vote without knowing what they are about, and the latter so ambitious that everything they attempt leads to factions; this is why Venezuela has never known successful free elections; and this has placed the government in the hands of men who were either indifferent to the cause [of independence], or incapable, or lacking in moral sense."[2]

Six years later, made wiser by the experience of war and fearing the consequences in various Spanish American countries of the power vacuum created by the termination of the old order, Bolívar unsuccessfully advised the Venezuelan Congress to give the republic a constitution that would take into account its history, its lack of maturity, its social conditions: "Our destiny has always been purely passive, our political existence has never been real, and it has been all the more difficult for us to achieve Liberty because [until 1810] we were relegated to a position even lower than that of slaves. . . . America was in every way dependent upon Spain, while at the same time Spain deprived it of the benefits and practice of self-determination. . . . Triply weighed down by ignorance, tyranny, and vice, the American people have not been able to acquire knowledge, power, civic sense. . . . An ignorant people is the blind instrument of its own destruction: ambition

2. "Memoria dirigida a los ciudadanos de la Nueva Granada por un caraqueño," December 15, 1812, published in *Proclamas y discursos del Libertador*, ed. Vicente Lecuna, Caracas, Litrografía y Tipografía del Comercio, 1939, 2 vols., vol. I, pp. 11–22.

More Home Truths

and intrigue take advantage of its credulity and inexperience, and men who lack any sort of political, economic, or civic knowledge accept figments as realities, mistake license for Liberty, treason for patriotism, vengeance for justice. . . . A spoiled people that secures its freedom soon stands to lose it; for it is in vain that [some of their leaders] will strive to prove that happiness lies in the practice of virtue; that the power of Laws—precisely by virtue of their inflexibility—is superior to that of tyrants, and that everything has to bow before the Good that stems from their rigor; that civic virtue, and not power, is the proper support for the Law; that the practice of Justice is the practice of Freedom. . . . Many nations, ancient and modern, have shaken off the juggernaut of oppression, but few indeed have been able to enjoy even a few happy hours of their new-won freedom; they promptly fall back into their old political vices: for tyranny is bred by Peoples, and not by Governments. . . . The more I admire the excellence of the Federal Constitution of Venezuela, the more I am convinced that it cannot be applied to this country. And, in my opinion, it is astounding that its model, as formulated in North America, continues to prosper and was not upset by the first difficulty or danger that threatened it. Even though the North American people offer a unique example of political and moral virtue; even though Freedom was its cradle; even though it grew up in Freedom and lives only in Freedom; even though, as we must admit, this People constitutes in many ways an example unique in the history of mankind, it is a wonder, I repeat, that a system as fragile and complex as the federalist system proved able to maintain itself under circumstances as trying and as delicate as those it met with. But whatever we may think of this kind of government and of its suitability to the North American people, I must say that it never occurred to me to equate the situation and nature of States as different as British America and Spanish America. Everyone agrees that it would be very difficult to apply to Spain the code of political, civil, and religious liberties of England. It would be even more difficult to apply the laws of North America to Venezuela. Montesquieu, in his *Esprit des lois,* states that laws must be adapted to the people for which they are made; that it would be a great coincidence if the legislature adapted to one nation were appropriate to another; that laws must be conceived taking into account the physical constitution of the country, its climate, the quality of its soil, its geographic location, and the size and way of life of its people; that they must take into account the degree of freedom that its character can accommodate, the religion of its inhabitants, their tastes, their customs, their habits. That is the Code we should consult, and not the Code of Washington."[3]

Our propensity as Latin Americans to be blind about ourselves is dramatically illustrated by our refusal to see that as early as 1812 Bolívar had lost all hope of governing Spanish America without a hand of iron. Another hero of Spanish America, the Cuban José Martí (1853–1895), pleaded the same case eighty years later: "Spanish America owes its inability to govern itself entirely to those of its leaders who sought to rule nations that have conquered their identity through violence with laws based on four centuries of freedom in the United States and nineteen centuries of monarchy in France. A decree formulated by Hamilton will not keep a horse of the pampas from bucking, nor will a pronouncement of Sieyès stir the thick blood of the Indian race. . . . Government must grow upward from the land itself. The spirit of a government must be based on the true nature of the country."[4]

The *caudillos*, the Latin-American tyrants, merely constitute the revenge of historical and sociological reality on an ill-conceived plan, the attempt to foist "utopian republics" on a foundation of historical elements inherited from the Spanish empire—an attempt made all the more senseless by the terrible episode of the war of independence, which intervened between the demise of the empire and the birth of independent republics.

The Trauma of the War of Independence

The destruction in Spanish America did not have quite the same scope as that in Haiti, which between 1791 and 1804 experienced crushing institutional breakdown, civil war, and extermination of the Creole dominating classes. But the situation was almost as extreme in many parts of the continent. Therefore, if Spanish America was not prepared for self-government before 1810, it was even less prepared in 1824, after the last army faithful to the King of Spain had been defeated in Ayacucho, Peru.

The war was pitiless, total, with no quarter given and no

3. Speech before the Venezuelan Congress, February 15, 1819, upon his installation in the city of Angostura, now Ciudad Bolívar.
4. *Nuestra América*, 1891.

respect for property, public or private. Venezuela lost half its population, Uruguay almost as much. In *Facundo,* Sarmiento contrasted the ruined state into which the Argentine Republic had fallen with the prosperity that prevailed in the Viceroyalty of Buenos Aires in 1810. In 1828, Bolívar commented, "Buenos Aires, Chile, Guatemala, and Mexico are lost."[5] In 1830 he wrote: "The situation of Spanish America has reached such a degree of horror that no leader can hope to maintain order for even a short spell of time, even in a single city. . . . There has never been a spectacle as horrendous as that of Spanish America, and it is even more depressing when we think of its future rather than its past. . . . Who would have dared imagine a whole population seized by frenzy and devouring its own race, as do cannibals? . . . The case is unique in the annals of crime, and the worst is that all this is irremediable."[6]

Laborers were pressed into the army; those who came back from the wars recognized no authority beyond their warlord. The Creoles were decimated either in war or in massacres. In 1814, almost the entire population of Caracas fled the city, terrified by the atrocities committed by the *royalist* camp after it destroyed the patriotic armies. Bolívar's uncle and godfather, Esteban Palacios, returned from exile more than ten years later; Bolívar, who thought him dead or lost forever, wrote to him in elegiac tone from Peru, on July 10, 1825: "I have learned that you are alive and back in our dear Country. . . . You must have thought on homecoming that you were living the dream of Epimenides: you have come back from among the dead to witness the ravages of inexorable time, cruel war, the ferocity of man. Now that you are back in Caracas, you must feel as a ghost come back from the netherworld, finding nothing as you had left it. You left behind a large and fine family, it was cut down by death; you left a budding fatherland that was beginning to feel the first stirrings of its activity, the first elements of society; and you find nothing but ruins . . . but remembrances of things lost. The living have disappeared; the works of men and the temples of God, the very fields have undergone the formidable tremors of an earthquake. . . . The fields, watered by the sweat of three hundred years of labor, have been parched by the conjunction of the planets[7] and the crimes of men. Where is Caracas? you will ask. Caracas is no more. . . ."

5. Letter to José Fernández Madrid, February 7, 1828.
6. Letter to General Rafael Urdaneta, October 16, 1830.
7. Bolívar is referring to the earthquake of 1812.

In 1800, Humboldt had admired the speed and safety with which a letter traveled from Buenos Aires to Mexico. Now communications were to be almost entirely severed for a century, made hazardous even between regions of a single country. In Mexico, thieves and highwaymen ruled the countryside until the last third of the nineteenth century, when a particularly crafty and brutal tyrant, Porfirio Díaz, conceived the plan of hiring the fiercest of these criminals for his own service, thus setting up a rural terrorist police that gave the government a monopoly in the realm of exactions. The established structures for production and financing gave way everywhere. Such capital as had been accumulated was destroyed or dispersed. The mines were flooded, the cattle annihilated by roving bands.

Although Peru had to endure the war for a shorter period than the other countries, and was probably the least affected, an Englishman visiting it said in 1826 that "the horrors which have attended the struggle for independence" had left the country in such a state of devastation that "the appearance [is] such as if the country had just suffered from one of those dreadful earthquakes which lay all in ruin and devastation. The lands are waste, edifices to be rebuilt, the population diminished, the government unstable, just laws to be established, new capitals to be raised, and tranquillity to be secured. The ground plan of improvement is not yet traced. . . ."[8]

Bolívar's uncle Esteban Palacios was only one of the many Spanish Americans who fled from the war by emigrating to the Antilles or beyond. After Bolívar, the best known of the Spanish Americans of the independence generation is the Venezuelan Andrés Bello. He had been sent to London as the Venezuelan republic's first diplomatic representative in 1810. When he returned to Latin America—not until 1829—he settled not in his native land, but in Chile, which was embarking on a less brutal and primitive political course than the other Spanish American republics. There Bello was able to pursue a career suited to his talents, working as legislator, critic, philosopher, historian, and grammarian, and becoming a dominant figure at the university. José María Vargas, a Venezuelan physician of the same generation, had no illusions about the restoration of the republic in 1813. When the patriots liberated him from a royalist prison, he went directly to England, and then spent

8. Quoted in Lewis Hanke, ed., *History of Latin American Civilization*, 2nd ed., vol. 2, p. 21.

ten years in Europe, perfecting his medical knowledge in Edinburgh, London, and Paris. He returned to Latin America in 1823, choosing not Venezuela but Puerto Rico, where the Spanish imperial order still reigned. In 1825—the year in which Bolívar learned of Esteban Palacios's return to Caracas —Vargas decided to return to Venezuela, which by then had finally been liberated from Spain and, he supposed, was also free of war. The *caudillo* who took over in Venezuela, following Bolívar's resignation as Supreme Chief of Colombia in 1830, made Vargas the President of the republic on the strength of his scientific reputation. But this civilian and man of science was promptly overthrown by the first in a long series of military coups d'état that Venezuela was to know in its history as an independent republic. When he died, in 1854, he was again in exile, this time in New York.

The Heritage of Spanish Mercantilism

Monopoly practices, privileges, restrictions placed on the free activity of individuals in the economic and other domains, are traditions profoundly anchored in societies of Spanish origin. Spain forbade access to its American possessions not only to all who were not subjects of the King and Emperor (which would not have barred Flemings, Burgundians, Milanese, Neapolitans, Sicilians, or Tunisians) but even at first to Spaniards from anywhere else on the peninsula than Castile, Andalusia, or Estremadura. These measures, and others of a similar kind, resulted in the establishment of an extraordinarily closed society in America. In New Spain, Humboldt met eminent Creoles who did not know that there were people in Europe who did not speak Spanish.

The discriminatory measures against individuals also extended to goods. It was not until 1776, when it became a viceroyalty, that Buenos Aires was permitted to participate in maritime trade. Until that time, the imports and exports of this Atlantic province were under the jurisdiction of the Viceroyalty of Peru, which meant that a cargo from Cadiz or Seville destined for Buenos Aires had to be landed at Portobelo on the Caribbean coast of Panama, carried across the isthmus on muleback, transported on the Pacific Ocean to Lima, again loaded onto mules, and taken across the Andes, to La Paz, and thence to the plain and the Atlantic Coast. When this astounding requirement was abolished, the price of imports in Buenos Aires dropped by two-thirds, and export of the locally produced leather and wool was possible for the first time.

To the retrograde, mercantile Spanish mind, the Middle Ages had remained the absolute model; this mentality neither understood nor approved capitalism, then in its earliest stages of development. Individual economic pursuits were viewed as almost sinful; at any rate, they constituted a reprehensible practice that deserved to be taxed at every turn of the road and at the crossing of every river. The permanent *alcabala* mentioned earlier, which exists on the most modern roads of Spanish America today, is a relic of the Spanish distrust of the free circulation of persons and goods. This is but one illustration of an all-embracing prejudice against everything that does not originate with the state, or is not authorized or supervised (that is, meddled with and hindered) by the state. The *alcabala* must be viewed as the very opposite of roadblocks in Anglo-Saxon countries, which are set up as temporary barriers when it is exceptionally necessary to filter traffic. In the Anglo-Saxon countries, citizens are normally free, and a restriction on free movement, or a restriction on freedom of any kind, requires both a just cause and the legal, non-arbitrary process of law.[9]

The British consular agent whose impressions of the aftermath of the Peruvian war of independence were quoted earlier,

9. So deeply rooted is the contempt for businessmen and work in Hispanic cultures that even Francisco de Miranda, normally a lucid analyst and quite willing to stress the advantages of liberty over despotism, failed to recognize in the Anglo-Saxon political institutions the link between, on the one hand, the guarantees of private property and the respect for trade and commerce and, on the other, the progress of liberty. During his stay in Boston in 1784, Miranda witnessed several meetings of the Legislative Assembly of the State of Massachusetts. His South American sensibilities were shocked at the presence of artisans of low birth, who often expressed themselves in homely fashion, in this hallowed Assembly where, he felt, significant *noble* questions should have been under discussion. The topics being considered appeared basely materialistic to him; the Assembly's popular membership scandalized, but did not surprise, him: "If we consider that the representatives need not be the best-educated members of the community . . . they are people who lack principles and education: one was a *tailor* only four years before . . . another an *innkeeper* . . . another a *blacksmith*." While in Boston, Miranda found that Samuel Adams shared his regret that the American Constitution rejected the concept of nobility. Luckily for the newborn country, Miranda's aristocratic attitude was as little widespread as was Adams's Jacobinism: "He seemed to be in agreement with me on two points that I made concerning the question. First of all I said to him, how can a democracy founded on *virtue* give no place to virtue, while it gives all honor and power to *property*?" (*Archivo* [*Viajes, Diarios*], Caracas, Editorial Suramérica, 1929, vol. 1, pp. 317, 314.)

also found that the practices of the republican government of this former Spanish viceroyalty contradicted its profession of faith in favor of free trade. "In their desire to obtain resources [the administrators of this government] conceived that the readiest mode of acquiring them was by the imposition of heavy duties; old prejudices prevented their believing that the income of a state will be progressively augmented by leaving merchants to derive the advantages which they expect from low profits on extensive dealings; and contemplating the [Peruvian] mines [worked by slaves] as yielding an inexhaustible supply of wealth, they saw not that the results of a liberal commercial system would prove the only sure means of securing an increase of trade, industry, capital, and population [and, therefore, fiscal revenue]. Prohibitions and absurd enactments met the fair trader at every step; he was obliged to abandon his speculations unless he became a party to the contraband system which others pursued; and he found that he could resort to it with impunity, as in case of detection, a bribe ensured connivance."[10]

Even today the economic development of Latin America reflects the methods and habits of the past; these tend to discourage tradesmen who attempt to limit themselves to fair business practices, and at the same time to encourage and favor unscrupulous trade practices, the selling of privileges, the corruption of civil servants, and fiscal fraud. Faced with this situation, the governments heir to the mercantilist Spanish tradition naturally tend to intensify controls, multiply restrictions, raise taxation, without ever considering that there may be as many corruptible men among those who enforce restrictions and regulations as among those who suffer them. As a result, whenever regulations are made more complex or wider in their application, chances of corruption grow greater, while it becomes more and more difficult for the ordinary man to get along without resorting to dubious practices even in the simplest matters, let alone in those that hold expectation of profit. In such a situation, the corrupt official will have every reason to encourage the proliferation of formalities, to multiply the complexity of export and import licenses, to demand special permits for every kind of activity, till breathing and bird watching are the only nonregulated occupations left. Each new restriction naturally provides an opportunity to offer or ask for a kickback. The honest civil servant is inclined to let cases

10. Quoted in Lewis Hanke, 2nd ed., vol. 2, pp. 21–22.

drag on or to bury them, for fear that the least display of alacrity will be interpreted as a reflection of corrupt involvement.

Parasitic Cities

Beginning with 1824, the Spanish American republics were obliged to enter the capitalist world's free market as importers and exporters, a role for which they were in no way prepared. When free trade prevails while governments are inept or corrupt and unable to exert basic checks—for example, on foreign indebtedness—imports tend to outgrow exports, and national expenditure goes beyond national income. Financial instability becomes chronic and leads to habits that feed the kind of galloping inflation characteristic of Latin America in the twentieth century. In this situation, the easiest course for the government is to balance the public budget by selling off national property and borrowing foreign capital at usurious rates. And it is not just interest rates that soar under such conditions; foreign bankers demand steadily higher commissions, some of which find their way, not infrequently, into the pockets of negotiators or government officials.

A split between urban, commercial centers and rural, producing areas characterized Latin-American colonial society and economy, particularly in export production. The cities took on the role of exploiters and supervisors, feeding on the countryside, while the agrarian world and the mines supplied slave-like laborers and subconsumers. This imbalance dated back to the empire; it was now reinforced by the new economic order, which favored the dominance of ports and capital cities over the hinterland. The tendency has gained momentum in the present day, leading to the development of such cities as Buenos Aires, which is the most striking example of macrocephalia in the subcontinent. (Montevideo, Lima, and Havana are also both port and capital; Caracas and Santiago de Chile are not properly ports, but are near the sea.) Urban parasitic society has undergone "modernization," aping the fashions of Europe and the United States, while the rural areas have continued to be bound by the habits and behavior patterns implanted by the conquistadors, the colonizers, and the churchmen of the sixteenth century.

It is in this disparity that one of the basic themes of Latin-American thought and literature originated: the city as an alien, cancerous growth preying upon the body of a tributary and backward rural society.

One of the most respected of Latin-American essayists, the Argentine Ezequiel Martínez Estrada (1895–1965), describes Buenos Aires in these terms: the city "brutally and blindly absorbs the wealth of the interior . . . which it devours like the giant it truly is. . . . It fattens on poverty, underdevelopment, ignorance, and loneliness."[11] Sarmiento, the reader will recall, argued that civilization was possible in Spanish America only when imported from abroad and implanted in the cities, to radiate outward from there. Yet he commented that Buenos Aires "drowns in its fountains the riches brought in by all the rivers: the unwilling tribute of the subject provinces. Only Buenos Aires derives profit from foreign trade; the power and the wealth are the capital's only. The provinces beg in vain that a little civilization, a little industry, and European population be allowed to trickle down to them. . . . But the provinces have had their revenge by sending the tyrant Rosas down to the capital, a worthy representative, an oversized return of the kind of barbarism with which they are replete."[12]

Those who knew Havana before 1960 and have gone back since Fidel Castro's take-over have seen how the countryside has exacted its revenge on the parasitic capital. In Asia, Phnom Penh underwent the same experience on a far more brutal scale with the triumph of the Khmers Rouges. Will other Latin-American cities experience the fate of Havana and Phnom Penh? Quite possibly. There is little to recommend the Spanish American hinterland, and I am far from idealizing it, giving way to some fascistic tellurism,[13] or reverting to the theme of the noble savage. But it is clear that the bloated capitals squatting among their impoverished provinces are symptoms of the deep disequilibrium of the soul and the structure of Spanish American society.

And city dwellers, whether city-born or recently arrived from rural areas, provinces, or foreign countries, are fashioned or refashioned by these inhuman cities, and therefore suffer (and inflict) alienation, having roots "neither on earth nor in heaven; feeling neither love nor sympathy nor affection of the unknown neighbor . . . not feeling that we are one people, that we have a mission, a task to accomplish, a destiny."[14]

11. *La cabeza de Goliat,* Buenos Aires, 1940.
12. *Facundo,* Chapter 1.
13. See pp. 88–91.
14. Ezequiel Martínez Estrada, *Exhortaciones,* 1957.

The Latin Americans

The non-Spanish European immigrants exemplify another kind of alienation. They have contributed greatly to many of the most positive aspects of Latin-American culture, and yet less than their potential, since neither they nor their children could help feeling, and being affected by, the society's lack of a common bond. If they had settled in the United States, they could have come to feel part of a solid and viable system, as did so many other Italians, Irishmen, Greeks, Central European or Russian Jews, et cetera. In Latin America they found themselves cut off from their home countries, "deprived of any inner discipline, torn up from the European societies in which they were born and where they had lived without ever being conscious of how profoundly they belonged; they are now outside of the moral framework that is afforded by a balanced and fulfilled collective life, and at the same time they would never find [in Latin America] that they had joined a new and different 'process of incorporation.' "[15]

This inability to become part of the whole, to feel involved in the collective destiny, which for Ortegy y Gasset is a sign of the decadence of Hispanic societies, manifests itself in Latin America even among emigrants from the most tightly structured and closely knit societies. And the isolation and lack of solidarity, leading naturally to excessively individualistic and selfish behavior patterns, are most pronounced on the higher rungs of the social and cultural ladder.

Ortega y Gasset's perceptive observation leads us to understand that the Spanish conquistadors and colonizers set the pattern for all later immigrants, whatever their origin. Little wonder that the lower levels of the pyramid of castes that constituted the Spanish empire in America never felt part of society, since they were effectively excluded from it. Except in one sense, which Octavio Paz pointed out but perhaps overemphasized: the Church was able to make them believe that the Christian brotherhood of men reserved a place for them, a niche in the cosmic order not without dignity. But these disenfranchised groups constituted an "internal proletariat,"[16] which at the first opportunity—the wars of independence— turned into a new and powerful force pushing toward disintegration.

15. Ortega y Gasset, "Intimidades," in *Obras Completas,* 3rd ed., vol. 2, Madrid, Revista de Occidente, 1954.
16. In the sense in which Toynbee used the expression: "An alien underworld, a mobid affection [of society], a group estranged from a dominant minority, a social element which in some ways is 'in,' but not 'of' any given society at any stage of such society's history."

Yet the lower strata of the Spanish American empire—the peasants who formed the bulk of the people of the Latin-American republics—could not imagine leaving Spanish American soil, uprooting themselves from the geographical setting in which their history was being played out. There are obvious reasons for this. None among these uneducated folk ever had elaborate pipe dreams of "returning home from the Indies." No village of Estremadura or Andalusia had seen them leave and none expected their return, whereas every Spanish settler dreamed of going home.

As If Each One of Us Were Alone on Earth

Because they do not quite identify with the society in which they live, the members of the Spanish American ruling classes in general do not give themselves wholly to that society. They are always potential exiles; in any case they are moral exiles, even if, generation after generation, they manage to keep their hold on the reins of power and see their families prosper. They keep bank accounts and real-estate investments abroad, while their activities, commitment, devotion, and civic sense are never entirely engaged in the country in which they live.

Many would like to think that this *egoism,* this way of behaving "as if each one of us were alone and unique on earth,"[17] is characteristic only of a few: the very wealthy who have made their fortunes in a more or less questionable way, like the Bolivian tin barons who are voluntary exiles and have allied themselves through marriage with European "high society"; or dictators who make a practice of plundering the public treasury before moving with their bounty to Miami, Madrid, or Paris. But this same pattern of behavior can be discerned in all who have reached a position of some power, however modest, and also in the groups, institutional or otherwise, that represent or support the interests of particular sectors of the community: the Church, the armed forces, the university, regional or political clans (the latter going under the name of "parties"), labor unions, professional organizations, et cetera.

We Latin Americans are not intrinsically different from others; and we are moved by the same motives as they. Other societies—and particularly societies that have not yet reached a high degree of political integration, or that have begun to see their cohesion decline—have experienced this phenomenon of

17. H. A. Murena.

individual, family, or clan egoism. But Latin-American societies are the only Western societies that *since birth* have lived in a state of disintegration. In other Western societies, men are, and feel, part of a distinct human group whose members are all existentially dependent on one another and on the land they call their own; they know their society to be part of a process that reaches out in time, embracing the past of their ancestors and the future of their descendants. These men enjoy a sense of nationality that we in Latin America have not been granted. The only other modern Western society comparable to us in this regard is Italy's; and that is why it was an Italian who wrote *The Prince*—a manual for tyrants, a compendium of the techniques required to weld together a fragmented society and to control it with a strong hand, as all Latin-American *caudillos* from Rosas to Fidel Castro have done.

The tyrant claims the lion's share of the national spoils for himself and his followers, both the power and the wealth, and forces the rest of the population to work without protesting; he himself determines the share of the benefits that will be allotted them. In Fidel Castro's case, as earlier in Rosas's, the terms of this apportionment are entirely arbitrary. But when we in Latin America are *not* dictated to by a tyrant who forces us to some kind of national solidarity, we often are concerned only with our own self-interest. We seem far more interested in what our country can do for us than in what we can do for our country.

An example: In Venezuela the Social Security system is admirable in theory, but in practice it tends to give the physicians, nurses, and other medical personnel far more than the supposed beneficiaries. This instrument of public welfare has resorted to strikes and political pressure, tolerated or even endorsed by political parties as a way of gaining influence over the medical sector. We have reached the point where an organization as basic to the welfare and development of a modern society as Social Security spends a disproportionate part of its budget on the payroll of its own personnel, and little on social and health benefits. To make matters worse, a number of physicians draw pay for working hours they manifestly cannot have earned, since they continue to maintain their private practices and often even their university posts.

Universities and University Clans

Much attention has been paid to the exactions that such power groups as the armed forces and the economic and political oligarchies have wrought on our societies, but little has been said of the way in which "good causes," such as the universities, have also managed to prey on the social body. Latin-American universities are symbiotic alliances of the professors and university students with political clans. It may be said that, possibly without exception, the Latin-American university systems draw far more resources from the nation than they ever contribute to it. Ivan Illich, in analyzing with his usual ferocity what might be called the racket of schooling, explained how in Latin America a vast proportion of the overall national educational budget is invested in a way that perpetuates and further accentuates social inequalities.[18]

The "mystique" of the Latin-American university is based partly on the fact that enrollment is free, and partly on the fact that the university is autonomous. This autonomy rests on the election of university authorities by an assembly made up of professors and students; on the university's discretionary use of the funds attributed to it out of the state budget; and on the inviolability of the university grounds, which are normally not under police jurisdiction (though this does not prevent *exceptional* raids in which the forces of order invade the university with varying degrees of justification and brutality).

The combination of these factors in the Latin-American setting has led to extremely low academic effectiveness, even as measured on the elementary yardsticks of actual teaching hours, total class attendance, the number of B.A.'s or Ph.D.'s in relation to enrollment, or—an essential point—the number of graduate degrees granted in disciplines for which society has a real need and in which there are suitable employment opportunities. When we move from these elementary indices to more sophisticated ones, the overall picture is nothing short of catastrophic.

Certain stubborn defenders of the Latin-American system of higher education excuse university practices (and even go so far as to praise them) because of their so-called revolutionary character (both teachers and students call themselves revolutionaries). But these spokesmen from within the academic community are not very convincing, as they derive too many benefits from the institutions they praise: fellowships, tenured

18. Ivan Illich, *Deschooling Society*, New York, Harper & Row, 1971.

chairs, travel expenses, sabbaticals, the subsidized publication of even the most mediocre books, special financial support for projects that need not even be remotely academic, the use of the university grounds as a sanctuary from which to plot armed subversion, and so forth. Even if we close our eyes to the identity of interests that exists between the university clan and the institutions it defends, the "revolutionary" argument cannot stand up to analysis, unless we grant that the destruction of existing society is a prerequisite for national progress. If this is what we believe, we must consider the progressive asphyxiation of Latin-American societies a worthy goal, and recognize that the universities have taken a number of measures in that direction. They have squandered funds that could have been utilized far better elsewhere—for example, in the field of preschool training; they have used their position of prestige in science and culture to endorse simplistic or even wholly false explanations of the continent's difficulties and possible remedies; they have encouraged wide, tacit complicity between teachers and students to lower academic standards; they have guided the young to fields of study that carry prestige in the university, but that after graduation are of use neither to them nor to society.[19]

In other words, if, in order to be "revolutionary," an institution has to help confound or destroy the society of which it is part, then there is no doubt that the Latin-American universities *are* revolutionary. But by this criterion, pornography and drugs, too, ought to be called revolutionary. No one so far has suggested glorifying them, or asking the state to grant increasing subsidies to drug addicts so as to allow young people from sixteen to twenty-four years of age to give themselves over to *this* kind of revolutionary activity.

Actually, we could well view the Latin-American university as a bastion of traditional privilege, an instrument in the service of a specific sector of the population. To this sector—by no means the poorest—it transfers more resources than that sector ever feeds back to society. Although enrollment is free,

19. In a television program I conducted, the leaders of the "university sections" of the four main Venezuelan political parties were interviewed. Each of these leaders criticized the excessive importance assigned to "social sciences" of dubious value in the general framework of higher learning. Each recognized that the university should guide the students to technological careers adapted to the country's real needs, in such fields as petroleum research, petrochemistry, metallurgy, agronomy, et cetera. I then asked them what their own specialties were, and found they were preparing B.A.'s in, respectively, sociology, economics, psychology, and diplomacy.

the students who enter the university, and certainly those who graduate, almost invariably belong to the middle class or the bourgeoisie. The proletarian masses whose name is so often invoked in defense of the university do not in fact send their children there, except as cafeteria workers or cleaning women. The university has never bothered to investigate whether some sections of the student body would be in a position to pay for their schooling. Thus, through higher education, society as a whole, including its poor, further subsidizes the middle and richer classes, which would be quite capable of paying their own way.[20] The diplomas and certificates that the children of these classes collect as they proceed with their years of higher education extend old privileges or bestow new ones. At the same time, a lack of diplomas blocks the upward social and economic mobility of those who are too poor to continue their education. The distorted values that make this system possible are further reflected in the scanty interest still shown today in preschool education, the only level at which a substantial financial input and a sustained effort could make a start toward equalizing opportunities. When the pie of public education is being cut up, the poorest classes never have a voice in the sharing, even though we are assured it is all being done with their good in mind. The "revolutionaries" do not make themselves heard in defense of the poor when it comes to preschool training; they are heard only in defense of the universities, which graduate the M.A.'s and Ph.D.'s who will some day reach important positions in society. And how could these in turn fail to show their gratitude toward the institution that duly certified their qualifications as physician, lawyer, or engineer, and thus made them once and for all members of the upper caste?

Not only has the autonomous Latin-American university worked to benefit and perpetuate a class; it has also been unable to imagine, let alone to launch, the new type of higher education that the changing social realities of the continent make so imperative. The universities have remained among the most backward of Latin-American institutions. As the constituent parts of the social organism in Latin America are uncoordinated or disjointed, it is possible for some to progress rapidly and to show a capacity for daring innovations. But this certainly cannot be said of the university, which plods docilely along the path of the traditional European model; witness its division into faculties and schools, its pattern of yearly gradua-

20. Ivan Illich, *ibid.*

tions, its inflexible programs, its commencements in medieval garb. And as soon as they have received their diplomas, most students abandon their defense of radical causes and their revolutionary views—supposing they ever were seriously revolutionary. For in a Latin-American university, it is just about as daring and heretical to be "revolutionary" as it is for a student in an Irish seminary to be a fervent Catholic. The brightest students, once they graduate, have only one aim in mind: to get as much out of society as they can. The free education they have received prepares them for it, and their diplomas enable them to play much the same role as did petty nobility under the *ancien régime*.

Latin-American universities must be viewed as playing the role of safety valves to the system. At very considerable expense, they allow the system unobtrusively to counterbalance centrifugal forces that might otherwise express themselves in a far more violent manner. Many of the potential, and actual, radical leaders of the student movement find their ambition and their thirst for power surfeited—after much rivalry and infighting—by the acquisition of chairs or deanships at the universities. The power of patronage attached to such positions, and the satisfaction of seeing their writing brought out by the university presses as books no one will read, leads the radicals to be content with merely verbalizing their revolutionary commitment.

In order to maintain their privileges, traditional Latin-American oligarchies have been forced to compromise not only with the *caudillos*, but also, more recently, with the middle classes. The university serves this second function by acting as a channel of upward mobility for the urban middle class, thus simultaneously replenishing the lower ranks of the oligarchies. It is through the university that the middle classes have a chance to practice self-expression before they have actually succeeded in integrating themselves more directly into the traditional, "orthodox" power structures. Thus the universities can be seen as the training grounds for the "new men" needed to renew the political staff of the state. But at the same time, the university has failed to play the role for which it was intended: that of producing the new crop of administrators, scientists, and technicians required by a modern nation.

The function of producing these essential technocrats has been delegated too extensively to foreign institutions, in particular to the North American universities, to which all families that can afford it usually send their children. The young men who may expect to accede to leadership within their generation generally belong to families that take the privilege of foreign education for granted, or else are among the gifted few who have earned fellowships on their own. The best education for a young man from this favored group is to do his undergraduate work at home (in addition to the B.A., this would include the so-called doctorate, a degree that does not require unduly long studies or exacting research). There he establishes lifelong friendships with his peers, whom he will be encountering at every step in his career. From there he goes on to the United States to complete the higher education that he needs if he is to capitalize on the advantage he has over the simple sons of the middle class. Also, he will acquire fluency in English, without which a man cannot "get to the top" today, either in Latin America or anywhere else.

The Intellectuals

The Latin-American universities also provide a forum and a way of life for a significant number of those who are called "intellectuals"—a term, as I have already said, that is far more broadly applied among us than among societies with more carefully compartmentalized structures.

Achieving an understanding of the intellectuals' role is complicated by a number of factors. The intellectuals are, almost by definition, men who can give eloquent, seemingly lofty expression to their own phobias or self-justifications, and make them correspond—or appear to correspond—with the views then current among other members of the ruling classes. So-called intellectuals have been apologists for the men in power; they have been the secretaries of all the *caudillos;* in one way or another they have been part and parcel of the ruling classes in the true meaning of the term. The question of their significance as a group touches upon the interpretation of the continent's past and present reality—with all the difficulties this entails.

Foreign observers who have been satisfied with a cursory first impression of Latin America usually express their surprise at the great influence they perceive intellectuals as having in our national life. They see in this proof that Latin America is more open to the "spirit," more concerned with "culture," than other Western societies that are merely efficient and materialistic. These foreign observers and intellectuals are delighted to find so many of their Latin-American peers—novelists, essayists, poets, artists—occupying high posts in government or the Foreign Service, in larger proportions than in other countries. Actually, the writings and the academic record of these men are mostly mediocre; if they have gained a certain renown, it is in most cases due to the low standards of the society in which they so distinguished themselves. In countries that are suffering from a chronic penury of executives and in which a public man's image is improved by his "having letters" (provided his literary vocation isn't too real and exclusive), these intellectuals' education automatically gives them access to membership in the ruling classes. Many of them have successively been active as novelists, poets, essayists, orators, historians, philosophers; once they have been made ministers or ambassadors they have reached their true goal, toward which their "intellectual" activity was only a ladder.

No doubt Latin America has produced a number of remarkable intellectuals who have also been men of action, the foremost among them being Bolívar and Sarmiento, as well as admirable thinkers, novelists, and essayists, such as the Argentines Ezequiel Martínez Estrada, H. A. Murena, Jorge Luis Borges, and Ernesto Sábato; the Mexicans Octavio Paz, Carlos Fuentes, and Juan Rulfo; the Guatemalan Miguel Angel Asturias; the Chilean Pablo Neruda; the Uruguayan Juan Carlos Onetti; the Venezuelan Arturo Uslar Pietri; the Cuban Alejo Carpentier; the Peruvians Cesar Vallejo, Luis Alberto Sánchez, and Mario Vargas Llosa, and the Colombian Gabriel García Márquez, to mention only a few of our contemporaries. But of those men who have been both intellectuals and men of action, most have been primarily effective in action. The influence of their ideas when they were critical or running counter to accepted opinion has been very weak; some others, naturally, have been conformist and demagogic. The handful of pure intellectuals who have aimed toward serious literary creations have expressed very lucid demands, of themselves as well as society. But they are not very numerous, and they have been subject to difficulties, pressures, temptations that often prove irresistible. Below these lies a plethora of timorous and impotent opportunists and sycophants, who throughout Latin-American history have made their way by becoming latter-day imitators of foreign literary and intellectual trends. Thus we have had our own late harvest of romantics, positivists, symbolists, Freudians, and surrealists; and today we are afflicted with a full quota of Johnny-come-lately Marxists.

More Home Truths

In discussing present-day Marxists, I am not speaking of the few honorable men (now very old) who were converted to Marxism at a time when it was a misunderstood, outlawed, and ruthlessly persecuted sect, rather than the intellectual coterie it is today; I must also make exception of those in the new generation whose deeds and words show them to be sincerely committed. For the rest, the "new wave" of so-called Latin-American intellectuals have taken to Marxism much as the cat takes to the fireplace corner: that is where the warmth is, and where they can feel coziest and most at ease with themselves and with society.

Latin-American governments, even those reputed to be rightist and authoritarian, tend to be rather tolerant, or even indulgent, toward Marxist intellectuals of this ilk—as long as they refrain from acting out the philosophy to which they pay lip service. The tolerance ends when the Marxists take the road of political activism; for instance, at the time of the post-Castroist uprisings, when events forced the intellectuals' hand, slogans they had formulated carelessly drove them to take more of a stand than they may have wished. And in the Southern Cone (Argentina, Chile, and Uruguay), a savage backlash of anti-Communism has in recent years turned into paranoid, murderous persecution of persons with the faintest left-wing leanings. But in a sense, even rightist governments have good reason to be fairly tolerant of Marxist intellectuals, those meek apostles of mythical revolution. In "normal times," habitual invocation of the outside demon of imperialism serves to explain away all difficulties, and the Marxist contention that Latin America will be redeemed "come the revolution," without too much effort on our part, lightens everybody's sense of guilt and frustration and veils over everybody's shortcomings.

"On my altars there are no saints, only a map of Latin America. A *guerrillero* is not merely a man with a gun, he is also the Latin-American citizen who has fought for the liberation of our land from the time of European invasion in 1492 till our own days," a Latin-American intellectual (the Argentine painter Alfredo Portillos) says characteristically. And these words seem full of significance, for they appeal to our collective Latin-American neurosis, whereas Luis Alberto Sánchez's admonition goes unnoticed: "The term 'religion' refers not only to man's connection to God, but to his search for some entity or concept that will help him remedy his inability to understand his own destiny; it follows that Marxism is as much an opiate for the people as Christian Deism."

The Latin Americans

In the meantime, "while waiting for the revolution," Latin-American intellectuals with Marxist leanings do not feel obliged in any way to share the privations of the common people in whose name they claim to be speaking. They do not even feel they must lead frugal lives. They gladly accept the good things to which they believe themselves entitled, as members of the Latin-American privileged classes. With but a few exceptions, they have no scruples about making forays outside their professional fields in the artistic, literary, or academic world and accepting—or actively seeking—appointments in the administration and government of the "prerevolutionary" state whose destruction is a basic tenet of their philosophy. They feel that they have become incorruptible since they have understood the meaning of history. The privileges they enjoy, even the luxury in which a few of them live, cannot alter the fact that in the struggle between good and evil, they have, once and for all, chosen the side of the angels.

9

The Forms of Political Power in Latin America

"Caudillismo"

The basic political problem of independent Spanish America is that the different republics have not succeeded in replacing the institutional equilibrium that disappeared, between 1810 and 1824, along with the Spanish empire. The challenges peculiar to the second half of the twentieth century—the radical changes in mass expectations caused by new developments in communications; the demographic explosion caused by the sudden decrease in mortality rates, particularly infant mortality; the ideological virulence of the Marxist–Leninist–Third World view of life; and, more recently, the military and economic power of the countries that endorse that ideology— these challenges have revealed the fragility of even those policies and institutions that earlier had been thought of as lasting and solid, such as those in Argentina, Chile, and Uruguay.

Mexico is the only Spanish American country that in the last fifty years has not experienced any changes of government by civil war or military coup d'état. On the other hand, it experienced at least forty-six irregular changes of government in the first quarter century of its independence. In Venezuela, no fewer than fifty civil wars occurred in less than one century (from 1830 to 1902), one of which, the so-called Federal War, or "the long war," which lasted from 1859 to 1863, was as cruel and bloody as the wars of independence had been half a century earlier. In Bolivia there have been one hundred and sixty civil wars or coups d'état from 1835 to the present: an average of more than one a year.

Broadly speaking, various societies will react in a like manner to like stimuli. Faced with arbitrary rule, with insecurity,
with the lack of a stable and adequate judicial and institutional framework, men will be driven to seek refuge within a
heavily centralized, pyramidal system of social relations, under
the leadership of a tyrant.[1]

The societies within the Spanish American republics broke
up and dissolved when faced with the institutional vacuum
that resulted from the wars of independence—a vacuum that
developed at the very start of disturbance. Each single country,
each region, even each village, was able to re-establish peace
only by appealing to a *caudillo* for protection.[2] It may be said
that a primitive feudalism developed; it was natural for this
kind of social structuring to emerge, for it reinforced the existing pattern of the haciendas, the virtually autonomous social
units on which the agricultural economy was based even before the fall of the Spanish empire.

At the start, there were as many *caudillos*, or war lords, as
specific geographic conditions permitted, each lord exerting his
authority over a limited territory. Strong men emerged among
them and brought larger areas under their control, so that a
regional structuring emerged; this led to nation-wide rule by
supercaudillos, each suppressing or subduing regional caciques, much in the manner in which the kings of medieval
Europe subdued or eliminated lesser feudal barons.

Arturo Uslar Pietri has argued that the *supercaudillos* developed as a natural response to existing conditions: "Rosas,
Páez, Porfirio Díaz, Juan Vicente Gómez were the products of
the land, of tradition, and of historic necessity. They owed
their immense power to the fact that they incarnated the reaction of a rural world that had severed its connections with the
Spanish empire in the hope of implanting republican and liberal institutions that had no roots whatsoever in the past. The
historic *caudillo* was the native reply to the power vacuum.
Latin America saw the emergence of a form of social organization that was contrary to the republican ideas that had been
fashioned in Europe, but that perfectly suited the American
economic and social structure. . . . Men like Don Porfirio or
Rosas emerged because they reflected the thoughts, the inclination, the deep feelings of the majority of their people; in the

1. This is why Communist countries have reinvented a *caudillismo* of
their own, known as "personality cult."
2. *Caudillo* means "chieftain." *The Dictionary of the Spanish Royal Academy* defines the word literally as "the chief of an armed band."

fullest sense of the term, they were their spokesmen, their representatives, the symbol of the dominant collective feeling of the time."[3]

There is little new in this interpretation. Bolívar had said much the same thing in his own way, and so had José Martí. Many other Spanish Americans pointed to the same explanation, either to deplore it, or to use it to justify their own position. This made an essentially sound interpretation appear ambiguous and distasteful. Many who have quoted Bolívar[4] have done so to justify themselves or their leaders or *caudillos*. The Venezuelan dictator Marcos Pérez Jiménez, who ruled from 1952 to 1958, took as motto a sentence of Bolívar's, "The best government is that which gives the people the greatest social security and the greatest happiness," in order to convey the impression that the Liberator would have endorsed the excesses of his, Jiménez's, regime—the suspension of public liberties; prison, torture, exile, or death for opponents of the regime; the theft of public funds; the absence of all moral sense—as preferable to the risks and pitfalls of democracy.

In 1908, just before his regime collapsed, the Mexican *supercaudillo* Porfirio Díaz stated: "I believe democracy to be the one true, just principle of government, although in practice it is possible only to highly developed peoples. . . . Here in Mexico we have had different conditions. I received this Government from the hands of a victorious army at a time when the people were divided and unprepared for the exercise of the extreme principles of democratic government. To have thrown upon the masses the whole responsibility of government at once would have produced conditions that might have discredited the cause of free government."[5]

Citizens active in public affairs had three choices: (1) They could oppose the "telluric" forces incarnate in the *caudillos*, which would have been a suicidal stance; (2) they could withdraw into anonymity; (3) they could collaborate with the *cau-*

---

3. "El caudillo ante el novelista," *El Nacional*, Caracas, May 11, 1975.
4. Or even Miranda. Being not a *caudillo*, but a European career officer and a *philosophe* of the Enlightenment, he led the first Venezuelan Republic to disaster in 1812. "Trouble, all these people can do is to make trouble," the Precursor exclaimed, witnessing the growing gap between the illusions he had formed in the United States, England, and France, and the pitiful troops of the republic, manned by illiterate *peones* and led by overexcited Creoles unable to agree among themselves. Bolívar's criticism of the first republic (see pp. 197–200 of this book) refers to what Miranda simply and directly called "disorder."
5. Interview with the American journalist James Creelman, *Pearson's Magazine*, March 1908, quoted in Lewis Hanke, ed., *History of Latin American Civilization*, 2nd ed., vol. 2, pp. 295–96.

dillos and so hope to accede to the higher positions of government.

Those who chose the third of these options and felt embarrassed about their choice welcomed the positivism of August Comte, Taine, Renan, and Le Bon, which was beginning to have influence in Latin America. In this philosophy they saw an apology for their position; they certainly did not use positivism as a tool for the objective understanding of the phenomenon of *caudillismo*. Instead of criticizing the government for being personal, arbitrary, and brutal, these men enlarged on the merits of absolute rule, contrasting it with civil war or anarchy, which they presented as the only possible alternatives. The few who did not choose to collaborate with the *caudillos* criticized those who did for having become lackeys of power. No doubt they had, as have those who walk in their tracks today, serving the new *caudillos* in the modern mold, like Fidel Castro in Cuba. A friend of mine, a writer who has long been, and continues to an extent to be, an admirer of the Cuban Revolution, admitted in private in 1974 that on each successive visit he has made to Cuba since 1960, he has grown more concerned with the government's tendency to resort to personality cult, arbitrary rule, and the pyramidal pattern of authority that characterized the darkest and most unproductive periods of Spanish political and social life in the nineteenth century. The Cubans themselves whisper that they are governed by *sociolismo* (a pun on the word *socio*, which means "partner" but also "crony" or "accomplice"). Another admirer of the Cuban Revolution in its early stages, the Uruguayan Angel Rama, one of the most intelligent and cultured of Latin America's intellectuals today, wrote: "*Caudillismo* and paternalist dictatorship are forms of government characteristic of Latin America; they are still widespread today, covered over by a seemingly modern terminology that helps give a sheen of persuasive universalism to forms as old as our independence. Reading Régis Debray's *Revolution Within the Revolution?*, I was surprised to find the same old formula of *caudillismo* being re-exported back to us dressed in the language of the Paris Ecole Normale. We had thought *caudillismo* so much a local product that it could not be cast in the intellectual mold of Marxism. This tour de force simply proves the resilience and pervasiveness of *caudillismo*. However upsetting it may be to intellectuals seduced by ideas come from Europe, the fact is that even those societies of our continent that claim to be most modern in matters of ideology have fallen back on *caudillismo*.

The Forms of Political Power in Latin America

The proof has been given that the living reality of Latin America is still prone to the kind of government that concentrates all power in the hands of a providential leader."[6]

A Venezuelan of an earlier generation, Pedro Manuel Arcaya, one of whose accomplishments was to have assembled for his personal use the best library in Venezuela prior to 1940, recorded in his memoirs a description of Venezuelan provincial life before the end of the nineteenth century. He vividly portrayed how the citizenry had only just recovered from one civil war when another came sweeping down like a hurricane, killing off men and cattle, destroying everything in its wake. Arcaya raises the question of whether it is not better to be governed by a *supercaudillo* such as Juan Vicente Gómez (who ruled from 1908 to 1935) than to experience a series of such calamities. A man such as Gómez will resort to whatever means—terror, exile, persuasion—he may feel necessary to destroy his *subcaudillos* or force them to submit; once he has established unquestioned authority, however, he will go on to enforce a period of peace.

Bloody and protracted civil wars have frequently resulted from the collapse of institutional order; it is natural for a strong, autocratic regime to emerge, and for the people to be tolerant of its philosophy for the sake of the new-found stability. Thus Russia put up with Stalin, and Spain with Franco.

We should also note that in Latin America, the *supercaudillos* have been the real artisans of our precariously founded nationhood. They succeeded in establishing a system of feudal, personal loyalties over the national territory as a whole; they created the modern, centralized professional armies, and eliminated the armed bands of irregulars that had controlled provinces or regions; they further unified the nation by building the telegraphic networks that allowed news and instructions to be received and relayed rapidly, and the railway facilities and roads that in a few days could dispatch loyal troops, with all their equipment, to the borders of the country—an operation that previously took months.

If we look at the matter from this angle, Bolivia appears as the most unfortunate of the Latin-American countries. It has known an endless series of petty dictators, each of whom in turn managed to seize power and hold it for a brief spell with a maximum of corruption and brutality, but none of whom was endowed with the gifts of the stabilizer, pacifier, and builder

6. "Una remozada galería de dictadores" (A rejuvenated series of dictators), *El Nacional,* Caracas, June 1, 1975.

that were displayed in other countries by such absolute rulers as Rosas, Juan Vicente Gómez, or Porfirio Díaz; none retained control long enough to be called a *caudillo*.

This is not to say that these efficient dictatorships were in any way pleasant to witness let alone to endure. In *Facundo,* Sarmiento related how, between 1835 and 1840, almost every man in Buenos Aires experienced one or more terms of imprisonment. Rosas made a practice of having men jailed in groups of two or three hundred, chosen at random. When they were released two or three months later, their places were taken by others. What had these people done? Nothing at all: this system of arbitrary arrests was simply Rosas's way of teaching proper obedience. The Venezuelan *caudillo* Gómez filled his subjects with such terror that when he died, no one dared publicly to display relief, for fear that the tyrant's demise had been yet another ruse staged by the old fox, who, besides everything else, had acquired a reputation for sorcery and extrasensory perception. Several days passed before people dared show any of their feelings, and almost two months went by before the political consequences of his disappearance from the public scene became manifest. Even then, the system instituted by this *supercaudillo* maintained itself without too much trouble, no doubt partly because of the shrewd and flexible tactics of his successor, the Minister of War, but mainly because of the horror instilled by practices of the late government—such as suspending opponents by the testicles or executing them (as was done with at least one prisoner) by hanging them by the lower jaw from a meat hook. The prevalence of this kind of cruelty filled all Venezuelans who had reached the age of reason by 1935 with fear of the state and its police, a fear that continued even when Gómez's regime of terror came to an end.

The Consular Caudillos

The Spanish American *caudillos,* from the time of independence to the last third of the nineteenth century, found a power base primarily in the class of large landowners. These came to play the role of powerful vassals, whose fidelity the tyrant could count on as long as he maintained the double policy of guaranteeing their privileges while keeping them in terror of himself. Ambitious rivals occasionally emerged from this class, to foment the kind of revolution whose caricatured portrayal, in a comic and folkloric vein, constitutes one of the particularly humiliating aspects of the stereotyped view foreigners have of Spanish America. But once the United States had clearly defined its imperialistic vocation, with the Spanish-American War and the Panama affair, no *caudillo* could rise to prominence in Latin America for over half a century without understanding that henceforth power was to be based primarily on North American support. Once a *caudillo* had understood this and acted on it, his rule was assured, under North American protection.

The Dictionary of the Spanish Royal Academy defines a *cónsul* as a "person accredited by a foreign State to protect its nationals and interests in the country to which he is accredited." Thus consular *caudillos* developed, such as Gómez, who was tacitly delegated by the United States in much the same manner as Rome had delegated Herod to be King of Judea.

Porfirio Díaz, who governed from 1876 to 1910, was another consular *caudillo*. He deliberately extended exorbitant privileges to foreigners and to foreign investors, ostensibly to promote the modernization and unification of the Mexican nation (an effort in which he was largely successful, to Mexico's continuing benefit), but also to secure the protection of the investor countries, primarily the United States.

As United States "consul" in Mexico, Porfirio Díaz, after many years of service, merited an interview with a North American newspaperman. In this conversation, details of both his cruelty and his submissiveness to foreign powers are candidly presented, alongside a discussion of the positive aspects of his rule. The author concluded: "There is not a more romantic or heroic figure in all the world . . . than [this] soldier-statesman, whose adventurous youth pales the pages of Dumas, and whose iron rule has converted the warring, ignorant, superstitious and impoverished masses of Mexico, oppressed by centuries of Spanish cruelty and greed, into a strong, steady, peaceful, debt-paying and progressive nation.

"For twenty-seven years he has governed the Mexican Republic with such power that national elections have become mere formalities."[7]

Before Porfirio Díaz, as he himself said, "neither life nor property was safe." With Díaz, Mexico has risen "among the peaceful and useful nations." Before Porfirio, "there were only two small [railway] lines. . . . [Now] there are more than

7. This quote and those that follow are from James Creelman, in Lewis Hanke, 2nd ed., vol. 2, pp. 293–303.

nineteen thousand miles of railways . . . nearly all with American managers, engineers and conductors. . . ."

Before Porfirio, the mail, carried aboard horse-drawn stage-coaches, was slow, costly, irregular, and unsafe. On a regular trip between Mexico City and Puebla, for example, the mail was frequently the object of two or three holdups. Creelman pointed out—perhaps with some exaggeration—that the national mail network now covered all the national territory, and had become inexpensive, safe, and rapid. Porfirio had the sparse, inefficient telegraph network extended to 75,000 kilometers in good working order. In his own words: "We began by making [damage to telegraph lines] punishable by death and compelling the execution of offenders within a few hours after they were caught. . . . We ordered that wherever telegraph wires were cut and the chief officer of the district did not catch the criminal, he should himself suffer; and in case the cutting occurred on a plantation the proprietor who failed to prevent it should be hanged to the nearest telegraph pole. These were military orders. . . . It was better that a little blood should be shed that much blood should be saved. The blood that was shed was bad blood; the blood that was saved was good blood."

Creelman went on to describe how one billion two hundred million dollars in foreign capital were invested in Mexico thanks to Díaz. In 1908, new investments reached the astounding total of two hundred million dollars a year. "The cities shine with electric lights and are noisy with electric trolley cars; English is taught in the public schools . . . [and] there are nearly seventy thousand foreigners living contentedly and prosperously in the Republic. . . ."

But what earned Díaz the gratitude of the United States was his punctiliousness in the settlement of Mexico's foreign debts. The United States attached particular importance to the repayment of debts by Latin-American states neighboring on the Panama Canal, for reasons discussed in Chapter 3. Creelman related that the price of silver, which at the time was Mexico's main export, dropped sharply just then, and that Don Porfirio's advisers pleaded with him to suspend the repayment of the country's foreign debt. "The President denounced the advice as foolishness as well as dishonesty, and it is a fact that some of the greatest officers of the government went for years without their salaries that Mexico might be able to meet her financial obligations dollar for dollar. . . . Such is Porfirio Díaz, the foremost man of the American hemisphere."

We may question the sincerity of this grossly flattering article, and expect the author to have been well rewarded for it. But we would then have to conclude that Don Porfirio also bought off Elihu Root, the United States Secretary of State, who formulated his admiration in the following terms: "Of all the men now living, General Porfirio Díaz, of Mexico, [is] best worth seeing. Whether one considers the adventurous, daring, chivalric incidents of his early career; whether one considers the vast work of government which his wisdom and courage and commanding character accomplished; whether one considers his singularly attractive personality, no one lives to-day that I would rather see than President Díaz. If I were a poet I would write poetic eulogies. If I were a musician I would compose triumphal marches. If I were a Mexican I should feel that the steadfast loyalty of a lifetime could not be too much in return for the blessings that he had brought to my country. As I am neither poet, musician nor Mexican, but only an American who loves justice and liberty and hopes to see their reign among mankind progress and strengthen and become perpetual, I look to Porfirio Díaz, the President of Mexico, as one of the great men to be held up for the hero-worship of mankind."[8]

The power of consular *caudillos*—among whom Anastasio Somoza of Nicaragua and Rafael Leonidas Trujillo[9] of the Dominican Republic were second-rate specimens—fed on itself. The sale of concessions to foreign investors and the economic activities that directly or indirectly resulted from them brought money to the national treasury; this allowed the consular *caudillos* to offer their officers better pay, their troops better arms, and their partisans greater spoils—all this while repaying the national debt. Porfirio, who brought the system to its point of perfection, offered foreign investors advantages so great that they alone would almost have sufficed to motivate and justify the Mexican xenophobia that followed and that has endured ever since. The United States' support of these consular *caudillos,* so profitable to American interests in the short run, was soon to create wide resentment and difficulties of many sorts in Latin America, which no doubt will continue to erupt in the future.

8. Quoted by James Creelman in Hanke, 2nd ed., vol. 2, pp. 302–03.
9. Franklin D. Roosevelt, who was more lucid, or perhaps more wary, than Root, was once asked to withdraw American support from Trujillo because he (Trujillo) was "a son of a bitch." "Yes," said Roosevelt, "but he is *our* son of a bitch."

The Mexican System

The "positivist" apologists of the Latin-American tyrants felt assured that after a few decades of "peace, order, and work" (the motto of Juan Vicente Gómez) the different countries of the continent would learn to live in civil peace and be ready for democracy. They argued that before Porfirio's accession to power, Mexico had experienced sixty years of bloodshed, but that after benefiting from his rule, it would be blessed with an era of "justice and liberty." This was Root's hope as well.

But in 1910, Mexico became the scene of an explosion of violence unparalleled since in Latin America; indeed, the introduction of more lethal weaponry has made such outbreaks all but impossible without foreign intervention.

Mexico lived in a state of revolution for some twenty years; not until 1929 was a centralized authority able to assume effective control over all the national territory. That year the different *revolutionary* factions were reunited into a single party, which at first was called the National Revolutionary party and then, in 1938, Party of the Mexican Revolution; since 1946 it has had the paradoxical but appropriate name of Institutional Revolutionary party (PRI).

The Mexican system, as it has come to be called, has been criticized on the grounds that it is not a true democracy, but rather an oligarchical democracy, a "directed democracy," rife with graft, entailing a strong dose of "constitutional" lying and hypocrisy, in which little relation exists between what the government says and what it does. At the same time, we must recognize that the Mexican government is not basically tyrannical; it is merely *strong*. And the smoke-screen double-talk it practices may well be, along with other related subterfuges, one of its political virtues, distasteful in a way, but politically successful because it corresponds to Latin-American idiosyncrasies.

Spanish American countries seem willing to tolerate a wide breach between words and deeds. They have produced millions of speeches, issued thousands of press releases, party platforms, manifestoes, parliamentary resolutions, student demands, professional-association statements, thousands of laws and decrees, and hundreds of constitutions. The smallest of Latin-American republics is sure to have been the source of more codes of law than Great Britain.

As we have witnessed, countries frustrated by their lack of

real power find in rhetoric a form of compensation that satisfies those who practice it and those who listen to them. It is worth noting that Juan Vicente Gómez, the Latin-American *caudillo* most satisfied and secure in his power, remained a very discreet, even a taciturn, *caudillo:* he was not interested in being hailed as an intellectual or a leader of international stature. But he was an exception. Usually Latin-American leaders chafe at their relative insignificance on the international scene, even when they are unquestionably the master at home, and tend to drown their self-doubts in endless oratory. And this is all the more true of men on the lower rungs of power.

The Latin-American masses, at the bottom of the social ladder, may not be able to express their feelings, but they expect their leaders to speak for them; they are ready to follow a leader who knows how to fit words to the dreams that lie deep in their collective psyche. Demagogues can thus make their way on the steppingstones of this basic, pervasive psychological need: witness Juan Domingo Perón.

The most remarkable feature of the Mexican system is that it has made revolutionary rhetoric the chief and permanent fulcrum of a political machinery controlled by neither a demagogue nor a *caudillo,* but by a "common man" (these days usually a technocrat) who will hold the presidency for a single six-year term.

Mexico has virtually a one-party system. The PRI does not seek to learn what the people want, but claims to interpret the popular will through symbolic elections in which it invariably claims for itself over ninety percent of the votes; each President in turn is the absolute leader, a virtual monarch for the set term of his rule—but no longer. The other cogs of power, such as Congress or the judiciary, may be seen as stage props to varying degrees, dependent on the President's will. The same holds true of the armed forces, which in other Latin-American countries constitute such a steady threat to stability. The news media either are directly controlled by the government or keep their criticism within limits.[10] The private sector of the economy exists in symbiosis with the government and the PRI, as do labor unions and the farmers' associations.

In fact, the PRI has succeeded in controlling, directly or

10. The government has the means to exert different forms of pressure on the media it does not control directly. For example, it holds a monopoly on the import or manufacture of newsprint.

indirectly, all the special-interest groups of Mexican society, as well as all shades of political opinion except the extreme right, the Manchester liberals,[11] and the Maoist, Guevarist left.[12]

This is not to say that all sectors of the population are satisfied that they have proper hearing or representation, or that the basic social problems have been solved. The peasantry still lives in poverty, and migrants from rural areas crowd the shantytowns that surround the main cities, while millions of Indians lead a marginal existence in Mexican society. But relations between the different interests within the country, and the apportioning of appointments within the system, are carried on in an orderly and acceptable manner, under the supervision of the PRI.

The secret of the system's viability and longevity—qualities rare on the Latin-American political scene—lies in two factors: the President cannot seek re-election (this is an absolute rule that so far has been scrupulously respected); but he is all-powerful during his tenure, and practically appoints his successor.[13] When he hands over the presidency to the new incumbent, he does so without any reservations. The newcomer will be the one, new, shining star in the political firmament; he will need to fear no rivals, and will not allow anyone else to share the public limelight with him.

As in Sieyès's *Tiers Etat*, this new Sun President, who until his nomination was nothing, now suddenly is all. His nomination as candidate by the PRI, and hence his certain election to the presidency, is not made public till the very last moment, and he himself traditionally plays a discreet role till that time; it is said that he is "in hiding." Once his selection as official candidate has been made public, he sets off on what appears to be a classic electoral campaign, through which he becomes

11. The reference is to the Manchester school of Cobden and Bright, the "Apostles of Free Trade."
12. In recent years, the students have constituted a source of trouble for the system. But, as in other countries of Latin America, students stop dissenting as soon as they graduate from the university; each then goes his or her own way to further personal ambitions.
13. Mexican political scientists are reluctant to admit this. They make the perfectly well founded observation that there are limits to the President's freedom in choosing his successor. He could not, for example, nominate his wife, as did Governor Wallace of Alabama. But however we look at the question, the Minister of the Interior is almost invariably nominated as the PRI candidate. If the President holds out hope to other ministers, it is in order to keep his options open and to stave off a premature transfer of power. Nor is there a single case on record of the new nominee's *not* being a member of the outgoing President's Cabinet; we may say that the President is assembling candidates for his succession when he selects his Cabinet.

known to people and solicits the broad support of which he definitely stands in need. For this plain, uncharismatic citizen, whose name until the day before was still quite obscure, must now make himself recognized as the new embodiment of the perennial revolutionary rhetoric. He achieves this by donning the mantle of nationalism, egalitarianism, anti-imperialism; he becomes the champion of the Third World, of the native (the noble savage), the peasant, the worker, et cetera. His inauguration marks his apotheosis as the newly anointed standard-bearer of the revolution, in neat coincidence with the final setting of his predecessor's sun.

Common sense dictates a double task for the ruler: he has to control the social body, and at the same time he has to induce the various, largely centrifugal component forces of society to be tolerant of and patient with his leadership. If we grant that the process of government, through its very operation, tends with time to arouse discontent among the governed, the Mexican pattern of ruling out from the start the possibility of renewed tenure for the President has much to recommend it, for it allows outsiders or contenders on the fringes of power to hope that some day their moment will come. Whether this hope proves founded or not is not the point here. The fact is that the ambitious are far less tempted to force a "noninstitutional solution," as a *Putsch* is called in Latin America.

We could say, more bluntly, that the swarm of men who have derived profit from the existing regime, and who naturally clustered in widening circles around the outgoing President, are in due course forced to relinquish their positions—and to do so in good will, as it were, without conflict—and hand over power to the swarms forming around the new leader.

But we should not overlook the positive aspects of the Mexican system. Mexico has experienced nearly fifty years of stability, from 1929 to the present, while other Latin-American countries have been prey to far worse governments, or, like Chile and Cuba, victims of national tragedies. At the same time as it makes for stability, the Mexican pattern prevents the sclerosis of power—as was witnessed, for example, at the end of Porfirio Díaz's rule, when an unduly extended term of office led to blatant gerontocracy.

Some may argue that the Mexican model would not have such favorable results but for the nearness of the United States. The formidable neighbor to the north may exacerbate problems in the Mexican national psyche, but revolutionary rhetoric keeps these from becoming unbearable. And the United States also stimulates economic development, through the massive influx of North American tourists and the steadily growing export of Mexican manufactured goods. A substantial quantity of these goods are produced by North American firms attracted to Mexico by the lower wages, by trust that Mexico will maintain good relations with the United States, and by preferential trade agreements. (Mexico chose not to join OPEC in order not to be automatically deprived of the advantages that a new law on foreign trade, passed in 1974 by the United States Congress, grants "developing countries" other than OPEC members.) The common border also provides an opportunity to help relieve population pressure, through clandestine emigration to the United States. This "geographic privilege," already operative under Porfirio Díaz, has gained further momentum since 1940, when Mexico started capitalizing on the United States' formidable war and postwar expansion. Thus it has found in its proximity to the United States a significant, and possibly a decisive, factor for economic growth and political stability.

The Military "Party"

I have noted that one of the chief successes of the Mexican political system has been the effective neutralization of the military, and this at a time when the development of increasingly powerful weapons has caused armies throughout the world to play an ever-greater role in political affairs. In Latin America, there have been two distinct ways in which military men have reached the presidency. Formerly, successful *caudillos*, men without formal military training, automatically became "generals" and chiefs of the armed forces through the same process that carried them to supreme power. More recently, career officers have become President simply by happening to hold the highest rank at the time the armed forces intervened "institutionally." I have already analyzed the first process in my study of *caudillismo*, and will now examine the second.[14]

The first armies of independent Spanish America were those, perforce improvised, of the wars of independence. At

14. Fidel Castro rose to power in the first of these ways. This is another reason he can be more readily understood if examined within the framework of Latin-American *caudillismo*.

the same time, the old order and stability were being destroyed, which caused the emergence of *caudillismo*. From approximately the middle of the nineteenth century, at different rates in the various countries, regular armed forces were to emerge, which invariably ended up wielding excessive influence on political affairs. Nor could this have been otherwise in ill-structured, undisciplined nations, in which a ruling class worthy of the name hardly existed, in which the middle classes had emerged only recently and were timorous and indecisive, and in which the popular masses were quite unable to imagine that they would ever play a role in decision making. In this relative vacuum, the armed forces came to constitute a dominant institution—more effective, or less ineffective, than others. The military had the advantage of sharing a sense of values that encompassed discipline, unity, *esprit de corps*— and of being able to transmit clear and concrete instructions in an organized and effective manner. Thus they were committed professionally to certain socially useful attitudes that were far from widespread in Latin-American societies. In recent years, they have even become, or claim to have become, more proficient than many civilians in disciplines that, although unconnected to the military profession, are included in the curriculums of the war colleges. Note that military schools have not experienced the difficulties and setbacks of the civilian universities; they are the only institutions of higher learning that have not had to suffer the assaults of the Castro-Guevarists and that have therefore maintained or even improved their academic standards. Furthermore, graduates of the military academies frequently also study civilian disciplines and become qualified sociologists, physicians, lawyers, psychologists, anthropologists, and so on.

In the pursuit of their career, officers know that their professional advancement is contingent on their steady adherence to a program of continuing education; and while their professional viewpoints and ambitions are naturally shaped by the traditions and prejudices of their profession, the more intelligent among them learn from war games to consider issues from a wide strategic angle. Thus, though they are not basically different from other Latin Americans, or superior to them, their training and the theoretical problems they have had to face at all levels—particularly at general-staff level— prepare them to regard political questions in a global context.

Latin-American officers belong to a sort of international freemasonry. They attend advanced courses and seminars in various institutes in the United States, Europe, and Latin America, or at the Center for Anti-Subversive Tactics, which the United States has set up in the Canal Zone. These meetings, along with others that are organized by the Inter-American Reciprocal Assistance Treaty, allow officers from different nations systematically to compare their views and methods. The mutual distrust that understandably exists among members of less homogeneous Latin-American professional groups is much less prevalent among the military of different nations.

It could be argued that the armed forces of each of the Latin-American countries other than Mexico, once they have become professional and institutionalized, constitute to all practical purposes another political party: no doubt a special kind of party, but in any case a permanent element of the political scene. They thus become a "spare tire" party, the nation's last resort when civilian political structures prove unable to surmount a crisis, or to rally contending elements under a single workable authority.[15] In this sense, military intervention in politics may be viewed as an "institutional" step, rather than as a "noninstitutional," outside force, as is usually claimed: a predictable step to which the nation resorts whenever it requires exceptional measures to regain its balance, or to clear the ground for a new redistribution of power.

The Venezuelan crises of 1945 and 1948 exemplify these two situations. In 1945, the country's system of government was immobilized by the oligarchy that had inherited control of the state from Juan Vicente Gómez's protracted regime and was resolved to stay in power. This oligarchy failed to understand that after the Second World War it was no longer possible to repress the ideas and aspirations of the new middle class—or to take for granted the passivity and obedience of the workers and peasants, who were now being worked on by Aprist teachings spread by university students and graduates from the middle classes and the provinces. The armed forces stepped in, allowing the Venezuelan Aprist party, Democratic Action, to assume power and initiate an ambitious project of social, economic, and institutional reform. But three years later, the party's unwillingness or inability to let other groups play a role in the government led to its political isolation. All

15. "Latin-American militarism should not be blamed on the military. It is due to our [civilian] political movements that have not been able to understand our respective countries, and have created [power] vacuums. These vacuums have then been filled by the only organized institution that exists in the Latin-American countries." (Carlos Andrés Pérez, President of Venezuela, press conference, Mexico, March 22, 1975.)

other sectors in the country came to view Democratic Action's too-exclusive approach to governing as a threat, a step toward a one-party system that would display all the shortcomings, but none of the strengths, of the Mexican system. The military stepped in once again, and cut short this threat, real or imagined. Democratic Action made a comeback as the governing party eleven years later; by then it had developed into a much more mature movement, able to take a new approach to the task of governing. This time it drew on the participation of other groups, and a much more stable political system resulted, even though this second chance coincided with the Cuban Revolution, so unsettling to Aprism as a whole.

An interesting variation of this pattern occurs when a military dictator brought to power by a coup d'état forgets his position of "delegate of the armed forces" and tries to act as a *caudillo*, the dictatorial leader of the armed forces. In such a situation, the army usually topples the would-be *caudillo* first, then withdraws to its barracks, and leaves overt political action to the civilian parties by re-establishing political and civil rights and creating the preconditions for free elections.

This description, which explains the need for the "military party" and summarizes its pattern of action, applies to the period of one-half to three-fourths of a century that separated the foundation of professional armies in Latin-American countries from the watershed of the Cuban Revolution. Castro's success has led the Latin-American military to reconsider precisely what elements of a crisis constitute a threat to their unity or even their existence—and call for a *Putsch*. To understand how much this question means to them, we must remember that not only their instinct for survival, but also their *esprit de corps* and ideology, lead them to view the armed forces as the very heart and cornerstone of the nation. The lessons of the Cuban Revolution—in which the army was dissolved, and its officers were dragged to trials reminiscent of Roman circus games and condemned to death or imprisonment—were not lost on them. They began detecting signs of an impending constitutional crisis—which would implicate them and drag the army into a general collapse of the political system—not only in the familiar power vacuums that had triggered their take-over in the past, but in a wide range of governmental actions or nonactions as well.

A parallel could be drawn between these "new armed forces" and the "new Church," which I discussed in Chapter 6. Like the Church, the Latin-American army commands have started to face the question of their institutional survival in a new global political context, which elsewhere (i.e., in Cuba) has led to uncontrollable and irreversible change. Not surprisingly, the military have displayed much less subtlety than the Church in their maneuvering, and have appraised the situation in tactical terms, and in a regional rather than ecumenical framework. The Church operates in much easier and more flexible conditions. It is free to try to adapt itself to the most radical changes, renege on former commitments when it finds it has sided with a hopeless cause; it can even, when it wishes, establish contacts at the highest level with the "enemy," and negotiate with him as with an equal. It can welcome, or discreetly encourage, individual commitments, and flirt and play along with the "revolution"; it can even allow the preaching of "new wave" policies, for it retains the right at any time to suspend its priests, place them under an interdict, or excommunicate them. But the armed forces know no such flexibility. If they act, it must be in a straightforward manner that commits the institution as a whole, taking on responsibility openly and absolutely, with all the risks this entails. Within these limitations, however, the armed forces have several options, varying in strategy from the Brazilian to the Peruvian pattern of action, which I shall now discuss.

The Brazilian Model

Well before 1964, the Brazilian Army command had made up their minds on how to lead Brazil to the great future the country had so long been promised but never had reached—a situation that inspired the cruel joke that Brazil was, always had been, and always would remain a country with a great future. The army command developed a clear blueprint for its takeover and future policy, under the influence of a group of high-level civilian lecturers at the War College. These were men who had succeeded in staying aloof from the political disorders that followed the suicide of the civilian *caudillo* Getulio Vargas in 1954, and also from the attendant period of financial irresponsibility and galloping inflation. The conclusion they reached was that, far from allowing itself to be goaded into confrontation with the United States, Brazil should seek to become a major economic and military power in Latin America, friendly to Washington and able to serve as a stabilizing pole and a center for anti-Soviet influence, economic and political.

They were convinced that the United States would look favorably upon Brazil's emergence on the scene as a major power, able to relieve the United States of some concerns in this part of the globe. Thus, once Brazil was properly governed, stable, and practicing an *ad hoc* foreign policy, it could hope to be a Western bastion in the South American continent, drawing active assistance from the United States. One might even imagine Brazil extending its influence to the western coast of Africa and, through Portuguese-speaking Mozambique, to the Indian Ocean.

In this connection, I must repeat the observation stressed in the first pages of this book: that generalizations about Latin America are not applicable to Brazil. No Latin-American country other than Brazil could project itself into the role of a great world power. And yet Brazil shares its Iberian origins, as well as its historic development and its national character, with the rest of the continent. Now, the policies of civilians constitute one of the areas in which the Portuguese-speaking nation shows the fewest affinities with other Latin-American countries, and where there is the least sympathy, understanding, and communication. The policies and actions of Brazilian civilian leaders such as Getulio Vargas, Juscelino Kubitschek, Janio Quadros, or Joao Goulart were difficult to understand in Caracas, Lima, or Buenos Aires. But Goulart's elimination by the Brazilian armed forces was something Spanish Americans readily understood, and with which the military of other Latin-American countries could readily identify. For the first time in the twentieth century, the armed forces of a Latin-American country were seizing power without expressing or even implying any intention of returning to "normal" political processes after a certain length of time, a limitation that was often agreed to beforehand. Thus they put an end to the consecrated pattern through which the primacy of the Constitution was upheld—even though elections usually served the purpose of bestowing on a *de facto* President the legitimacy of constitutional recognition. Goulart's replacement was something very different: the junta that was taking over categorically refused to promise elections, even at some indeterminate future date.

The second new and surprising element was the Brazilian military's firm and immediate resolution to proscribe the whole stratum of high civilian personnel that had manned the key posts of the state in the last decades, thus creating a break, a kind of political *cordon sanitaire,* between past and future political leadership.

Thirdly, the "revolutionary" military government undertook the ruthless repression of any pro-Soviet political action, whether open or clandestine, in the nation's life, including the universities.[16]

Finally, the new military leaders and their civilian advisers ("technocrats" such as economists Roberto Campos and Delfín Neto) initiated a new plan of economic recovery. Some have disingenuously argued, and others misguidedly believed, that this plan sought to foster the primacy of the private sector. On the contrary, it was proposed to strengthen the *public* sector of the economy, which was already very powerful and extensive. It emphasized a program of government guidance that aimed primarily toward controlling inflation, while stimulating and guaranteeing savings and attracting the foreign investments needed to step up exports.

This "Brazilian revolution," as it is called, was conceived by men who viewed the nation's problems in their totality. Today, after having watched the new policy in effect for twelve years, we would be foolish to deny that it has been fairly successful, in its own terms and deliberately chosen policies, particularly if we bear in mind developments in other Latin-American countries.[17] The military government's financial policies have given the country the impetus it required for economic growth, and have come close to reaching the targets the government set itself. The interior provinces and all the country's borders have been opened up to travel from the settled coastline by a vast new road network. Until the slowdown of the economy that resulted from the fourfold increase in the price of oil in 1974 (Brazil is a big oil-importer), expansion had progressed at a rate of 10 percent per annum, or more. Inflation was finally brought under control and stabilized at a figure that, although still very high (20 to 25 percent a year), is predictable and manageable. This stabilization has been achieved through a system of readjustments in prices, wages, credits, and bank interest rates that deserves to be widely studied— particularly now, when an inflation rate of 20 percent is no

16. This repression has been called Brazilian "fascism." The Marxist–Leninist–Third World ideologists apply this term of opprobrium to any government that tends to oppose pro-Sovietism—whatever its position may be on other matters. Correspondingly, they carefully keep from applying the term to any government, however militaristic, repressive, or chauvinistic, whose overall policy happens to serve Soviet strategy.

17. In the same way, we may call the Mexican system a success. It is interesting to note that Brazil's adoption of the principle of not renewing the presidential term of office is obviously based on the success this practice met with in Mexico.

longer characteristic only of Latin America. Universities have been renovated, their productivity has been improved, and priority has been given to scientific and technological training.

At the same time, to check the desperate and violent resistance of the extreme left to its political death sentence, the government has resorted to methods comparable to those used by the most brutal *caudillos*. From 1971 on, the government might have allowed itself to be less repressive, but did not think it expedient (or possible) to dismantle its police apparatus, in which torture and arbitrary treatment had become institutionalized practices. It would seem that in our day only a repressive regime, of one ideological tinge or another, is able to enforce strict curtailment of the purchasing power of the majority of citizens, a limitation that is required for accelerated capital accumulation and rapid economic growth.

Between 1964 and 1969, the real earning power of the lowest-paid Brazilian workers fell by 30 percent, while the average earnings of university graduates rose by 50 percent. No doubt this, too, had been planned and worked out prior to the military coup d'état, and constitutes an essential element of the general design of what has been called the Brazilian model.

Peronism

From 1966 to 1970, Argentine officers under the leadership of General Juan Carlos Ongania made an attempt to institute a government on the Brazilian model. They were unsuccessful, for a number of reasons. Argentine society was far less pliable; it had already reached a higher level of culture and consumer expectation than Brazil; unlike Brazil, Argentina no longer seriously thought that as a nation it had a great destiny; finally, it had been deeply shaken and intoxicated by the fascist demagogy of Juan Domingo Perón. By 1970 the Ongania government had clearly failed to make Argentina accept the Brazilian formula, and was therefore replaced by another military government, this time of the "constitutionalist" model described earlier: an interim regime designed to transfer power to civilian politicians through elections. In this case, the process resulted in Perón's restoration in September 1973, as elected President.

The example of Argentina, clearly the most successful Latin-American country, is proof of the difficulty Latin-American culture experiences in overcoming its characteristic neuroses, particularly its inferiority complex vis-à-vis the United States.

Argentina was foremost among Latin-American nations in admitting as self-evident the political, social, and economic advancement of North American society compared to its own, and in attempting to adapt North American institutions, laws, and even attitudes and behavior patterns, as a means to its own development. Argentines saw themselves as especially well adapted to this approach, and came to flatter themselves that they were about to succeed. I have already mentioned that the "classic" Argentine Constitution of 1853 was so closely modeled on that of the United States that Argentine jurists faced with constitutional problems have occasionally appealed to North American precedents. Argentina also followed the United States in implementing a policy of open immigration; like the United States, it admitted on favorable terms the European capital it needed to finance the infrastructure of its ambitious agricultural development, its railway construction, its ports and cold-storage facilities. Like the United States (and unlike any other Latin-American country), it vigorously encouraged popular education. And Argentina was properly rewarded for all this with a spectacular economic and cultural surge. By 1910, one hundred years after independence, the country appeared more European than Latin American, entirely free of the slowdown and hopelessness in which the rest of the subcontinent lived. To Argentines' thinking, their country was on its way to becoming equal and even superior to the United States.

However, this policy, taken over from a very different society, ultimately did not suffice to erase a deeply rooted cultural difference. For Argentina the period between 1860 and 1910 constituted a half century of illusion as well as of achievement: the country succeeded in achieving a resemblance to the United States, but in fact it resembled the United States only as a hothouse plant resembles its wild sister flourishing in its natural habitat. The Argentine hothouse, the milieu in which the Argentines felt they were building a "southern colossus" able to rival the United States, was in fact an oligarchic democracy whose ruling class was allied to enormously wealthy cattle interests.

The Argentine plant grew so well that it ended by smashing through the glass panes of its hothouse; and out in the native air, exposed to universal suffrage, oligarchic democracy became chaotic democracy, full of inner contradictions, demagogical, ineffectual, incapable of holding in check the factions and the forces of disintegration that are characteristic of Hispanic societies. In such circumstances, and in spite of its prosperity, Argentina failed to make the transition from rapid growth and capital accumulation to a wider distribution of wealth and power. In 1933, the United States responded to its great crisis very appropriately, with Franklin Roosevelt's New Deal. Argentina failed to meet the same challenge with a suitable response; instead it experienced a series of convulsions that started with a military coup d'état in 1930, led to Perón (1945), and has not ended yet.

The United States was not immune to the virus of fascism, but in the North American context Mussolini's and Hitler's gospel proved attractive only to a minority. Roosevelt, an embodiment of the United States' genius for political self-renewal, rose to the occasion; he conceived a policy that halted the prevailing, self-destructive *laissez faire* and gave guarantees to the labor movement (already deeply rooted in the States—a native son in no way alienated from North American society as a whole).

By contrast, fascism held a great attraction for Argentines, especially army officers like Juan Domingo Perón, who had been military attaché in Rome and spent a long time with Mussolini's Alpine troops. Fascism offered a political alternative that not only was radically different from the crushed illusion of successfully emulating the United States, but also was actively anti–North American, antidemocratic, anti-Communist, populist, and nationalist. Here was a "philosophy" able to soothe the wounded pride of a frustrated country.

From 1939 on, Argentine industry had grown rapidly in response to the war situation, which prevented the import of European and North American manufactured goods. This industrial boom was further stimulated by the government through a policy of financial and political support. By 1943, there were more workers employed in industry (the very great majority in Buenos Aires) than in agriculture or ranching. The situation was propitious for Perón. He may not have been the only Latin-American officer seduced by fascism, but he was the only one who had Argentina as an operational field and who displayed the daring and political acumen to capitalize on an aspect of fascism or Nazism that is not always sufficiently emphasized today: its ability to galvanize crowds through a mixture of unabashed demagogy and grossly chauvinistic nationalism. Besides, once he was in power, Perón, like the other fascist demagogues, showed himself ready to give some substance to his promises to the industrial workers: he improved their working conditions, and gave them higher real wages and a populist style of government.

After the military coup of June 1943, Perón was made Director of the National Labor Department—an undersecretaryship others had turned down. From that apparently modest power base, he set about strengthening the existing labor unions and creating new ones. He also instituted a control system that benefited the unions protected by the Labor Department (that is to say, by himself). As Director of Labor, later as Minister of Labor and Social Security, then as Vice President, he showed his readiness to settle issues in favor of the working man. As one labor leader put it: "Finally, here is an official who does not automatically side with management, but shares our concerns, resolves our problems, and even teaches us how to watch over our interests!" Within the government, Perón steadfastly made himself the spokesman of factory workers, recommending labor reforms, housing developments, health and social security programs, and so forth. In two years, he became the most powerful man in the military government. The officers around him grew concerned, and in October 1945, he was dismissed and imprisoned.

Evita Duarte then came into the limelight. Perón's mistress and a third-rate actress, she showed a real sense of leadership at this critical juncture and organized an enormous demonstration. The workers who took part (*los descamisados*, "the shirtless ones") occupied the heart of Buenos Aires and refused to vacate it as long as Perón was not released. On October 17, Perón was freed; he was unmistakably in control of a new political situation. His first move was to marry Evita; then he announced his candidacy as the head of a new party in the presidential elections scheduled for February 1946. At first he called his organization, whose political platform was a loose adaptation of Mussolini's Fascism, the "Labor party"; later he gave it the name of Justicialismo.

Perón earned the Church's support by suggesting that the "new Argentina" would encourage a close alliance between the Catholic faith and the state, to check the secular free thinking propagated by foreign liberal and Marxist influences which had been poisoning the fatherland in the last years. The United States Ambassador inadvertently brought more popular votes to the Peronist cause, through public statements announcing his government's displeasure with the growing success of a notable sympathizer of the Nazi-Fascist Axis. Perón's triumph at the elections was legitimate, shattering, unassailable. He easily won the presidency, while his party took two-thirds of the seats in the House and all but two in the Senate.

At the time of Perón's accession to the presidency, Argentina had accumulated enormous financial reserves, due to an exceptionally favorable balance of trade during the five years of the Second World War. But in record time he succeeded in turning that surplus into a deficit, through his policy of stimulating consumption and promoting economic activities that flattered Argentine ultranationalism but were costly and unproductive. He nationalized public services; the railways, which until then had been making profits under private (foreign) ownership, were soon burdened with skyrocketing operating expenses and in the red. Wages and other benefits for industrial workers were increased by decree, without any consideration of productivity. Consumption was subsidized. To pay for all this, as well as for an extravagant project of industrial self-sufficiency, heavy taxes in the worst Spanish mercantile tradition were placed on the sectors to which the economy owed its prosperity—namely, agriculture and ranching. In general, the relation between costs and sales prices was artificially restructured, to the immediate material and psychological benefit of the *descamisados*.[18] This earned Perón the lasting support of unionized workers in Buenos Aires, who still call a pleasant spring day a "Peronist day."

But Argentina has been practically ungovernable ever since. The crisis that crippled President Isabel Perón's[19] mandate, in June and July of 1975, can be traced to yet another effort by a post-Peronist government to rescue the country from the economic unrealism into which her late husband had plunged it between 1946 and 1950.

Evita Perón died in 1952; when he lost her, Perón lost part of what, without any doubt, had been a shared charisma. Although popular in its origins, Justicialismo, like all forms of fascism, tended to be repressive, pretentious, and obscurantist.

---

18. One of the negative and irreversible consequences of Perón's economic policy was to heighten the tendency, ever-present in Hispanic and particularly in Spanish American societies, toward giving up the productive fields of agriculture and ranching for industrial, commercial, and administrative city-based activities. Buenos Aires boomed and became more than ever the parasitic capital of a hypercephalic nation.
19. Perón's second wife, who was his Vice President, inherited power on his death in 1974.

It now became a brutal police regime. The daily *La Prensa,* Argentina's great paper and one of the foremost in the Spanish language, was banned because of its opposition to the government. Public administration set records for corruption; the state's incessant interference in private business inhibited the development of any significant economic activity outside government "protection." Galloping inflation began to erode the earlier, spectacular rise in the real wages of industrial workers. Even Perón's "ultranationalism" turned against him when he tried to salvage the badly threatened economy by granting oil-prospecting rights to foreign corporations. The Church had been alienated earlier; now the armed forces resolutely turned their back on him, when certain of his friends started talking of the creation of paramilitary brigades comparable to the Nazi SS.[20] It is difficult to say whether these Peronists were speak-

20. Thousands of Nazi officers, including Adolf Eichmann, received a friendly welcome in Argentina after the defeat of Hitler's Germany. Peronist fascism naturally had an anti-Semitic aspect, and stressed that Argentina had let itself be contaminated by diverse "cosmopolitan" elements—in particular by the large Jewish minority. The following "poetical" incitation to pogroms appeared in the Peronist magazine *El Caudillo* as late as May 1975:

Today is the day we break everything.
Nine o'clock in the evening is the right time.
You are invited to come and destroy the enemy outposts.
When everything is burning, they'll know whether we meant business or not.
Let the fire join the cries, the cries the night, the night the smoke, the smoke the neighborhood, the flames the flames. Let us be fire.
The world remembers only that which is brutal and great.
You will be paid a reward for every usurer who runs away in fear.
Bring the torches, the whips, the chains, the tar, the pipes, the bottles, and to be sure, the weapons.
The neighboring kilns will supply the bricks as usual.
Throw stones! Let them fly!
Hurry! They will hit the mark!
Let a thousand bricks fly toward the sky,
Each one seeking its own target,
Each on its own trajectory, going through store windows, splintering the panes, the bricks have the floor!!!
For those Jews who die of fear, without being touched,
There will be a double reward.
We recommend piling up at street corners the contemporary horrors that go under the name of art.
Don't get the pyres mixed up.
Don't get them confused.
Order is what we want.
To each thing its own stake . . .
Let us carefully apportion our diverse and motley hate.
Let us separate our black and white hatred.
Fire! Fire everywhere!
Let us fire our hatred red-hot.
Our masterly hatred will run the moneylenders from the temple,

ing seriously or in jest, but the Argentine officer class had not forgotten Hitler's success in subduing the Reichswehr. In September 1955, a military coup d'état removed Perón from power, on the grounds of excessive administrative corruption. The *descamisados* staged a few weak demonstrations in favor of the dictator, under the pitiful slogan: "We want Perón, honest or crooked." Perón temporarily disappeared from the scene, but the irresponsible and corrupt trade-union system he had set up lived on to plague later governments. From his exile, Perón assiduously cultivated and encouraged the most diverse factions at home, leading each to believe that it would eventually have his special blessing when he returned to power.

More of the Same

Many groups took the bait, including the Marxists—not only the orthodox Communists, but also, starting in 1959, the Castroists and the Guevarists. Because Perón had been anti–North American, and the United States had been anti-Peronist, the Castroists came to look upon the President in exile as a kind of messiah, and upon his delegate, Héctor Cámpora, as his prophet. They seemed to have forgotten the style of Perón's government from 1946 to 1955, as well as the successive stops he made during his exile, which took him from Stroessner's Paraguay to Pérez Jiménez's Venezuela, with a brief stopover in Panama (where he met María Estela—"Isabelita"—Martínez); then to Rafael Leonidas Trujillo's Dominican Republic, and finally to Franco's Spain, where he settled in 1960.

By 1973, the Argentine armed forces had convinced them-

That they may have nowhere to come back to. . . .
They have sucked our blood and they have fleeced us.
It is right that they should pay with their blood.
Let us encircle the [Jewish] neighborhood. None will be allowed to leave
    without prior notice,
And proper permission.
Feel free to plunder, requisition, do anything you wish. . . .
May a thousand cudgels come down, a thousand skulls crack!
Impure books will be burned separately.
All around, post bills to tell people what is going on.
Let everything be destroyed. Then we will level the ruins. . . .
In the morning, we'll meet at street corners. Cheer the fatherland,
Sing songs of hope. Shake off the dust a bit. Say good-bye. Take up our
    place in the ranks again.
Breathe in deeply. Go home again!

selves, or had let themselves be convinced by Perón (who certainly offered them guarantees), that there was only one way out of Argentina's permanent political crisis: Peronist participation in the elections. In Madrid, Perón entrusted his flunky Cámpora with the task of wearing his colors at an election whose outcome was not in doubt. On election day, May 25, 1973, Cámpora appeared at the balcony of the Pink House surrounded by Presidents Allende of Chile and Dorticós of Cuba. On the square below, flags proclaimed: "Chile, Cuba: the Argentine people greet you." Hundreds of Latin-American Marxists of lesser stature than Allende or Dorticós had come over as to a new Mecca, and assembled that same evening amid the crowd that surrounded the Villa Devoto prison, waiting for Cámpora's government to issue its first order, which was the unconditional liberation of the hundreds of underground fighters: Montoneros ("leftist" Peronists), members of the People's Revolutionary Army (Guevarists).

Cámpora left the scene when he had fulfilled his limited assignment and had made possible the transition from military government to Perón's return; in leaving, he took on himself responsibility for any "softness" toward the Marxist *guerrilleros* who for so many years had defied military power. In October, new elections gave the presidency to Perón, with 62 percent of the votes, as compared to Cámpora's earlier 52 percent. Three months later, at a press conference at the Pink House, a 29-year-old leftist Peronist journalist, Ana Guzetti, asked the President this question: "What will be the government's stand concerning the police groups that are even now busy murdering the members of revolutionary organizations?" Amid the general consternation, and not hiding his anger, Perón replied: "Can you prove what you say?" "The recent murders of popular and labor activists prove it, Mr. President," Ana Guzetti insisted.

On the spot, and in front of the journalists, Perón gave the order to "profer charges against this young lady." "Mr. President, I am a Peronist activist," said Ana Guzetti. "Congratulations, you certainly know how to hide it," replied Perón. *El Mundo*, the newspaper that employed Ana Guzetti, was suppressed soon after this on the charge of "encouraging guerrilla activities." The young journalist found herself unemployed when *La Calle*, another newspaper where she had found work, was banned for reasons of "state security." During a mammoth demonstration somewhat later, Perón expressly disavowed the slogans carried by Montoneros and members of the People's

Revolutionary Army, who left the demonstration in protest. This put an end to the illusions of those who seriously believed that Perón had switched from fascism to Communism during his stay in Franco's Madrid.

These details need to be filled in to make clear that the AAA (Argentine Anti-Communist Alliance), the rightist terrorist organization that, working hand in hand with the police, is still murdering left-wing activists, was not the "post-Peronist" creation of José López Rega, Perón's trusted astrologer and his gray eminence in his last years—an excuse offered by some in the hope of preserving Perón's image (and Evita's) for posterity. The organization was part of Perón's system of repression; and Perón himself was a brutal and unscrupulous demagogue, one of the most pernicious false heroes of our Latin-American history.[21]

The Difficult Task of the Democrats

Political leaders and statesmen committed to the ideals and achievements of the liberal revolution are not quite absent from the Latin-American scene. But their limited reputation, as compared to that of the *caudillos*, demagogues, and tyrants, serves to prove how little respect the world pays to decency and moderation in politics. In his *Decline and Fall of the Roman Empire*, Gibbon mentioned Augustus's advice to his successors to keep within their inherited boundaries. This counsel of moderation was followed by his immediate successors, but transgressed after the accession of Trajan. Gibbon commented, "As long as mankind shall continue to bestow more liberal applause on their destroyers than on their benefactors, the thirst of military glory will ever be the vice of the most exalted characters." As long as men reserve their praise, their admiration, and their romantic longings for murderous leaders who dispense with civilized political conduct in the name of "revolution," while dismissing true democrats as

21. Ana Guzetti was kidnapped on April 29, 1975, following Perón's death, presumably by the AAA. It seemed certain she would never be heard from again: since the end of 1973, a shocking number of disappearances or murders of left-wing activists has been recorded in Argentina, more than matching the high number of murders, kidnappings, and other acts of terrorism by the extreme left, which has since gone underground once again. An "insurrectional focal point" was started in Tucumán Province, about five hundred kilometers north of Buenos Aires. Ana Guzetti unexpectedly reappeared alive: her captors had only beaten her.

"mere reformers," Stalin will have more followers than Léon Blum, Clement Attlee, or Walther Rathenau; Fidel Castro and Perón will be "in," and Rómulo Betancourt, Eduardo Frei, Rafael Caldera, and Carlos Andrés Pérez will be "out."

The European or North American reader may not even be familiar with these four political figures: they are the most recent exemplary democratic, "reformist" leaders to have held power in Latin America. Frei, who was President of Chile from 1964 to 1970, and Caldera, who was president of Venezuela from 1969 to 1974, are the two most remarkable Christian Democratic leaders of the Western Hemisphere. Betancourt and Pérez have been Presidents of Venezuela, the former from 1945 to 1947 and from 1959 to 1963, the latter since 1974; both are social democrats.

Following the death of Juan Vicente Gómez in 1935, Rómulo Betancourt, who is now nearly seventy years old, set out to create the Venezuelan Aprist party, Democratic Action, which for the last thirty years—alternately in power and in legal or underground opposition—has dominated the country's political life, defined its aims, and helped Venezuela progress toward them. In his youth, Betancourt was attracted to Marxism-Leninism, but later he switched to the views of Haya de la Torre,[22] which he felt were far more adapted to the Latin-American situation. Like Haya, Betancourt refused to give the Comintern the kind of servile obedience that the orthodox Communists demanded. He felt not only that automatic alignment with Comintern directives was humiliating, but also that a policy that was dictated from abroad, and did not take into account the cultural diversity of nations, was bound to fail. Communists had no standards of judgment beyond the party line that the Soviet Communist party handed down. And since, in 1935, Venezuela lacked a proletariat and was governed by a feudal oligarchy tied to North American power, an orthodox Communist party enfiefed to Moscow would have been as powerless and as ill-adapted to the local reality as a polar bear in the tropics. Some day, perhaps, the general precepts of Marxism-Leninism might apply unadapted to Venezuela. But in the meantime, and as far as could be foreseen, the only sensible policy—and, indeed, the only policy consonant with true Marxism—was to recognize local conditions as they were. This would involve trying to bring about the reforms required on the basis of a wide coalition, grouping peasants, workers, intellectuals, university students, and progressive business

22. See pp. 115–19 of this book.

managers: that is to say, any groups or individuals sincerely interested in contributing to modernization. The time was ripe; though Venezuelan society had remained basically rural and feudal, it had been traumatized by the sudden emergence on the national scene of a modern, dynamic industrial sector, the oil industry, which was run by foreigners mainly for their own profit, and which contributed greatly to the development of militant consciousness in the nation.

The contractual arrangements that controlled the exploitation of oil wells showed no concern for the national interest; they represented Venezuela's greatest scandal in Juan Vicente Gómez's day and immediately thereafter. Here was an issue that could be used to unite the great majority of the nation. The political program of the Democratic Action party rejected the system of concessions, through which North American and Anglo-Dutch corporations reaped nearly all the benefits deriving from the oil industry and practically controlled the economy and the life of Venezuela. Betancourt and Democratic Action knew that it would have been utopian to strive for nationalization of the oil industry in the immediate future. But as early as 1943 they saw that they could take advantage of a Congressional debate on new (and less unfair) legislation to reduce the privileges of foreign corporations.

The political order that succeeded the Gómez government crumbled in October 1945, quite suddenly. If Gómez's heirs had been able to maintain their regime this long, it was only because of the state of helplessness in which the country found itself following twenty-seven years of terrorist tyranny —a helplessness further complicated by the peculiar conditions prevalent during the Second World War. No doubt the most repressive and brutal aspects of the Gómez dictatorship had been eliminated after his death in 1935, but ten years later, control of the political and economic system was still in the hands of the same coalition of landowners and military— albeit a more "liberal" wing of the same oligarchy. At a lower echelon, young officers of the professional armed forces created by Gómez were consumed with frustrated ambition. These men established contact with the Democratic Action party, which had been officially founded in 1941, after having existed subterraneanly for several years. It represented the only political force of any significance that had not compromised itself by cooperating with the existing power structure that the young officers wished to eliminate.

Betancourt at first refused to play a role in a military coup d'état. With the consent of the lesser leaders of Democratic Action, he tried to obtain from the government a promise of constitutional reform that, within a reasonable time, would lead to presidential and legislative elections based on bona fide universal suffrage. When the government gave a scornful reply, it was promptly overthrown.

Rómulo Betancourt became provisional President. The future promoter of OPEC (Organization of Petroleum Exporting Countries), Juan Pablo Pérez Alfonzo, was appointed to the Ministry of Commerce and Industry, responsible for the oil industry as well as for such questions as the price of beans and the size of nails. Strange as it may seem, Venezuela, the world's third-largest petroleum producer and its largest exporter, did not have a ministry specially concerned with oil; it continued to depend for petroleum statistics and other basic data on the foreign corporations.

A profile of Pérez Alfonzo published by the New York *Times* in November 1973, when the price of oil rose by some four hundred percent, stressed that this Venezuelan Aprist, far more than any Arab sheik or Persian shah, was responsible for launching the cartel of oil producers; at the same time, OPEC received the most adverse coverage in the press of the oil-importing countries. In fact, OPEC's action only proved that oil had for years been priced at an absurdly low level, to the short-term advantage of the richest and most industrialized countries in the world. This imbalance played an important role in further stimulating advanced economies, without providing just compensation to the poorer countries that were nominal owners of this scarce raw material.[23]

The New York *Times* coverage was good journalism, but

23. From the point of view of the oil-exporting countries, the only criticism that can rationally be made of the readjustment of the price of oil on the international market is that it was so sudden that it drew the attention of the rich consumer countries too dramatically to their dependence on foreign oil producers. They then began to display some interest in the welfare of the OPEC countries in the future, when there would be less demand for oil as a fuel, or—to take the extreme case—when oil as a source of energy would have been altogether superseded by nuclear power. Their concern must be considered suspect, for it would never have occurred but for OPEC. Anyone unduly worried about the distant future should be reminded of Lord Keynes's dictum: "In the long range, we will all be dead." Furthermore, oil is not just, or even primarily, a source of energy; it has far more varied and interesting uses in the petrochemical industry and it seems highly improbable that it will lose its usefulness. The long-term problem, rather, is how to extend the productivity of the wells, to make the best use of this nonrenewable natural resource. Within orthodox economic theory, there is no better guarantee for this than high prices.

perforce stated the issue only superficially. Pérez Alfonzo could not have been effective had he not been part of a political project that was elaborated in Mexico in 1924 by the Peruvian Haya de la Torre and introduced in Venezuela in 1945 by Democratic Action. From 1959 on, Venezuela worked to persuade the other oil-producing nations—each of them weak when acting in isolation—to join forces, and to elaborate a common plan of action that would in due course allow a group of small countries jointly to confront consumer groups in the great industrialized nations of the West and Japan. In the same years, the Latin-American Communists, carried away by the success of the Cuban Revolution, attacked more viciously than ever such men as Haya de la Torre, Betancourt, and Carlos Andrés Pérez, branding them as "traitors and running dogs of imperialism," and throwing themselves heartily into armed struggle, urban terrorism, and the furthering of "insurrectional focal points." They scorned OPEC, since for them the only correct policy for oil-exporting countries was the total stoppage of all oil exports to Western powers. And if this met with reprisals—economic or military—from the industrialized nations, so much the better! The ultimate aim, the true revolutionary path, was the creation of more Vietnam-style confrontations throughout the world. Any mechanisms for negotiation, for mutual adjustment, for a continuation of cooperation and interdependence between advanced capitalist countries and Third World countries (including the OPEC countries), could only be the despicable invention of the "traitors to History," comparable to the equally despicable endeavor, on the part of "petit-bourgeois," democratic, reformist labor unions to improve the standard of living of workers, rather than let them live in misery and hasten the revolution through a general strike.

For several years, the multinational oil companies and the principal oil-importing countries failed to take OPEC seriously. But in 1973, a number of factors suddenly turned in favor of the oil-exporting countries. A false buyers' market had existed until that time, loaded in favor of the large importers. The price of crude oil had been artificially pegged down to such a low level that the importing nations were able to raise more income from local sales taxes on gas than the exporting countries from the sale of their only natural resource. Overnight the situation changed to a seller's market. It suddenly became clear that oil had always been underpriced at the source; that it was a nonrenewable resource, the demand for which had been increasing at runaway rates, precisely as a function of the artificially low prices. The low pre-1973 price level was particularly absurd in light of the much higher price, and very short current supply, of other forms of energy.

The sudden correction of this situation showed Venezuela that its interests had been far better served by Rómulo Betancourt and Democratic Action than Cuba's had been by Fidel Castro and the Communist party. Strategically, and as an example of how a developing country can gain control of its own natural resources, the nationalization of the Venezuelan oil industry is far more significant than Fidel Castro's expropriation of the United States–owned sugar industries.[24] Venezuela was able to achieve this result without "Vietnamization," and this is why its palpable success failed to satisfy the Communists. They do not view the nationalization of foreign-owned basic industries as a worthwhile economic goal in itself, or as an affirmation of national sovereignty, but only as a means of confrontation by which to effect a break between the developing countries and the non-Communist, developed countries—a step in the grand strategy of world revolution.

Rómulo Betancourt: The "Anti-Castro"

In January 1959, when Fidel Castro entered Havana, Rómulo Betancourt had just been elected President of Venezuela, after being in exile for ten years. We should step back to those years and look briefly at the reasons for the overthrow of Democratic Action in November 1948, by the same young officers—majors and captains—who had ushered the party into power in 1945. After three years of Democratic Action government, these officers had come to feel that the crafty Betancourt had got the better of them: that they had borne all the risks, while Democratic Action had ended up controlling all the power. Labor unions had proliferated and were becoming aggressive, as were the members of Democratic Action, and by contagion, the civilian population, the "rabble." The respect and fear that the military uniform had traditionally inspired in Venezuela were vanishing. Perhaps—the officers thought in 1948—this Rómulo Betancourt had been, or still was, secretly

24. The Venezuelan nationalization of the foreign oil concerns became law in August 1975, when Congress ratified the bill proposed by President Carlos Andrés Pérez two months earlier; take-over of operations went into effect on January 1, 1976.

a Communist? At the very least, he was trying to institute indefinite one-party rule in Venezuela, on the model of the Mexican PRI. The officers came to doubt their own political acumen.

The fact is that, under Betancourt, questions of public interest were for the first time in memory discussed freely and democratically, in the streets as well as in the media (Congressional debates were even broadcast over the radio). After having been muzzled throughout fifty years of *caudillismo,* Venezuelans were stirred and unsettled to an unprecedented degree by this new-won freedom.

The practice of free speech in our subcontinent easily degenerates into personal vilification designed to bring about military intervention against the current government; far less often does it press for reform or enlighten public opinion. In 1945, Betancourt was only the fourth civilian President in Venezuelan history, except for some insignificant figures delegated by *caudillos* to play interim roles. Of the three who preceded him (all before 1892), two had been overthrown by military coups d'état. The fifth civilian President, who immediately succeeded Betancourt's provisional presidency in 1948, received three-quarters of the vote in the first election in Venezuela to have universal suffrage and a secret ballot. The new President was an intellectual, the novelist Rómulo Gallegos, chosen by Democratic Action to symbolize its rejection of the past and the start of a new era. But Gallegos was not a politician. He imagined that because, as President, he was commander-in-chief of the armed forces, he would be immune from a coup d'état; for a *Putsch* would constitute a betrayal of which the Minister of War could not be capable.

One of the first objectives of the 1948 coup d'état was the assassination of Rómulo Betancourt, but he managed to escape, take refuge in a foreign embassy, and go into exile. Neither his prestige nor that of Democratic Action was diminished by the ruthless repression that lasted until January 1958. By then, the armed forces had grown tired of the political incompetence of the military dictator they had installed, who was forgetting that he owed his position to them and was starting to play *caudillo.* They staged a coup of the kind I discussed earlier, aimed at re-establishing a new civilian legitimacy, restored civic freedom, and, in December 1958, called an election. This was easily won by Betancourt and his party.

In the interval between Betancourt's electoral victory and February 1959—date of his inauguration as President—Fidel

Castro became the biggest news story not just of Latin America but throughout the world. No Latin-American leader had ever been in this kind of spotlight before.

At first, everyone, including the United States, acclaimed Castro as an authentic hero, a revolutionary social democrat, a *guerrillero* David who had vanquished the Goliath of the armed forces, a radical Catholic reformer, a young Hercules set to clean the Augean stables of Cuban politics.

Betancourt remained skeptical. He had met Fidel in Havana, when the Cuban was only a student terrorist—an idealist, no doubt a courageous man, but also an adventurer and an egomaniac. There was no telling how he would develop, now that he had seized power.

In fact, after a few months, the new democracy in Venezuela was caught between two fires. On one side were the old enemies of democracy and liberty in the Caribbean area, the most wily and ruthless of whom was the Dominican dictator Rafael Leonidas Trujillo; on the other were the Venezuelan Castroists, many of them former members of Democratic Action attracted by Fidel's wonderfully insolent defiance of North American imperialism, and therefore eager to renounce social-democratic, reformist, Aprist ways and to commit themselves to the revolutionary shortcuts advocated by Fidel and Che.

Trujillo, as usual, went straight to the point. He provided the bitter, right-wing enemies of Betancourt and Democratic Action with the means of assassinating the President. In June 1960, a bomb shattered Betancourt's car, killing the general commanding the President's military household, who was sitting in the right front seat. The President, just behind him, received a severe shock, and his hands were badly burned when he tried to open the doors of the blazing car. He nevertheless refused to take any sedative, and insisted on being immediately released from the hospital to return to the presidential palace. Two hours after the attempt on his life, he spoke to the country on radio and television; his hands were heavily bandaged, and his pronunciation was blurred because of his swollen, charred lips, but he was fully in control of himself and of the situation.

Anyone who believes Communist propaganda on the supposed repressiveness of Betancourt's government should know that when the authors of the bombing were apprehended, they were tried under due process of law and received relatively light sentences. At no time were they ill-treated. So lax were the conditions of their imprisonment that one of them was able to escape by jumping out of the window. Their sentences were reduced for good conduct or through grace or amnesty,[25] so that *ten years later, all were free men.*

Although steadily opposed to all that Trujillo stood for in Caribbean and Latin-American politics, Venezuelan Communists were at this particular juncture (1960) unremittingly hostile to the successful social-democratic reformer who so consistently had bested them. Their hatred of Betancourt was fueled by their regret that, paralyzed as they were by having to follow the erratic course of Soviet orthodoxy, they had not seen in Fidel Castro, prior to his triumph, anything more than a "petit-bourgeois adventurer," whose antics ran dangerously counter to the popular-front line reintroduced by Moscow in 1955.[26]

By contrast, the Communist party had been a model of moderation in the interregnum between January 1958 (when the military dictator Marcos Pérez Jiménez was ousted by his fellow officers) and Betancourt's election in December. During those eleven months, the Communist party played the role of ardent defender of democracy, and followed a popular-front soft line. Its members had pinned their hopes on helping to elect a candidate who, they felt, could be maneuvered into policies carefully tailored to profit Soviet aims without unduly provoking the United States.

Now, in 1959 and 1960, they were beginning to understand that they might well have let slip a unique opportunity when they failed to attempt to seize power during the interregnum. With a degree of boldness, they might have assumed the leadership of a loose, "progressive" coalition quite uninterested in any democratic electoral mandate—a pattern that would have paralleled Fidel's during the early months of 1959. We will never know whether they would have been successful in installing a "dictatorship of the proletariat," as Fidel Castro was to do one year later in Cuba. But after Fidel's success they thought that they might at least have made the attempt. Having missed their chance, they now resolved to apply the strat-

25. The leaders of the Castroist-Communist insurrection against Rómulo Betancourt's Aprist government were also free by 1970. Some are now Congressmen, others newspaper editors, leaders of legal political parties, professional associations, or labor unions; university teachers, well-placed artists and writers. Compare this to Cuba, where thousands of people were shot and hundreds of thousands exiled, and where *tens of thousands* of dissidents are still in jail, including men like Huber Matos, the hero of the Sierra Maestra, condemned to twenty years of hard labor for having questioned Fidel Castro's pro-Sovietism.
26. See pp. 123–24 of this book.

egy of the insurrectional focal point, based on the Cuban example. Fidel Castro, in his attempt to start a generalized revolutionary process in Latin America, was perfectly conscious of the strategic importance of Venezuela and its oil, and provided Venezuelan Communists with all the help he could—sending arms, money, and even a group of Venezuelan *guerrilleros* trained in Cuba and officered by veterans of the Sierra Maestra.

Today everyone has agreed that this gambit was deplorable, including those who took part in it. The violence that ensued was almost as costly as an all-out civil war. There were innumerable terrorist attacks, and much bloody skirmishing and fighting, both in the cities and in certain rural zones that had been selected as insurrectional focal points. Sizable insurrections broke out in a period of five weeks on two naval bases, led by officers who either had been secretly active in the Communist party for a long time or had been won over by the Cuban Revolution.

Betancourt had to spend most of the time during his nearly five years of government holding Venezuelan democracy together. He had to reckon not only with attacks from within, but also with a widespread, international slander campaign, which was meant to present him to the world as the "anti-Castro," which he certainly was, and as a monster of repression who had sold out to the North Americans, which he was not. Betancourt and the Venezuelan people should be understood as sharing the Aprist search for a truly Latin-American policy, progressive without being subservient to the Soviet strategy elaborated in 1920.[27] Hence the need, from the Communist point of view, to discredit Betancourt and his party by any and all means, including distortions and outright lies.

The pro-Castro, anti-Betancourt propaganda campaign was particularly virulent in France, which, for reasons rooted in its own character and history, was drawn to the Cuban Revolution. Castro's success proved that there were limits to North American power, and pointed to a certain ambiguity in the North American "anticolonialist" stance; France's humiliation in Indochina was not long past, and the dream of *Algérie française* was in the process of being liquidated. The French press was unanimous in its pro-Castroist reaction. *L'Aurore* and *Paris-Match,* as well as *L'Express, Le Monde, Les Temps modernes,* and of course the Communist *L'Humanité,* all viewed Fidel Castro and Che Guevara as the avengers of

27. See pp. 108–12.

France's humiliations. Such an endorsement, when given by the right, was totally irrational—but the right is by definition visceral and nonrational. The liberals, "the men of good will," were in sympathy with Castro, from bias or misinformation. And naturally, the many who feel the world is a little better off with each new American setback, and with each success of Soviet foreign policy, greeted Fidel and El Che as the apostles of the rising anti–North American revolution in Latin America. Jean-Paul Sartre, in his 1964 letter to the Swedish Academy refusing the Nobel Prize, saw fit to make an allusion to the heroic (Communist) Venezuelan *guerrilleros* and the horrible (social democratic) Venezuelan government. In his eyes, Betancourt had committed the crime of failing to declare his solidarity with the Cuban Revolution, as another Latin-American social democrat, Allende, was to do much later, out of vanity and weakness. The crime of which Sartre accused Venezuela was that of defending itself against an utterly unjustifiable insurrection imported from abroad. Sartre entirely ignored the fact that Venezuela had just begun to enjoy an era of liberty and popular reform, and had made considerable progress toward freeing itself from foreign economic dominance. Significant reforms attest to this purpose: Venezuela's membership in OPEC, the final suspension of further petroleum concessions to foreign corporations, and the setting up of a national oil company that some fifteen years later was to help make possible the full nationalization of the oil industry.

Betancourt succeeded in defeating the insurrection toward the end of his tenure. The next elections (1963) were won by a Democratic Action candidate (Raúl Leoni), and those of 1968 by the candidate of the main opposition party, the Christian Democrat Rafael Caldera.

The 1973 elections brought another Aprist candidate to the presidency, Carlos Andrés Pérez, Rómulo Betancourt's Minister of the Interior during the most trying moments of the Castroist-Communist insurrection twelve years earlier. He is Venezuela's President today. Pérez, like Betancourt, was called names that would far more aptly have suited the present Chilean ruler, General Pinochet, and, even more, Fidel Castro. But Castro is exempt from such opprobrium: when he disregards basic human rights, on a much larger scale, and with effects far more lasting than the Chilean dictator, he does so in the name of the Revolution.

Under Pérez's presidency, the aims set by the Venezuelan Aprist movement for the country have very nearly been reached. Citizens have been given their basic civil rights; financially, the country is very prosperous; income from oil has quadrupled, and the oil industry has come under state control. This last point has earned the praise of the Soviet press and of Fidel Castro. Communists are realists, who know that fallen martyrs such as Allende can be put to good use, but that live rulers are far more immediately interesting—especially when, like the Venezuelan social democrats, they have proved tough and durable.

The Chilean Experience

"In one hundred and fifty years of independence, Chile had succeeded in evolving a common national sense of values shared by the great majority of citizens. This common ethos was communicated within the family, in school, during military service, in the office . . . throughout the whole of social life. It was a common code that provided the mental foundation of the Chilean people . . . to an extent unparalleled in any other [Latin-American] countries.

"A historical conscience progressively developed which was clearly perceived by the *soul of the nation*. Chileans were convinced that theirs was a great country, strengthened by ethnic homogeneity, by a demanding system of education, by a spirit of tolerance that so far had reigned for one hundred and fifty years. Except for brief spells, the country had been governed by democratic regimes. The house of representatives had functioned from the start of independence and was one of the oldest in the world. Positions of public trust were filled by election, and this process lent legitimacy to leaders as well as to their policies. The Chilean educational system enjoyed a well-earned prestige; soon after independence, scholars from abroad, such as Andrés Bello, Sarmiento, Humboldt, Courcelle-Seneuil, and many others, had taught at Chilean universities. . . . The primary and secondary education systems had enlisted the assistance of German, French, English, and Spanish educators. The armed forces were modeled on the German, and later on the North American model, the navy underwent British training. In short, the country had the foresight to open itself to the outer world and to take advantage of the cultural assets of the West. The Chileans were patriotic, intelligent, well educated, courageous, skilled negotiators; they had a reputation for humor, and for a manifest openness to new ideas; above all they were respectful of their constitution and of the law. They respected religious opinions different from their own. Their civic sense had earned them the nickname of 'The English of Latin America.' "[28]

It is remarkable that this eulogy to the Chile we have lost came from the pen of one of the main actors in the political drama that in three years, from 1970 to 1973, put an end to the order he was praising. For Gonzalo Martner was in charge of national planning throughout the administration of Salvador Allende, a man who at his inauguration as President was given charge of the country described by Martner, and who, three years later, handed to posterity the Chile Pinochet governs today.

Of course, Martner's purpose in proposing his full argument was quite different. He was trying to prove that Chile's national tragedy was due not to Allende and his collaborators, including Martner himself, but to the unjust and perverse resistance of *others*. He placed the blame on opponents, from inside and outside, of Allende's attempt to transform Chile into a Communist country though he had had only a very slim electoral victory, and was stretching to the breaking point the limits defined by the Constitution. These limitations on Allende's power and his "tolerance" of opposition were in no way gracious concessions on his part, as has been argued, but were due to Chile's legal framework and to the pluralism and tendency toward law abidance that Martner recognized as typical of pre-Allende Chile.

But, as Jean-François Revel said in commenting on Allende's performance, "a statesman worthy of the name should not be surprised to find that his enemies oppose him"; he cannot complain that "those I sought to destroy failed to give me their support."[29] The same European and North American "progressives" who had vilified the Aprists Rómulo Betancourt and Carlos Andrés Pérez, from 1959 on, because they would not allow Venezuela to follow in the footsteps of Cuba or Vietnam, now applauded the Aprist Allende when he foolishly adopted the pose of a "second Fidel," though this involved a course of action that by 1970 had lost all attractiveness and relevance, and was less justified in Chile than in any other

28. Gonzalo Martner, *Chile, mil días de una economía sitiada* (Chile, a thousand days of siege economy), Caracas, Universidad Central de Venezuela, Facultad de Economía, 1975, pp. 178–79.
29. "Faut-il se taire?" (Must we keep quiet?), *L'Express*, Paris, no. 1213, October 21–27, 1974, p. 54.

Latin-American country. The society described by Gonzalo Martner hardly needed to yield to the enticements or the interference of the distant, primitive Cuban adventure, already discredited by more than ten years of personal dictatorship and subservience to Soviet world strategy.

Salvador Allende failed to secure the absolute majority of the vote required for election to the presidency on the popular ballot. He obtained 36.2 percent of the votes, slightly more than the Conservative candidate, Jorge Alessandri (34.9 percent), and the Christian Democratic candidate, Radomiro Tomic, ran a poor third (27.8 percent).[30] In Chile, when no one candidate received an absolute majority, Congress was called upon to make the final choice between the two candidates who had polled the highest percentage of votes. In the 1970 electoral bind, the Christian Democrats could have allied themselves to the Conservatives and elected Alessandri without violating either the spirit or the letter of the Chilean Constitution. This situation paralleled the French elections of 1973, in which the partisans of Chaban-Delmas preferred to give their votes to Giscard d'Estaing, rather than to François Mitterand, who had polled the strongest minority vote in the first ballot. The French and, until 1970, the Chilean constitutional systems both aimed at defining a consensus solution, in a democratic spirit of compromise and agreement. Alessandri proposed an arrangement of this kind to the Christian Democrats. Frei, the Christian Democrat who enjoyed the greatest prestige and was accepted not only by the majority of his party, but also by a majority of his countrymen, had been barred from the 1970 presidential race, since the Chilean Constitution ruled out the immediate re-election of an outgoing President. And the Conservatives viewed Tomic's position as so close to Allende's, so far to the left, that they concluded that a candidate of their own would be more attractive, and would draw a plurality of votes.

This calculation miscarried by a narrow margin. It now seemed probable that, in line with an unbroken tradition, Congress would ratify Allende's plurality, and thus select a President who would surround himself with men quite ready to bury Chilean democracy. To prevent this, Alessandri proposed to the Christian Democrats an arrangement that was in agreement with the letter of the Constitution, and quite in line with

30. Six years earlier, the Christian Democrat Eduardo Frei had polled 57 percent of the popular votes against 38.5 percent for Allende, who, in 1964, was already the candidate of a Socialist-Communist coalition.

the "British" genius for intelligent compromise that Martner attributes to pre-Allende Chileans: he asked the Christian Democratic Congressmen to help elect him, in return for which he would immediately resign, thus creating a situation in which Frei would again be legally entitled to run, and would doubtless beat Allende by polling more than 50 percent of the popular vote.

The Christian Democrats turned down this solution, after heated discussion, and thus must bear a considerable burden of responsibility before history: this proved to be their last opportunity to forestall the coming tragedy. Allende himself would have other opportunities to avoid disaster, but he, too, neglected them.

Eduardo Frei's had been a sound government, widely representative of his country as a whole and very much in the progressive and sophisticated tradition of Chilean democracy. Frei was aware that he owed his election in 1964 largely to the support of the Conservatives, who had agreed not to enter a candidate of their own for fear of splitting the anti-Allende vote and opening the door to his Marxist Popular Unity. Frei nonetheless put into effect a series of reforms that can only be described as Aprist.[31] He "Chileanized" the copper mining and refining industry, with the government acquiring 51 percent of

31. Some Chilean or Venezuelan Christian Democratic political theorist should undertake a study to show in what way the two Christian Democratic regimes in Latin America (Frei's in Chile and Caldera's in Venezuela) differ from Aprism. The most notable difference seems to be the social origin and the schooling of the leaders (as well as their idiosyncrasies, which are accidental). The Christian Democratic leaders practically all stem from the middle bourgeoisie; their higher social origin is reflected in a better formal education; they have attended Catholic schools and colleges, and owed their early political commitments not to the influence of Marx and the Mexican Revolution, but to that of enlightened priests, the papal encyclicals that dealt with social problems, and the work of such Catholic writers as Jacques Maritain and Emmanuel Mounier. The ultimate aim of their political action is a millenarian dream, a society that will combine Christian solidarity with an ill-defined but nonoppressive collectivism that they refer to as to the principle of "communal property" (propriedad comunitaria). But when they came to power, their concrete measures of reform and their conception of national goals were practically identical with what Haya de la Torre had been proposing since 1924. In their youth these Christians had viewed Marx as the devil incarnate; now, like the Aprist social democrats, they openly endorsed some theoretical aspects of the Marxist–Leninist–Third World perspective. Following the death of Pius XII, they saw in the flexible policy the Vatican adopted vis-à-vis Marxist ideology and the Communist empire an encouragement to synchronize their action with the development of Marxism–Leninism–Third Worldism in Latin America and throughout the world. This position, in line with world trends, has greatly increased their recently won popular acceptance.

ownership; he launched a significant and well-conceived program of agrarian reform and encouraged a policy of industrial growth and diversification, as well as a more equitable distribution of wealth. His government, which was too radical for the Chilean right, was too moderate for the left wing of his own Christian Democrat party. That Frei's policies met with opposition from the extremes of the political spectrum indicates that he stood in the centrist mainstream of Chilean politics, and that he gave his country a sound and realistic political orientation based on the realities of Chilean, Latin-American, and world politics between the years 1964 and 1970.

The divergences between the centrist-oriented Frei and the leftist Tomic, and the desire, natural in any group, to shake off the authority of a leader too long in power, led the Chilean Christian Democratic party to turn down Alessandri's proposal. As soon as the result of the popular vote was known, Tomic rushed to congratulate the Marxist candidate in front of photographers and journalists, as if his triumph were already a certainty. Frei was not in a position to censure Tomic: this would have seemed self-serving and counterproductive in the climate of civic courtesy that then still dominated Chilean politics. All that Allende's opponents could do was to place certain conditions on his ratification by Congress, by way of a constitutional reform protecting freedom of expression, education, and worship, and guaranteeing governmental noninterference in military affairs. Before this, no one in Chile had thought that such special guarantees were necessary. The fact that they were now rushed through shows how general was the conviction that Allende was committed to subverting the open, democratic society in Chile, which was based on the rule of law, tolerance, and mutual respect, and to replacing it with a Marxist-Leninist society largely structured on the Cuban model.

Even then Allende could still have saved Chile—and himself. Tomic's victory over Frei in the final Congressional vote that gave Allende the presidency implied that the Christian Democrats were willing to cooperate in the evolution of Chilean society toward democratic socialism during Allende's presidential term. This agreement provided the new President with a basis for a tacit alliance with Tomic's party on the many issues about which they were of one mind. No doubt such an alliance would have led to disaffection on the extreme left wing of the Popular Unity coalition, as well as on the right wing of the Christian Democratic party. And had Allende followed this wise course, international opinion would not have hailed him as a "revolutionary." Like Rómulo Betancourt and Carlos Andrés Pérez in 1960 to 1963, he would have been berated as a "traitor to the proletariat" and accused of "selling out to imperialism," et cetera. He might even have had to repress some shows of violence by the extreme left, comparable to those the social-democratic Venezuelan government had had to face ten years earlier. But he would still be alive today, and Chilean democracy with him. And the world would never have heard the name of General Pinochet.

Oil on the Fire

Allende apparently never gave even cursory consideration to the possibility that the Christian Democratic party might be ready to meet the new administration halfway. From the very first day he showed himself uncompromising, unreasonable, and condescending. He may have adopted this stance out of vanity and weakness of character, giving in to Guevarist fashion ("one, two, three . . . many Vietnams"). In any case, his actions show that he did not think of himself simply as a President within the country's democratic, reformist tradition, but, rather, as being destined to achieve a social and institutional break with the past, a *revolution*. It was usual in Chile for a new President to try to conciliate those who had not voted for him, to put aside partisanship and take on the role of "the President of all the Chileans." Allende launched his presidency by refusing to abide by this tradition, and announced that he would not be the President of all the Chileans, but would start from the principle that Chilean society was characterized by an unbridgeable class conflict; he intended to be a partisan in that conflict.

True to his word, Allende put into practice, or allowed others to put into practice, a number of measures designed to "awaken the conscience of the people," that is, deliberately to exacerbate the class struggle.[32] He was fully successful in this, but successful beyond his hopes, drawing *all* Chileans, not just the "proletariat," into active, violent confrontation. After three years of his rule, 40 percent of the Chilean population had

---

32. Witness an astounding "state visit" by Fidel Castro in 1971 that lasted almost a full month, during which he traveled from one end of the country to the other, haranguing the crowds as if he, not Allende, were the President of Chile.

come to argue passionately that the other 60 percent constituted an impassable obstacle to the nation's progress and happiness. No doubt Allende had succeeded in creating considerable "class consciousness" among those 40 percent. But the
other 60 percent can hardly be blamed for viewing with alarm
the future as "insects" (Lenin) or "earthworms" (Fidel Castro) that awaited them if Popular Unity effectively succeeded
in its stated purpose of irreversibly revolutionizing Chilean society.

This is how the country described by Martner was transformed into an unrecognizable Chile, in which the majority
were so desperate that they greeted the coup d'état of September 1973 with joy and relief; even today this segment of the
population would for the most part be found more willing to
put up with the regime of General Pinochet than with the
prospects held out by Allende. As for Allende's achievements,
only one seems unquestionable: he did succeed in convincing
all Chileans that, in accordance with Marxist theory, class conflicts admit of no compromise, and that one part of society can
hope to progress only by destroying the values, beliefs, and
way of life of the others. But this scenario can be played out in
reverse and to the detriment of the "proletariat." The proposed
victims, foremost among them the officers of the armed forces,
can take the initiative if convinced that they are acting preven-
tively and in self-defense.

Allende and his collaborators carry the full responsibility for
that outcome. The pro-Allende rhetoric in Chile and throughout the world during the years 1970–73, and even more the
interpretation given to events after the September 1973 military coup, suggests that the Popular Unity movement acted
democratically, almost naïvely, while it was in power, and that
it fell victim to its own exemplary patience, to its resolve to
respect legality when faced with unscrupulous enemies. Indeed, the regime may have tried to follow legal forms—but
only because Chilean institutions and traditions would have
tolerated no other approach. Popular Unity had no choice but
to proceed indirectly and stealthily in its attempt to transform
the presidency, with its limited constitutional power, into a
Marxist-Leninist dictatorship. At no time was the Allende government as candid as some would have us believe.

If Allende stayed as close as he could to the letter of the law,
while acting as much as possible against its spirit, it was not
out of principle, but in order to insure the support, or at least
the neutrality, of the armed forces. All the while, he allowed

the foundations of Chilean democracy to be sapped by indirect, nonlegal channels. And even those disingenuous tactics, while accepted (or inspired) and supported by the Communist party, were openly criticized as too soft by some members of Popular Unity, and even by some important figures in the Socialist party of which Allende was the nominal leader. Carlos Altamirano, Secretary General and real boss of the party, openly urged the government to prepare for the inevitable civil war that was in any case needed to lay the bases of true revolutionary power. The extreme left of Popular Unity—consisting of the small parties Movement of the Revolutionary Left (MIR), Organized Vanguard of the People (VOP), and Unified Popular Action Movement (MAPU)—shared this perspective. As Régis Debray imprudently revealed in 1971,[33] Allende himself privately admitted that only tactical differences existed between himself and Fidel Castro or Che Guevara: unlike his Cuban friends, he was obliged temporarily to respect "bourgeois legality," for reasons specific to the Chilean situation.

The systematic erosion of legality belies the propaganda presenting the Popular Unity government as a model of democracy. The steady deterioration of Chilean democratic institutions has been most authoritatively analyzed by ex-President Eduardo Frei, in a report to the World Union of Christian Democracy.[34] In this report, Frei stressed that throughout the period under discussion, Popular Unity remained a minority group in Congress, in city governments, and in local, professional, and farmers' organizations. He pointed out that by 1973 Allende had lost the majority he had initially secured in the industrial and mining unions, including those of the copper mines, which are Chile's principal asset. In popular polls, the highest percentage of votes ever attained by the Allende coalition was 43 percent (in March 1973). "The degree of the government's tampering with these elections knew no precedent in Chile's history: it made use of the State's administrative machinery, used enormous financial means, and exerted pressure . . . including violence, not to mention documented fraud affecting at least 4 or 5 percent of the votes, the government having printed thousands of false identity cards."

Allende's partisans, being a minority, were perforce limited

---

33. *Entretiens avec Allende* (Conversations with Allende), Paris, Maspero, 1971.
34. Report dated November 8, 1973, addressed to Mariano Rumor, President of the Italian Christian Democratic party and of the World Union of Christian Democracy.

in the means they could use to convert Chile into a dictatorship. Yet, Frei continued, they "openly flaunted the laws, never hesitating to disregard legal decisions. Whenever they were defeated at a union or student election, they refused to recognize the majority decision, and set up a parallel organization endorsing government policy, which the government from then on protected while it persecuted the other organization sprung from legitimate elections. . . . In their attempt to gain control, they even envisaged replacing Congress with a 'Popular Assembly' and setting up 'popular tribunals,' some of which were actually functioning [by the time of the coup d'état]. . . . They also presumed to modify the educational system so as to replace it with a training program in 'Marxist consciousness.' "

Frei went on to describe the resistance with which the majority of Chileans soon met these measures, and the growing discontent among opposition parties, unions, other popular organizations, professional associations, the press, and so forth. The Church attempted to remain neutral, and even sought to establish institutional cooperation with the government, comparable and parallel to that of the armed forces, but finally balked when Allende sought to place education squarely at the service of Marxist ideology.

The Supreme Court *unanimously* found the executive branch guilty of refusing to recognize the decisions of the courts. The Inspectorate of the Treasury denounced a number of actions and decisions of the executive as illegal. For three years the majority of Congressmen formulated grievances against the executive. To top it all, when constitutional reforms were approved, President Allende refused to promulgate them, and persisted in his refusal even though the judiciary arbitrated the quarrel in favor of the legislative branch.

According to Frei, by mid-1973 it could no longer be doubted that the Popular Unity minority government had resolved to install a totalitarian dictatorship, and that it was progressively moving in this direction: "The parties represented in the government no longer hid their purpose. The Secretary General of the Socialist party openly called on the soldiers and sailors to disobey their officers and incited them to rebellion, as did other parties in power [the MIR, the VOP, and the MAPU]; they did this so clumsily that the Communist party itself . . . manifested its disagreement even though its position . . . did not differ in regard to the ends to be reached, but only as to the means to follow.

"Two more key facts have to be taken into consideration:

"(1) Once the new Allende administration had taken over, thousands of representatives of the [violent] extreme left from all parts of Latin America converged toward Chile. . . . Tupamaros from Uruguay, *guerrilleros* from Brazil, Bolivia, and Venezuela and from all other countries. The Cuban Embassy became a veritable ministry with a staff that outnumbered . . . the total number of employees working at the Chilean Ministry of Foreign Affairs in 1970. . . . Men known throughout the continent for their guerrilla activities were promptly integrated into the civil service, spent their time mostly on paramilitary instruction; they set up guerrilla training camps on Chilean territory to which even members of the armed forces were denied entrance.

"(2) The accelerated smuggling of weapons of all sorts, not only automatic rifles, but also heavy arms such as machine guns, high-power bombs, mortars, antitank guns of recent models, ambulances, and a full complement of logistical communications equipment . . . et cetera. The Chilean Army had never seen hardware of this sort, produced in the Soviet Union and Czechoslovakia. [The infrastructure of] a full-fledged parallel army was thus set up. What democracy could survive such a situation?"[35]

None, of course, and the answer to Frei's rhetorical question is that Chilean democracy was doomed, one way or another, from the moment the Christian Democratic party rejected Alessandri's proposal and opened the door to Allende's election to the presidency in 1970.

From the Breakdown of the Economy to the Breakdown of Democracy

Only considerable economic success could have persuaded Chile to put up with the political abuses of the Popular Unity government, but the Allende administration proved utterly inept in economic matters. When Frei left the presidency, Chile was standing by all its international obligations; it had accumulated reserves amounting to five hundred million dollars—an unprecedented figure; during the last two years of Frei's mandate, the country had contracted no foreign debts other than those destined for capital investment. When it was learned that the Christian Democrats would cast their votes for

35. *Ibid.*

Allende in the final congressional vote for the presidency, the economic situation immediately took a turn for the worse. And responsibility for this economic deterioration, which began even before Allende's inauguration, lies with Popular Unity: this was the natural reaction of a free-enterprise system that had just learned it would soon be cornered and throttled by an incoming government.

Allende's first economic measures included a general wage increase, the freezing of prices, the setting of an unrealistically high fixed official rate of exchange for the national currency, and a considerable increase in public expenditures, largely invested in the acquisition of private enterprises. The appropriation of private businesses was carried out at a steady pace through a variety of means. The stock market panicked, so that the government was able to acquire control of many corporations by buying up their shares at nominal cost. Other corporations, whose shares were not quoted on the stock market, were disrupted by endless strikes, which were organized to justify the state's interference on the basis of reactivating production. Agriculture experienced the same kind of strangulation as private industrial activity. As was to be expected, the copper mines, which represented practically the single source of foreign exchange, were expropriated; the state took over the 49 percent of the stock still in foreign hands, and assumed direct control over their administration.

These measures led to a sudden rise in the purchasing of consumer goods, both domestic and imported, at artificially low prices, which were in fact subsidized by the state through the arbitrarily high rate of the Chilean escudo, supported by a hemorrhage of foreign-currency reserves. Naturally, this at first created a feeling of euphoria; productivity remained low, but employment figures and production rose temporarily. The real purchasing power of salaries rose by nearly 30 percent.

But this mini-boom during the first months of 1971 reflected only the dissipation of reserves, the spending of wealth built up in previous years. During the second half of the year, the discrepancy between production costs and prices, further compounded by the stagnation or actual decline of production in industry, agriculture, and cattle breeding, inevitably resulted in shortages and in the development of a black market. In 1970, the last year of the Frei administration, Chile had had a positive balance of payments of 91 million dollars; in 1971, there was a deficit of 315 million dollars. In November 1971, after a year of the Allende administration, Chile had to declare itself insolvent and asked for a moratorium on its foreign debts.[36] One month later, the artificial value of the escudo began to crumble: the Central Bank of Chile could no longer support the national currency. In one year, the government had doubled the amount of paper currency in circulation to finance its programs.[37] Private investments, national and foreign, had fallen to zero. The state had invested its assets mostly in nationalizing existing sectors of production; it had added practically no new sources of production to the economy. A majority of the professional and highly skilled members of society were by now shaken and demoralized; a large number were in opposition to the government. Many chose to emigrate (26 percent of the country's engineers, for example).

The seriousness of the economic crisis that Allende had created soon became apparent. Inflation had at first been artificially contained, while unbearable pressure built up on the Chilean escudo; but in mid-1972, prices exploded. Between June and December of that year, the consumer price index increased fourfold; this figure was to double again before Allende's fall. Besides, this index was purely theoretical. Many of the goods it listed could only be found on the black market, at prices that were much higher than listed and that truly reflected the deterioration of the currency. In September 1972, industrial production began to drop in absolute terms—a trend that continued until the end. Agricultural and livestock production in the third quarter of 1973 was 25 percent below what it had been before Allende's rise to power.[38]

36. It is true that following the expropriation (without compensation) of the North American mining companies Anaconda and Kennecott, certain foreign sources of credit, including the World Bank and the Export-Import Bank, stopped extending loans to Chile; but it is wrong to point to this as the chief cause of Allende's economic difficulties. Bankruptcy was rendered inevitable by the economic measures Allende took early in his tenure, in particular by his sudden stimulation of consumption while production leveled off. Further, the Popular Unity government succeeded in securing such sizable loans abroad (from other Latin-American countries and from Western Europe) that Chile's foreign debt rose by 800 million dollars in three years. The Chile of Popular Unity had difficulties raising loans in the Communist World: these countries contributed only 9 million dollars in loans in 1970 and barely 40 million in 1973. (See Inter-American Committee on the Alliance for Progress [ICAP], *Internal Efforts and Foreign Financial Needs for Chile's Development*, Washington, D.C., 1974.)
37. In September 1970, at the end of Frei's mandate, the free market rate of the dollar was 20 escudos; at the time of Allende's fall, a dollar was worth 2,500 escudos on the black market.
38. One stroke of ill luck for Allende between 1970 and 1972 was to see the average price of copper fall from $0.64 to $0.49 per pound; but in 1973 the price rose to $0.80 per pound—and even this near-doubling in the price of Chile's chief export could not stop the national bankruptcy.

As for the copper mines, the Popular Unity regime had hoped that once this key industry was taken over by the state, the "super earnings" that had supposedly been kept secret by the foreign companies would suddenly appear. In fact, the state administration not only proved inefficient, but also had to meet the miners' demands for higher wages and improved conditions, which they had been led to expect instantly by decades of Marxist propaganda; in this as in other sectors, the "Chilean road to socialism" found itself encouraging higher consumption at a time when production and productivity were falling. In May 1973, the government made a belated effort to peg the rate of increase of miners' salaries down to that of the price index; the result was a disastrous strike that lasted two and a half months, and a miners' march on Santiago.

The first serious crisis of the Chilean Marxist experience had occurred the year before, in 1972, when the truckers staged their first strike. The government described this as a truck owners' lockout. In fact it was a gesture of despair on the part of thousands of small truckers, owners of only one or two vehicles, who were threatened with ruin by the government's resolve to set up a state transport company. This strike sparked off the "class consciousness" of Chileans who disagreed with the new administration's orientation. What had begun as a limited strike soon spread to taxi and bus drivers, tradesmen, doctors, nurses, dentists, airplane pilots, engineers, and even farmers. The Christian Democratic party, by now thoroughly aroused, gave its full support to this nation-wide explosion of discontent. It is said that the CIA provided financial aid to the truckers—which is perfectly possible, as is the allegation that it supported the opposition newspapers, which the government was attempting to ruin by reducing, and later by suppressing, advertising. Such acts of interference in the domestic affairs of a foreign country, intolerable as they are in themselves, should be viewed in conjunction with the matching interference from the other side, which Frei mentioned in his letter to Mariano Rumor. The Chilean Marxist experience can rightfully be blamed for having created a climate of civil war in which dirty tricks had become commonplace; and this in a country that until then had been a model of decency in the never-very-innocent field of politics.

Be that as it may, the government lost the strike and was forced to give a number of key posts in the Cabinet to military officers before the truckers and other workers agreed to return to their jobs. This concession gave Allende a reprieve that he could have used to redress the situation. But he failed to take advantage of the opportunity, hoping that the parties constituting the Popular Unity coalition would secure an absolute majority in the March 1973 parliamentary elections. Frei described the tricks and the probable fraud that the coalition used at the polls; even so, Popular Unity did not win more than 44 percent of the votes, and Allende thus lost any hope he may have had of achieving a majority, either of the popular vote or in Congress.

At this point the Communist party proposed to consolidate the ground secured thus far; they felt that Popular Unity should agree to give way on a few issues in order to secure the greater part of the nationalizations and the other measures it had rammed through. But once again Allende let himself be convinced by the irresponsible, radical elements of the Socialist party, the MIR, the MAPU, and the VOP. Only two days after failing to win the majority, the government made public the education reform mentioned earlier, eliminating any school not directly controlled by the state, and transforming primary education into an instrument of Marxist indoctrination. As might have been expected, this project unleashed a political storm. For the first time, the Catholic Church openly manifested its opposition to a measure proposed by the Allende administration. Thousands of students demonstrated in the streets of the main cities. The military leaders, who had left the Cabinet after the elections, also expressed their disagreement. Allende had to suspend the decree. But his fate and that of Chilean democracy were sealed. On June 29, the first, isolated, and clumsy attempt at a military uprising was soon checked by the armed forces themselves, without a shot's being fired. But Allende lost his head and rushed to the radio and television, to exhort the workers to counter by seizing all factories. In one day the number of large industrial firms under state control increased from 282 to 526; production and productivity fell to a new low.

In July the truckers again went on strike, and did not return to work until the government fell in September. Even before these new crises, the Chilean economy had reached an annual rate of inflation of 323 percent. Once again Allende appointed generals to key positions, in the hope of neutralizing the armed forces while waiting for some miracle. Or perhaps it was not exactly a miracle that Allende was looking forward to: on August 7, Naval Intelligence reported the discovery of a plot to lead the sailors of Valparaiso and Concepción (the two main naval bases) in an uprising. The plot was uncovered and aborted. Naval Intelligence formally accused the Secretary General of the Socialist party, Senator Carlos Altamirano, as well as the leaders of the MAPU (Oscar Garretón) and the MIR (Miguel Henriques). On September 9, Altamirano openly admitted this charge but justified himself on the grounds of "awakening the sailors' conscience" to their officers' reactionary opinions. At the other extreme of the military hierarchy, the government had been attempting to divide and politicize the armed forces by promoting the officers they viewed as supporters, and by depriving of their commands or retiring those they supposed to be opponents of the regime.[39]

Democracy and Marxism-Leninism

The events in Chile that culminated in the overthrow and death of Salvador Allende had a world-wide echo; some have drawn from this tragedy the conclusion that freedom is an obstacle to the reform of social and economic structures in favor of the masses; they argue that the democratic system intrinsically involves a certain duplicity, in that it allows the participation of Marxist ideas in the general political controversy, but is ready to use any means to keep Marxists from governing if they happen to be duly elected. This argument is utterly misleading, and can only be arrived at by inverting the roles of culprit and victim. The lesson to be learned—once again—from the Chilean drama is that Marxism-Leninism is basically incompatible with democratic government. Democracy is by its very nature a system in which power is shared, distributed, dispersed. It is founded on the principle implicit in all democratic constitutions, that power must never be concentrated; and this principle in turn postulates a respect for the opinions, ideas, interests, and even the prejudices of minor-

39. Information on exactly what occurred in Chile between 1970 and 1973, though scattered, is available. There is no excuse for those who form an opinion on this matter without endeavoring to know the facts: these are readily available, even in the versions of sympathizers or militants who played an active role in Popular Unity. Paul E. Sigmund has drawn up a short and objective account in "Allende in Retrospect," *Problems of Communism*, Washington, D.C., May–June, 1974, pp. 45–62. For an alternative reading, divergent in interpretation although the facts themselves are not seriously in dispute, see "Showdown in Chile," by Andy Zimbalist and Barbara Stallings, in *Monthly Review*, New York, N.Y., vol. 25, no. 5, October 1973, pp. 1–24; and the special issue on Chile of *Latin American Perspectives*, Riverside, Calif., vol. 1, no. 2, Summer 1974.

ities. The spirit of democracy is not peremptory. It affirms the principle that neither public authority, nor the majority on which such authority bases its legitimacy, is invariably right on all issues, and that the opinion of the rest of society must therefore also be taken into consideration. It follows that in a democracy, the government must never commit the collective body of the people to an irreversible course, unless there is almost unanimous agreement that all other options have been eliminated.

This is why one basic article of faith in a democracy is a belief in the possibility of conciliating contending interests, among both individuals and social classes. Democracy is not so unsophisticated as to claim that there are no social antagonisms or tensions amounting to class struggle; but it holds that a workable compromise solution can always be found that will be acceptable to these contending interests—or at least preferable to the alternatives of civil war or tyranny. Such truly democratic solutions may never be perfect or fully satisfy any of the parties, but they have the merit of reducing hatred and intolerance as prime determinants of social actions. Thus they keep issues from being settled by resort to violence, the "divine judgment" that invariably gives victory to the strongest, and, as we have seen many times in recent history, condemns the weakest to subservience and extermination.

Marxism-Leninism, on the other hand, recommends exacerbating social conflicts (class struggles) by all possible means (as was done in Chile) until such time as, private property having been abolished, all conflicts have ceased, social classes have vanished, and antagonism has been removed from the social body.

According to this view, as long as the Peaceable Kingdom has not returned to us, and the lion has not lain down with the lamb, any kind of political or social concession to the "class enemy," unless intended as a tactical ruse, should be viewed as treasonable. For conciliation will only retard the inexorable, majestic progress of history to its ultimate fulfillment.

Many of our contemporaries, some of them quite well intentioned and respectable, have credited and continue to credit this fable, including the men who influenced Allende's policy while he was President of Chile. Democracy, which is undogmatic, admits that some minds may be seduced by this apocalyptic and messianic vision of history, and even allows that such ideas can play a role in improving human society, provided that they are propagated without violence. As a corollary to its own basic principles, democracy is committed to surrendering power to these men if they rise to the top through the electoral process, if they are able to convince a sufficient number of voters. This is what occurred in Chile, although Allende received only a narrow plurality of the popular vote, and secured his final selection by Congress by pretending to accept certain limits to his executive authority, even stricter than those defined in his country's democratic constitution.

But sincere Marxist-Leninists (or social democrats who become their servants, such as Allende) view such a situation as a tactical, intermediate position from which to conquer absolute power. If they used their legally won power within its prescribed constitutional limits and governed accordingly, they would be in violation of their political philosophy. To be true to themselves they must attempt to grasp all levers in the social process, and transform the mandate entrusted them by consent into absolute and permanent control. This ambition is utterly undemocratic. And if, besides, the Marxist-Leninists happen to misjudge the balance of forces within the society, as they did in Chile, they end up destroying their country's democracy.

Having accomplished this, they will then proclaim their attachment to the democratic process that they have just destroyed. But this is pure deceit, the bitterness of men who have lost a war, not the concern of men who had worked for peace. The Marxist-Leninist view of the matter was recorded once and for all by Lenin in his copy of Clausewitz's *On War,* where, next to the famous sentence stating that war is but the extension of politics through other means, he turned the formula around and stated that politics is the extension of war through other means; for war would be the natural state of mankind until the coming of the Marxist millennium.

The Peruvian Model

The Peruvian Army had traditionally been far less liberal in its attitudes than the army of neighboring Chile. Yet in 1968, it launched a political course in which some analysts have claimed to see a "Peruvian road to socialism."

Peruvian society was more backward than that of any other major Latin-American country. The racist, overbearing, intransigent Creole oligarchy that prospered even before independence had dominated the country ever since. This class did not look with favor upon emancipation from Spain; independence had to be imposed on Peru by the Argentines and the Venezuelans, who did not wish to see any vestiges of the Spanish empire left in the continent.

The Peruvian armed forces had always been a reflection, and until recently, an instrument, of this oligarchy. Coups d'état had been frequent, aimed at maintaining the social and economic *status quo* whenever the sheer ineptness of civilian politicians in power threatened the traditional power structure. The emergence of APRA in 1924, with its program of antioligarchic and anti-imperialistic reforms tailored to the Latin-American economic, social, and political realities, represented the only real threat to the *status quo* in all the history of Peru. This explains why the principal mission of the Peruvian Army after 1924 had been to bar APRA's way to power—a task they undertook particularly gladly because one of APRA's earliest exploits (in 1932) was the massacre of all the officers garrisoned in the city of Trujillo.

Victor Raúl Haya de la Torre, the founder and soul of APRA, returned from exile in 1931 and announced his candidacy for the presidential election. He won the election, but the armed forces immediately superseded him through a coup d'état, the first of several Haya would have to face in his tormented political career. Thirty-one years later, in 1962, after several periods of imprisonment, five years of political asylum at the Colombian embassy in Lima, and decades of exile, he ran again, was elected, and promptly overthrown by another coup d'état. After a year, the military government called for new elections, narrowly won by the architect Fernando Belaúnde Terry, a "technocrat" from the Popular Action party who turned out to be inept as both administrator and political leader, and who was, moreover, caught up in a scandal involving illegal oil concessions to a North American company.

APRA would doubtless have won the following elections, scheduled for 1969. The military did not want this to occur, but neither did they feel they could once again cancel the election ex post facto, as they had done in 1931 and 1962. In Belaúnde, they had hoped to find a non-Aprist civilian able to introduce the urgently needed program of economic and social reforms, and so remove the *raison d'être* of Aprism by stealing its thunder. By then, the Peruvian military had sincerely come to appreciate the need for this kind of social reform. As noted earlier, their professional training, which was quite impressive in itself, had been in recent years supplemented by graduate studies at the so-called Center for Higher Military Studies (CAEM), through which they had acquired a new insight into the political, social, and economic affairs of their country. Deeply impressed by the Cuban Revolution and the Alliance for Progress, they came to realize the extent to which they had been defending a stultifying conservatism that made them increasingly vulnerable in a changing world. There can be no doubt of the steady consultation and mutual influence between these Peruvian officers and their counterparts in Argentina and Brazil; like the Brazilian generals in 1964 and the Argentines in 1966, they had come to the conclusion that there was no political group (except APRA, which they hated) able to take charge and prevent a crisis that would threaten the unity, and even the continuation, of the existing armed forces.

They decided to step in, but this time not with the limited aim of assuring an interim rule between two periods of civilian government, as they had done in 1962. The formula no longer seemed applicable: that card had been played and lost. As the armies in Brazil and Argentina had done earlier, they now seized power nakedly, without any pretense of intending to turn it over to civilian leadership in the foreseeable future.

Peruvian military coups d'état had so far been simple, brutal, direct; they had been intended to salvage a social and economic order whose legitimacy was itself not being questioned. But here was something different. With this new intervention, the armed forces took over full responsibility for the conduct of political affairs, with the firm intention of implementing some of the same reforms that they had kept APRA from undertaking and that non-Aprist civilian administrations, one after the other, had been unable to put into effect. Thus this military intervention was frankly *political;* it employed basically political strategy and tactics; it had to refer and respond to the challenges present in the Peruvian, Latin-American, and global political contexts.

To understand the situation, we must consider the limited range of political and social forces that existed in Peru, besides the army, that could have been brought into partnership within the new government. There was of course the traditional oligarchy, whose instrument the military had been so far; but this was the very group whose power and prestige they were now set on destroying, so as to cleanse from their own image their collusion with traditional privilege. And the new military junta could turn neither to the second-string parties that had supported Belaúnde, nor to the high-level, independent "technocrats" who had served in his government, since it was specifically against Belaúnde that they had staged their coup. APRA was excluded by definition. Yet they stood in need of some civilian political endorsement in order to legitimize the take-over, to help forestall the pattern of rejection traditionally set off by military take-overs in all of Latin America, and particularly in Peru. Only one such group remained, the "Unity of the Left," which had been set up by the Peruvian Communist party to participate in the municipal elections in Lima in 1967, and which on that occasion had polled 15 percent of the capital's vote (whereas, for the country as a whole, the figure had never exceeded 5 percent).

The Peruvian general or, more likely, generals, who decided on this tactical alliance of the armed forces (now dubbed "revolutionary") with the Communist party ("the organized working class") hit upon a remarkably astute formula. The unexpected alliance with the Communists, who had so far been an insignificant group, paid considerable political dividends. Though few in number and ill-organized, the Peruvian Communists had considerable influence in the very intellectual, literary, and artistic sectors that might have been expected to oppose a military coup d'état. These influential groups now gave the military junta their endorsement. Even more important, international "progressive" opinion, instead of viewing the new regime in the stereotyped image of power-hungry, repressive, military Latin-American putschists, hailed them as nationalists, anti-imperialists, and Third Worldists.

When the time came to apportion the spoils, the military did not ignore the good turn the Communists and their international friends were doing them. The new leaders sincerely wished to push through a program of reforms, and they appointed Communists and fellow travelers to second-level executive positions to oversee the new measures. Thus they rewarded the Communists for their assistance while utilizing their services as zealous bureaucrats. The renewed political excommunication of APRA further endeared the military junta to the pro-Soviet international community, for reasons that are traceable to the years 1926–1927.[40]

This arrangement was to the advantage of both parties. To the Communists it gave psychological satisfaction, and to the military, a political advantage at the moderate cost of couching a whole series of their decisions in Leninist, Third World rhetoric. As some substance had to be given to such talk,

40. See pp. 114 and 117–19.

The Latin Americans

Peru's foreign policy came to reflect that rhetoric. The military government re-established diplomatic relations with Cuba, thus going counter to a decision of the Organization of American States that had thus far been broken only by Mexico. It developed commercial and technical exchanges with the socialist-bloc countries. It applauded the triumph of Chilean Popular Unity in 1970; and in 1971, Fidel Castro and Salvador Allende paid state visits to Peru. The Peruvian government undertook the nationalization of a number of North American concerns, some of which had a real significance while others were merely of symbolic importance. In this connection, Peru launched a bitter discussion with the United States government on the amount of compensation due American firms, and on the principle of compensation itself. The controversy, and Peru's having unilaterally decreed the extension of its territorial waters to a limit of two hundred miles, threatened the country with economic reprisals by the United States. The Peruvian government responded by publicly expressing doubts about the relevance of the inter-American system, and in particular of the Inter-American Reciprocal Assistance Treaty.[41] Peru now started purchasing weapons from the Soviet Union and Czechoslovakia and enlisting the services of Yugoslav technicians.

The military government's application of Marxist–Leninist–Third World rhetoric to foreign affairs led it to plead for the Third World's economic and cultural independence from imperialism and similar views. Only the style and vocabulary made their program different from that which the Aprists would have implemented, had democracy been allowed to function in Peru. But the Communist garb in which the secretaries to the military advisers dressed their policies earned them the wholehearted support of the world-wide pro-Soviet propaganda apparatus, for their contributions to "world revolution."

I am reminded of Stalin's cynical remark when he proclaimed, in 1924, that that feudal monarch, the Emir of Afghanistan, was "objectively revolutionary."[42] But no two historical situations are identical, and the Peruvian military from 1968 through 1975 cannot be equated with the Emir of Afghanistan in 1924. When they decided to assume power in 1968, the military leaders were fully aware of the sad role they had played for years as watchdogs of an iniquitous *status quo,*

41. See p. 51.
42. See p. 111.

and in reaction to this tarnished image promulgated a number of much-needed reforms. At the same time, they taught the military of the other Spanish American nations a new trick, which their Arab counterparts had long before learned from Nasser: in our time, world opinion is generally ready to welcome the most naked military grab for power, provided it wears the cloak of "socialism" and "anti-imperialism" and matches its dialectic with a few actions.

How to Stamp Out the Free Press and Be Congratulated for It

The new Peruvian regime's commendable reforms were balanced by other, less attractive measures, such as their destruction of the free press. The government instituted press control in 1970, and has since then liquidated the few remaining independent papers. These were confiscated with the promise that their ownership would eventually be handed over to deserving and representative "social groups" (workers, peasants, intellectuals, et cetera), a measure that supposedly would guarantee true freedom of information. This was of course only an excuse to suppress the independent papers while appropriating their printing facilities and well-established names. No Latin-American military leader had dared do this before except Perón, who confiscated Buenos Aires's *La Prensa* in 1951. The Peruvian military government claimed that the papers being taken over had been "in the service of reaction and imperialism," and thus made their assault on freedom of the press acceptable to "progressive" world opinion.

But another of the junta's actions sheds light on this particular hoax. In 1968, a few weeks after the overthrow of Belaúnde, the new leaders had published a book called *Why?* exposing the previous administration's failures: its economic and institutional mismanagement, its administrative corruption, et cetera. The book was entirely made up of extracts from the Lima press. One story that was omitted, although it had received ample coverage, was the exposure of a network of organized smuggling, discovered by journalists, which brought a military minister to trial and then to jail. The coup d'état cut short any further examination of this affair, which had threatened to compromise other leading military leaders who were now important members of the new ruling junta. Thus the government made use of the press to discredit the former regime, and then suppressed it on the pretext that it was "deceitful," "oligarchic," and "proimperialist."

Significantly, the first Lima paper to fall following the military coup was APRA's *La Tribuna*. Next came *Expreso*, confiscated in 1970 on the excuse that it was owned by the Minister of Finance of the government overthrown two years earlier. *Expreso* was handed over directly to the Communist party; this was one of the most significant and, from the viewpoint of propaganda, one of the most effective of the military government's gestures in favor of the Communist party.

Five influential dailies now remained outside the control of the government or of its docile Communist allies: *La Prensa*, *Ultima Hora*, *El Comercio*, *Correo*, and *Ojo*. The government started a campaign of intimidation and harassment against them, controlling the distribution of newsprint, pegging the sales price despite the rise in production costs, depriving the papers of the traditional benefit of governmental advertising, and encouraging labor troubles. On July 27, 1974, finding that these measures did not suffice to force the papers into complete submission, the government simply confiscated all five.

Formal direction of the newspapers was at first largely entrusted to Communists or Communist sympathizers. But this apparent delegation of power, like many other measures of the so-called Peruvian revolution, did not really give the Communists control, and all these papers now simply followed the official government line. When the time came, a year after the papers' confiscation, to hand over editorial control to representative "workers', peasants', professional, cultural, and educational organizations," the ministry simply announced the indefinite extension of the *status quo*, as well as a purge of all journalists—editors included—"who had not fully indentified with the revolution." It would seem that at this point the military government decided to curtail sharply the responsibility it had so far entrusted to the Communists. They had been useful allies in the early days, but now were not needed, and had even become a source of some embarrassment.

Generals and Intelligentsia

The sequence of events in Peru since 1968 shows how armed forces that were the most blatantly reactionary in Latin America could succeed in seizing power, governing effectively, and imposing policies with the full approval and support of the very groups that should by rights have been their most active adversaries. The Peruvian armed forces, as an institution, succeeded in making the world forget their steady support of an oligarchy whose myopia, social insensitivity, racism, and habitual exploitation of the downtrodden had earned its members the title of "Afrikaners of Latin America." The Peruvian military further managed to clear themselves of their share of responsibility in bringing about the inept regime of Fernando Belaúnde Terry. They managed to cover up the role they had played in his government, including their involvement in some rather shady affairs, such as the smuggling scandal referred to earlier and their implacable antiguerrilla repression in 1965. And this cleansing of their public image cost them very little. As we have seen, the Peruvian Communists shared the new military leaders' hatred of APRA, and readily agreed to serve them. In exchange for this they were given promises but little real power. Both on the domestic scene and outside, the Communists were satisfied to see the new leadership assume Third World, anti-imperialist rhetoric and a measure of opposition to Washington—a degree of opposition, we should stress, that was carefully gauged so as to fall within the limits of what the North Americans could tolerate. The new regime introduced some of the same urgently needed social reforms that had been implemented much earlier in other Latin-American countries by more honorable governments—governments that at the time had been denounced as reformist, inept, and even reactionary by the same propaganda machinery that now praised the Peruvian dictatorship.

The leftists who were attracted and enrolled as "fellow travelers" by the military government included a number of "intellectuals," a group that other Latin-American dictatorships had thought it necessary to persecute. The Peruvian generals preferred to enlist the cooperation of these men, by pretending to assume the rhetoric of anti-imperialism, or by initiating "cultural measures" that paid homage to the myth of the noble savage—for example, declaring the Quechua language an official language of Peru, on a par with Spanish. The government also granted a number of these former opponents administrative positions, which neutralized them and in many cases entailed their eager *collaboration* with the military dictatorship. Nearly ten years have passed since the Peruvian military set this course, and their political success has been phenomenal. In the political storm unleashed in Latin America by the

Cuban Revolution, they were viewed as prospective victims. Che Guevara undertook his Bolivian adventure of 1967 largely because Bolivia was at the heart of the South American continent, while neighboring Peru was supposed to be one of the weakest links of the imperialist chain, one of the countries that could be expected to be transformed most readily into a "new Vietnam." But in July 1969—hardly twenty-one months after Che's death—Fidel Castro buried the Guevarist concept of the "irrecuperability" of the military. In his "ten million tons of sugar cane" speech he declared that, in very little time, the Peruvian government had proven itself to be "objectively revolutionary."

Che Guevara, on the other hand, had remained until his death the implacable foe of the Latin-American officer class. Venezuelan *guerrilleros* who met him in Cuba in 1963 attempted to press on him the advisability of tactical alliances with progressive, nationalistic, patriotic officers—the thesis dominant among Latin-American Marxist-Leninists today. "El Che interrupted: In the Cuban Army there were some [officers] who could be described in those terms, but officers are all sons of bitches . . . all Latin-American officers have sold out. Their culture, their techniques, their education have been shaped by the Yankees. It is an error to entrust a revolutionary role to the military. . . . Class imperatives prevent any significant political conflicts from occurring within the army." When the Venezuelans pointed to the participation of certain "Castroist" officers in the uprising of the two Venezuelan naval bases in May and June of 1962, Che responded: "And tell me, Venezuelans, after those uprisings, what did these officers do? Did they take to the hills? And where are the weapons they seized? Did they have plans to take advantage of this insurrection? Let me tell you, the military like to do easy things such as staging bloodless coups or palace revolutions. In this country, too, when we were moving up from Oriente toward Havana, certain officers rose against Batista in order to save their necks and the system. But Fidel wasn't fooled."[43]

Fidel Castro may be right, and Che wrong. But it could also be the other way around. Castro's insight and instinct in conquering power and keeping it as a *caudillo* in his own country has been matched by his myopia in assessing the overall Latin-American reality. Che's previsions may yet be borne out, and the approach taken by the Peruvian military may prove to have been the one appropriate and effective way of neutralizing in

43. Rafael Elino Martínez, *¡Aquí todo el mundo está alzao!*, pp. 273–74.

Peru the "long march" that Régis Debray had predicted for Castroism in Latin America. Peru's was the most archaic and stratified society in Latin America; APRA, the only civilian political group that could conceivably have carried out the much-needed reforms, was disqualified. In such circumstances, perhaps no social force other than the "military party" could—paradoxically—have been expected to bring about change. The military's rule in Peru will come to an end sooner or later. It may then be remembered for having liberated the country from the individuals and the political power groups that had proved unable to open up Peruvian society between the years 1924 and 1968, and for giving the coming generation a new start. Who knows but that the country will be successful in evolving a democratic, nonmilitary, institutional government? But if such a trend is to develop, one of its harbingers will have to be the rebirth of an independent press.[44]

The Last Consular Caudillo

No Latin-American *caudillo* was able to impose his personal rule longer and more effectively than Porfirio Díaz, who owed his success to his alliance with the imperialist power of the United States. Now, as James Creelman clearly understood,[45] Don Porfirio was a man out of the ordinary, admirably suited

44. Developments in Peru since 1968, and in Portugal between the revolution of 1974 and the discomfiture of the Portuguese Communists and their military friends in late 1975, have some points in common, but also considerable differences. No doubt, the way in which the Peruvian military succeeded in softening world opinion by dubbing themselves "Socialist" served as an example to the Portuguese military. But the double allegiance—to the armed forces and to the Communist party—that characterized a number of Portuguese officers had no parallel in Peru. The officer corps in Peru, without exception, underwent strict and disciplined professional training. Portuguese officers, on the other hand, were shaken by the long colonial wars, and, besides, included a number of secret Communist party members—civilian cadre—who had been hastily trained as combat officers for the colonial emergency in Africa. When a double allegiance of this sort becomes fairly widespread in a military establishment, it can transform a military coup d'état into the spearhead of a "dictatorship of the proletariat." It is evident that such dual loyalty invariably works against the military establishment, since the true allegiance of such "red officers" is to the Communist party, which aims at the destruction of traditional armed forces. It follows that when sincere party members accept the army uniform, they do so only to work toward the dismemberment of the institution they are pretending to serve, and its replacement, in due course, by a completely different body, subject to the political control of the Communist party and staffed by a new officer corps.

45. See pp. 225–27.

to the primitive political environment of which he was a product. He was also the perfect representative of a fascinating human type: a primitive chieftain among his followers, the leader of the pack among lesser wolves; and therefore intriguing to mild, bookish men, who find little attraction in the "bourgeois" rulers of countries where power is traditionally exerted by civilized institutions.

It has been a major paradox for Latin America in the second half of the twentieth century that the ruler to receive most adulation, among us or in the rest of the world, should be a tyrant on the basic pattern inherited from our continent's history. Naturally, some of Fidel's popularity among certain types of European or American intellectuals stems from his attachment to the Soviet Union, and from the opportunity to orchestrate propaganda such a position automatically entails. But if we look beyond this, we find that his attraction is also based on the primitive character of his leadership, which harks back to patterns of governance long established among us. The most enthusiastic of his European admirers are to be found among members of the younger generation, who have no personal recollection of the kind of personal, tyrannical rule and political primitivism that Europe experienced in the period between the two world wars and until 1945. Thus the fact that Fidel Castro is primarily a traditional Latin-American *caudillo*, and, moreover, a *consular caudillo,* the agent of a major foreign power, tends to be lost. Castro's patron power is the Soviet Union, with which he dared to ally himself at a propitious moment. Here, again, we see an alliance that is profoundly humiliating to the consular *caudillo*'s country, but essential to him, since he owes the stability of his personal rule to his consular services.

Fidel Castro's political ideas during his early career as a student leader seem to correspond to a kind of Aprism; in his early anti–North Americanism, he shared the feeling prevalent throughout the continent as a whole. Nor was he the first Latin American to have sought power on the basis of an anti-imperialist platform. But most "anti-imperialist" Latin-American leaders who have made their way to the top have known very well that they could not stay in power without the support of the United States, and they built up a relationship with the North American embassy well before they became heads of state.

Fidel Castro acted no differently, but as he could not go to the embassy in Havana, nor the North American Ambassador to his headquarters in the Sierra Maestra, he made his contacts through American journalists and other emissaries. By the second half of 1958, it was clear that the United States had despaired of Batista, whose consequent "destabilization" might, and probably would, lead to a take-over by the Social Democrat Fidel Castro—with Washington's (guarded) blessings.

In 1959, his first year in power, Castro visited the United States, was interviewed sympathetically and at length by both press and TV, and had a meeting with Vice President Nixon in Washington. Castro's take-over was received with the active sympathy of wide and significant sectors of North American opinion. For many months, he enjoyed the support of many North Americans who knew Cuba and loathed Batista.

What brought about the coolness, and then the break, between Castro and the United States (or between the United States and Castro)? We might simply suppose that Fidel had always been a convinced Communist, a Soviet agent under orders to create in Cuba a situation that was embarrassing to the United States and of maximum tactical advantage to the Soviet Union; in this role he could be supposed to have attempted deliberately to provoke direct American military intervention, even if that threatened his own destruction. In this light, Castro's insistence on multiplying gestures of provocation toward the United States would appear, and could be explained, as planned and deliberate; his survival in power could be ascribed to Washington's lack of nerve. This hypothesis would be in line with Che Guevara's personal obsessions ("One, two, three . . . many Vietnams") but never, it seems to me, with Fidel's relentless hunger for personal power. Of course, one factor we must take into account here is Che Guevara's unmistakable influence on Fidel in making key decisions, such as the sudden confiscation of North American property, that determined future developments. But even so, I don't think the explanation of Castro's being a Soviet agent applies; he seems to be the very model of a *caudillo,* a man whose single purpose it is to conquer and hold absolute rule. Such a man has an almost unerring instinct for how to rise to power. He manages this through means that appear hopeless or impracticable to others. What he does may well be the reverse of what reason would dictate. Castro's simplest and safest course from the start would have been to reach an agreement with the North Americans and to make terms with the Cuban middle class, which was articulate, strong in numbers, and at first exuberantly pro-Castro. But this course would have forced him to share power, which he intended to wield alone. From January 1, 1959, the detailed meanderings of his course may have been unpredictable, but its ultimate strategic objective was set and pursued deliberately and methodically. It aimed toward removing any obstacles that might stand in the way of unlimited personal power. There were visible steps in Fidel's struggle for absolute control, some of them sordid enough. Witness the mysterious disappearance of Camilo Cienfuegos; the imprisonment of Huber Matos; Castro's order to reverse the acquittal of the military pilots accused of "war crimes" (these men were then found guilty in a second "trial," more like an auto-da-fé, conducted in the Sports Palace in front of thousands of spectators and TV viewers). Witness the executions, which at one point took place daily and had thousands of victims; the imprisonment of tens of thousands, many of whom are still in jail fifteen years later; and finally, the exile of hundreds of thousands of Cubans.[46]

These sequences of steps would at some point produce a fatal collision between Castro and the United States. But before this happened, Fidel dared to take an astounding, unthinkable step, a stroke of genius. He saw that his strength, both within his own country and abroad, was at its zenith, and knew that he could not hope to find in the United States support or even acceptance for his aims and methods. The United States was preparing for a presidential election, weakly governed by the outgoing President Eisenhower. Christian Herter had become Secretary of State following the fierce John Foster Dulles's death. Castro felt that in this situation the United States would hesitate to react in a crisis. He decided to play the most daring and risky card in the hand of diplomacy: an outright reversal of alliances. He carried it off successfully, and at the eleventh hour gained the protection of the other superpower.

The years that have gone by since have dissipated the lyrical illusion of a socialist island inhabited by noble revolutionaries walking in the footsteps of the noble savage, uncontaminated by Stalinism and capable of steering clear of it. The results of Communist rule in Cuba are perhaps even more disheartening

46. I should also mention the gradual estrangement of Che Guevara, and Fidel's encouragement of Che's adventures abroad—first in the Congo, then in Bolivia—and their tragic outcome.

than the application of Marxism-Leninism to Eastern Europe. The most telling sign of what is really going on, as in Eastern Europe, is the desperate desire of the supposed beneficiaries of the "new society" to escape to any country where an "old," more or less liberal society still exists. And how few Castroists from other Latin-American countries, exiled or expelled from home, such as survivors of the Chilean Popular Unity or "left-wing Peronists" threatened by the AAA (Argentine Anti-Communist Alliance), are tempted to settle in Cuba!

The punishment and humiliation that Fidel's government inflicts on Cubans who want to leave the country are worse than those the U.S.S.R. metes out to Soviet Jews who wish to emigrate to Israel. But even this price, and the serious risks and difficulties involved in *illegal* escape from the island, have not deterred hundreds of thousands of Cubans from fleeing from their native country and seeking shelter in *any* foreign country. Close to ten percent of the overall 1959 population now have gone to live abroad. If Cubans were freely permitted to leave, a much larger proportion would have done so.

Here is a criterion in terms of which we can reasonably judge all of the Marxist-Leninist political regimes the world has known up to now, including, of course, Castro's Cuba. They are the only political systems in recorded history that have forcibly had to block the flight of citizens, who are ready to leave everything behind, all their property and even their kin. And such exile is not the exceptional, painful decision of a small minority who are obeying certain principles, or are marked politically and must leave for reasons of personal safety, but the wild hope of millions.[47]

But Castro has achieved what he wanted. He rules Cuba as an absolute monarch, although his power is delegated to him by the U.S.S.R., and he governs under the Soviet Union's protection, as Herod governed Judea as the consul of Rome. His prestige has fallen in Latin America and throughout the world, but not as much as he deserves. For Castro continues to be the hero who defied the United States. This is why he still claims a place in the hearts of all who envy or fear the North Americans. In Latin America this motive acts more powerfully than anywhere else. Castro is the only Latin-American leader whose antagonism toward the United States is beyond doubt. A word

47. Even the German Jews, except for the most farsighted, refused to leave Germany, *their country,* after 1933—until it was too late to leave.

from him in favor of the social-democratic President of Venezuela, or of the military dictator of Peru, is of sure political usefulness to either. What is more, either of them, when Fidel condescends to approve, probably feels a secret thrill at thus receiving, from such an unquestionable authority, a certificate of good anti–North American conduct.

Index

Index

Index

Index

Index

Germany (*cont.*)
122, 241, 243, 244*n.*, 245,
287*n.*; West, 45, 94
Gibbon, Edward: *Decline and
Fall of the Roman Empire*,
247
Giscard d'Estaing, Valéry, 260
Godoy, Juan José, 157
Godwin, William, 130 and *n.*,
131
Gómez, Juan Vicente, 42, 88,
220, 223, 224, 225, 228, 229,
234, 248, 249
Goulart, Joao, 42, 237
Great Britain, 94, 101, 104, 111,
117–18, 147, 249, 261;
American colonies of, 21,
and *n.*, 22, 182, 183–84, 186,
189, 196–97; Marx on presence of, in India, 46–48, 102,
104
Great Colombia, 6, 19, 31, 70–
73, 77
Greece, 51; ancient, 9, 26, 46,
70, 95–96
Guatemala, 4, 42, 49, 52 and
n., 71, 88, 120, 159, 160, 162,
175, 201
guerrillas, 217, 246, 267; and
Castro, 125–26, 131–34; and
Guevara, 129–34, 282;
urban, 134–35
Guevara, Dr. Ernesto "Che," 17,
52*n.*, 56, 135, 139–40, 167*n.*,
254, 256–57, 265, 285, 286*n.*;
and guerrillas, 129–34, 282;
and insurrectional focal
point, 131 and *n.*, 132–33,
168; and Leninism, 112, 115,
131
Guevarists, 133, 135, 137, 230,
233, 245, 246, 263
Gulf Oil Corp., 146
Guzetti, Ana, 246, 247*n.*
Guzmán, Antonio Leocadio, 74

haciendas, 78 and *n.*, 184, 187–
89, 220

Haiti, 3, 18, 49, 189, 200
Hamilton, Alexander, 200
Havana, Cuba, 53, 55, 206, 207
Haya de la Torre, Victor Raúl,
115*n.*, 137; *Anti-imperialism
and APRA*, 117–18; and
APRA, 115–20, 135*n.*, 248,
251, 261*n.*, 275; and Com-
munism, 112, 115–16, 117–
20; *Remarks on Imperialist
Britain and on Soviet Russia*,
118
Henriques, Miguel, 272
Henriquez, Archbishop Silva,
169*n.*
Henry VIII, King of England,
11
Herter, Christian, 286
Hidalgo y Costilla, Miguel, 155
Hilferding, Rudolf, 104 and *n.*,
106, 108–09, 111*n.*, 195
Hispaniola, 13
Hitler, Adolf, 241, 244*n.*, 245
Hobson, John Atkinson, 104
and *n.*, 106, 108–09, 195
Ho Chi Minh, 111 and *n.*
Holland, xiii, 73, 94, 104–05,
249
Holy Alliance, 30–31, 71
Honduras, 4, 49, 52, 146
Hoover, Herbert, 38
Huaina Capac (Inca), 19
Humanité, L', 256
Humboldt, Alexander von, xiii,
176–77, 188, 202, 203, 258
Hungary, 43, 60, 123, 126, 128,
163, 165, 166

ICBM missile system, 37, 63
Illich, Ivan, 211 and *n.*, 213*n.*.
imperialism, 34, 61, 86, 90, 122,
138, 175, 182, 196, 217;
American, 20, 30, 44–46, 48,
53, 56, 86–87, 104, 113, 117–
18, 132, 138, 168, 254, 283;
European, xii, 31, 36, 45–46,
104, 113, 117–18; and Leninism, 100, 103–08 and *n.*,

Index

Index

Latin America (*cont.*)
92*n.*, 94, 102–03, 141, 145,
149, 151–54, 172–73; cultural
factors affecting, 56, 76, 88,
90–91, 100, 144–45, 147,
149–50, 172–76; democratic
ideas in, xiv, 32, 45, 50, 57–
58, 63, 67, 71, 77, 80–81,
96, 115, 121, 124–25, 136*n.*,
198, 220–21, 228, 240–41,
247–62; economy of, 7, 43–
44, 48–49, 53, 55, 57 and *n.*,
58, 61, 119, 188, 203–06, 219,
238; escapist literature of,
88–99; ethnic mix in, 3–4,
16, 91–93, 172–73, 191;
European influence in, xi–xii,
4, 16, 45, 84–86, 89, 144,
172, 176, 181–82, 191, 206,
208, 209; foreign investments
in, 57*n.*, 117, 119–20, 121,
146, 191, 225–27, 238, 240,
249–52, 257, 269*n.*, 278;
independent republics of, 40–
41, 48, 52, 57–58, 66, 69, 73,
75, 77–79, 142–43, 158,
197–200, 202–03, 205–06,
219–27; lack of progress in,
xiii, 6–9, 16, 20, 23–24, 29–
30, 37, 44–46, 48, 54, 56, 58,
61, 90–91, 98, 168, 190;
love-hate complex in, 50–51,
54, 61–65, 81, 86–88, 100–
01, 128, 240; myths in, xi–
xiii, 3–19, 29, 46, 51, 68, 103,
138–39, 173, 175–81, 197,
281; power groups in, 77–79,
95–98, 116, 119, 121, 125,
132, 143, 146, 150, 209–18,
274–76, 281; revolutionaries
of, xiii, 7, 15–17, 50, 74–75,
84, 117, 121, 125–35, 139–
40, 148, 167, 168, 175, 211–
14, 217, 254, 267, 282; self-
image in, xi–xii, 4, 6–8, 44,
50, 66–67, 79, 80, 94, 173,
200; society of, 185–94, 196,
206–20, 233, 243*n.*; Spanish

empire and heritage in, 4–5,
17–19, 21, 22, 25, 30, 45–
46, 48, 50, 68–69, 71, 77, 83,
85 and *n.*, 104, 108*n.*, 142,
149, 157, 172, 184–93, 196,
198, 200, 203, 206, 208–09;
terror in, 134, 224, 225–26,
239, 247 and *n.*, 256; and
Third World, 113–14, 138,
166, 174, 219; trade of, 188,
203–06, 207; wars of independence in, 25, 30–31, 67–
69, 74, 77, 81, 89, 142, 155,
157–58, 173, 175, 197, 200–
03, 208, 220, 232, 275; work
attitudes in, 192–93. *See also*
individual countries
Le Bon, Gustave, 222
Lenin, Nikolai, 106–09 and *n.*,
110–13, 114, 116, 119, 120,
195, 264, 274; *Imperialism:
The Highest Stage of Capitalism*, 104, 110*n. See also*
Marxism-Leninism
Leo XIII, Pope, 159–60
Leoni, Raúl, 257
Lesseps, Ferdinand de, 23, 33
Lewis, Oscar, 60, 174
liberals, 74–78, 87, 90, 173, 220,
242, 247–62; and Church,
76–77, 143, 158, 160–61,
164–66, 169
Lima, Peru, 19, 21*n.*, 59, 154,
203, 206, 275, 277, 279–80
Lincoln, Abraham, 197*n.*
Linowitz Commission, 64
London, Eng., 202
López Rega, José, 247
López Trujillo, Msgr. Alfonso,
168
Louisiana, 22
Lowenthal, Abraham, 63–64
Lowndes, William, 194
Lowy, Michel, 17*n.*
Lozowsky (Soviet Communist),
118, 138
Lunacharsky, Anatoli, 118

Index

Index

Index

Index

Index

Third International, 108–11
and *n.*, 113, 114, 115, 116,
117–20
Third World, 15, 46, 56, 61–62,
65, 91, 114*n.*, 131, 138, 166,
173–74, 178, 179, 195, 219,
238*n.*, 251, 261*n.*, 277; and
Communism, 109–12 and *n.*,
113–15, 116, 120, 122, 127,
163, 169, 170–71; and im-
perialism, 46–48, 100*n.*, 101–
08 and *n.*, 109–13, 171, 278,
281
Tocqueville, Alexis de, 69–70,
80
Toledo, Francisco de, 17, 153–
54
Tomic, Radomiro, 260, 262
Torres, Father Camilo, 129, 167
and *n.*
Toynbee, Arnold, 208*n.*
Trajan, Emperor, 247
Tribuna, La, 280
Trotsky, Leon, 118–19, 130
and *n.*, 131
Trotskyists, 59
Trujillo, Peru, 275
Trujillo Molina, Rafael
Leonidas, 37, 40, 42, 50, 227
and *n.*, 245, 254–55
Túpac Amaru (Inca), 17, 90,
154
Túpac Amaru II (Inca), 16–17,
18, 188
Tupamaros, 16, 86*n.*, 90, 134,
267
Turkey, 51

Ulloa, Antonio de, 176
Ultima Hora, 280
United Brands Corp., 146
United Nations, 56, 114; Economic Commission for Latin
America (ECLA), 34, 48*n.*,
56
United States, xi–xii, 4, 30, 52,
62*n.*, 85, 94, 120, 143, 172,
181, 206, 208, 236–37; Alliance for Progress of, 55–58,
64, 276; anti-Communism in,
146–47, 162, 166, 255; anti–
North Americanism, 20, 29,
35, 44–46, 50, 53, 86–88,
115, 124, 138–39, 173–74,
241, 245, 257, 281, 284, 287–
88; armed forces of, 22, 34,
35, 37, 39; Civil War in, 22,
36, 190, 194–95, 196; colonial, 21 and *n.*, 22, 26–29,
182, 183–84, 186, 189, 196–
97; contributions of, 44–45,
50, 57, 181, 206; and Cuba,
22, 54–57, 63, 64–65, 120,
121, 125–26, 127, 128, 254,
284–88; current Latin-
American policy of, 56, 60–
65; democracy in, 24–27, 29,
32, 38 and *n.*, 45, 50, 67, 69,
71, 80, 89, 144–48, 197, 199–
200, 204*n.*; development of,
22–25; Good Neighbor policy
of, 40, 51; imperialism of,
20, 30, 44–46, 48, 53, 56,
86–87, 104, 113, 117–18,
132, 138, 168, 254, 283; and
Latin-American dictators, 37–
38, 40, 58, 225–27; Latin-
American intervention of,
35–43, 121, 133, 270; Latin-
American investments of,
57*n.*, 146, 191, 249, 269*n.*,
278; Marshall Plan of, 51;
and Mexico, 49, 57*n.*, 60, 64–
65, 72–73, 81, 104, 231–32,
283; Monroe Doctrine of, 31,
32, 36, 38, 39, 72; New Deal
of, 241; and Panama Canal,
23, 33–39, 117; power and
success of, xiii, 6, 16, 23–24,
29–30, 32–36, 44–46, 50, 54,
61, 70, 71, 73, 80–81, 91,
97–100, 106, 114–15, 123,
168, 190, 248, 256; Protestant
ethic in, 144–49, 150, 161–
62; Revolution in, 17, 22, 25,
27–28, 172, 197; Roosevelt

Index

DEC 1977